SCOREBUILDER

for

Financial Accounting

Bruce A. Baldwin
Portland State University

1988
IRWIN
Homewood, Illinois 60430

©Richard D. Irwin, Inc., 1988

All rights reserved. No part of this publication may be
reproduced, stored in a retrieval system, or transmitted,
in any form or by any means, electronic, mechanical,
photocopying, recording, or otherwise, without the prior
written permission of the publisher.

Acquisitions editor: Frank Burrows
Project editor: Lynne Basler
Production manager: Ann Cassady
Printer: McNaughton & Gunn, Inc.

ISBN 0-256-06691-4

Library of Congress Catalog Card No. 88-80170

Printed in the United States of America

1 2 3 4 5 6 7 8 9 0 MG 5 4 3 2 1 0 9 8

PREFACE

SCOREBUILDER is a set of 700 actual examination questions previously used on introductory financial accounting examinations at colleges and universities all across the United States. The answer to each question is given and an annotated solution is provided that tells **why** the answer is correct.

Each question was originally written by faculty and staff trained in item-writing by the author. Also, each question has been psychometrically item-analyzed for difficulty and reliability. The difficulty index for each question is provided with the annotated solution and indicates what percentage of students answered the question correctly when it was used on a financial accounting exam.

THIS BOOK CAN HELP FACULTY AND STUDENTS IN SEVERAL WAYS.

Students often request faculty to provide copies of old exams or exam questions so that they can "sharpen their test-taking skills" or practice on "real questions" before an exam. Instead of having to reproduce old exams and distribute them, or instead of putting old exams on reserve in the library, faculty can save time by making *SCOREBUILDER* available in the bookstore. This procedure would allow faculty members to keep their actual exam materials confidential (allowing for reuse) while still giving students guidance in preparation for exams. All students then have equal access to exam preparation and review materials.

Second, faculty should recommend *SCOREBUILDER* to students wishing to challenge the introductory accounting course and want some guidelines as to what they should study or what type of problems they should be able to solve. A faculty member may state with confidence that *SCOREBUILDER* provides that information. This should be particularly helpful for students who studied accounting/bookkeeping in high school and wonder if they should challenge the first course.

Third, faculty could recommend *SCOREBUILDER* to students who took financial accounting some time ago, are now enrolled in managerial accounting, and need some "brushing up" on the basic mechanics of accounting.

A further use of *SCOREBUILDER* is by MBA students who might have taken their basic accounting courses some time ago. A faculty member might assign several "review" chapters from the text and recommend "self-testing" by the student in *SCOREBUILDER*.

There are many other situations in which *SCOREBUILDER* could be effectively used. The uses mentioned above are only examples of the ways that it has been productively used by faculty and students at my university.

THE DIFFERENCE BETWEEN *SCOREBUILDER* AND A STUDY GUIDE

A Study Guide and *SCOREBUILDER* are designed to help you in different stages of your learning. A Study Guide is most helpful in your day-by-day learning or in your chapter-by-chapter study. It is usually designed to "walk" you through each significant topic in each chapter. Chapter summaries, true-false questions, exercises, and fill in the blank items tend to be developmental in nature. That is, they are designed to prod your thinking and guide your learning.

SCOREBUILDER, on the other hand, is specifically designed to help you prepare for and maximize your score on exams. The multiple-choice questions are all actual questions used on prior elementary accounting exams. Test questions are often different from Study Guide questions since the objectives differ. Study Guide questions are usually designed to **help you learn**...test questions are designed to **measure** how much learning took place.

You will find, then, several different types of exam questions in *SCOREBUILDER*. Some measure your ability to recall facts; others measure your ability to apply concepts or procedures to given data. Still other questions measure the **depth** of your knowledge by rearranging facts into unfamiliar patterns and asking you to analyze, evaluate and integrate. Most Study Guide questions simply don't do this.

SPECIAL NOTE TO STUDENTS

The purpose of this book is to help you achieve better scores on your introductory Financial Accounting examinations. Careful study of the materials herein can contribute to that goal in two ways. First, by working through the questions and then reviewing the annotated solutions before an exam, you can find out which topics you have mastered and which topics still need a little work. (Most learning psychologists agree that studying old exam questions is an effective and efficient method of quickly identifying concepts or procedures that could use some further work.) When you find a weak area you should return to the relevant section of your textbook for more study. Sometimes, however, the annotated solution may be enough to establish the tested concept or procedure in your mind.

The second way this book can help you is by improving your test-taking skills. If your instructor gives examinations that are at least partially of the multiple-choice format, you can profit by practicing on these questions. Even if you instructor does not use multiple-choice questions, you will find *SCOREBUILDER* to be good exam preparation. Many of the problem-type questions contained herein could just as easily be presented on an exam in a "free-response" format. That is, the same question/problem could be asked without a set of possible answers being suggested. The skills necessary to master multiple-choice questions are often used to master "free-response" problems. These questions should give you insight into the level and complexity of questions that your instructor might ask on an introductory accounting exam.

The purpose of *SCOREBUILDER* is to help you maximize your exam score. It is **not** a substitute for other learning activities. Before trying to use it, you should have read the textbook chapters carefully (perhaps several times); worked and checked the homework assignments; maybe have worked through the Study Guide; and absolutely, positively attended **every** single class session. If you've done the necessary groundwork, *SCOREBUILDER* will help you maximize your test scores.

Good luck as your prepare for your accounting exams!

ACKNOWLEDGEMENTS

Many of the questions in *SCOREBUILDER* were written by the author, but most questions (or ideas for questions) were originally suggested by others. At the risk of unintentionally omitting someone, the following persons have contributed significantly to this book.

Viva Ashcroft
Arizona State University

Pete Bergevin
University of Nevada--Las Vegas

J Buckhold California State University--Chico	Janice Stemmler Carr Cal Poly--San Luis Obispo
Tom English Boise State University	Severn Grabski Michigan State University
Hassan Hefzi University of Arkansas	Dave Hansen Linfield College
Kumen Jones Arizona State University	Ed Kasky St. Joseph's College
Jodah Khalsa California State University--Fullerton	Steve Limberg University of Texas--Austin
Doug Lower Arizona State University	Loren Margheim University of San Diego
Allie Miller Temple University	Steve Roark University of Arkansas
Vickie Ruble University of Idaho	Dennis Togo University of New Mexico
Steve Wheeler Florida State University	Larry Wiggs Mesa Community College
George Violette University of Massachusetts	

Jim Rowan assisted the author by writing first draft annotations for many of the questions. The completed manuscript was read (and every problem worked) by Linda McCurry, Carol Randall, and Connie Kline.

In spite of the encouragement and assistance of others, however, all errors and omissions remain the personal responsibility of the author. Please communicate such information and comments to me. Thank you.

Bruce A. Baldwin
Portland, Oregon

TABLE OF CONTENTS

CHAPTER ONE: PERSPECTIVES — ACCOUNTING OBJECTIVES AND COMMUNICATION

PART A: The Objectives and Environment of Accounting

1. Limited liability is a feature of what form(s) of business organization?
   a. corporation
   b. proprietorship
   c. partnership
   d. both a proprietorship and a partnership

2. One of the following is **not** an advantage of the corporate form of business organization. Identify it.
   a. access to large amounts of capital
   b. continuity of life
   c. unlimited liability
   d. ease in transferring ownership

3. Which of the following types of business entity have (has) the disadvantage of double taxation?

         I. proprietorship
         II. partnership
         III. corporation
   a. I only
   b. II only
   c. III only
   d. both I and II
   e. both II and III

4. The accounting rule that prohibits a corporation from including the president's personal automobile (that is not used for business purposes) as a corporate asset is the:
   a. conservatism rule.
   b. accounting cycle rule.
   c. separate-entity rule.
   d. operating cycle rule.
   e. asset ownership rule.

5. The **primary** purpose of accounting is to:
   a. measure and report financial information of economic entities.
   b. facilitate decision making.
   c. certify the accuracy of accounting records.
   d. provide for internal control over financial transactions.

6. The foundations for the "basic accounting model" in use today were originally developed in what part of the world?
   a. Europe
   b. Africa
   c. South America
   d. Asia
   e. North America

7. The term GAAP refers to:
   a. generally accepted accounting principles.
   b. generally accepted auditing procedures.
   c. general auditing and accounting processes.
   d. general accounting associates program.

8. The best protection currently available to the public to assure that financial statements present a fair representation of the company is:
   a. have the president of the company sign a sworn statement that the financial statements are a fair representation of the company.
   b. have an audit performed by an independent CPA.
   c. have an audit performed by the company's internal auditors.
   d. have the financial statements reviewed by the Board of Directors.
   e. have the financial statements examined by the General Accounting Office of the United States.

9. Accountants perform many different kinds of services. The activities that have as their primary purpose the verification of financial statement information is called:
    a. cost accounting.
    b. consulting.
    c. management advisory services.
    d. auditing.

10. As part of the audit function, an independent CPA must:
    a. examine all business transactions of the entity.
    b. report any illegal activities of the entity to the proper legal authorities.
    c. express an opinion on the financial statements.
    d. prepare the required state and federal tax returns.

11. Which of the following is **not** included in management advisory services performed by an independent CPA?
    a. Design and installation of control systems.
    b. Preparation of tax returns.
    c. Preparation of business forecasts.
    d. Preparation of cost effectiveness studies.

12. The audit or attest function performed by the CPA in public practice:
    a. lends credibility to financial reports.
    b. assists management in designing and installing accounting systems.
    c. involves submitting periodic reports to the Securities and Exchange Commission and accepting responsibility for the reports.
    d. involves the accumulation of data concerning the cost of manufacturing products.

13. The private-sector organization that took over the APB's function of establishing and improving accounting standards and principles in 1973 is the:
    a. FASB.
    b. AICPA.
    c. AAA.
    d. SEC.

14. The Financial Accounting Standards Board (FASB):
    a. is a government regulatory agency.
    b. sponsors and encourages the improvement of accounting teaching and research.
    c. deals primarily with tax reporting problems with the Internal Revenue Service (IRS).
    d. is a private sector organization that develops accounting standards.

15. There are five important groups in the United States predominating the development of financial accounting concepts and practice. Which of the following is **not** considered to be one of those groups?
    a. The Government Accounting Office
    b. The Securities and Exchange Commission
    c. The American Institute of Certified Public Accountants
    d. The Financial Accounting Standards Board
    e. The Financial Executives Institute

16. Which of the following organizations was founded around 1900, has a membership limited to certified public accountants, and has as two of its major interests professional development of its members and the development of accounting standards?
    a. SEC
    b. AICPA
    c. FASB
    d. AAA

PART B: Communication of Accounting Information

17. Which financial statements cover a period of time?
    a. Income Statement and Balance Sheet
    b. Balance Sheet and Statement of Changes in Financial Position
    c. Income Statement and Statement of Changes in Financial Position
    d. Statement of Changes in Financial Position and Statement of Assets, Liabilities and Owners' Equity.

18. A business had the following transactions, among others, during January. Which transaction represented an expense for January?
    a. Purchased a typewriter for $300 cash.
    b. Paid $2,000 in settlement of a loan obtained three months earlier.
    c. Paid a garage $200 for automobile repair work performed in November.
    d. Purchased $60 of gasoline on account for the delivery truck. Account will be paid during February.

19. Assume you are examining a financial statement which indicates it is "At December 31, 19X2." That heading tells you the statement is the:
    a. balance sheet.
    b. income statement.
    c. statement of changes in financial position.
    d. ledger.

20. Under generally accepted accounting principles (GAAP), revenue is most commonly recognized when:
    a. a sale is made.
    b. the product is manufactured.
    c. cash is collected from the sale.
    d. the goods are delivered to the customer.

21. Assume that each of the following events occurs on January 1, 19A. Which **one** would result in revenue being recognized at that date?
    a. MK Apartments receives $500 for rent covering the months of February, March, and April.
    b. Billy B. Company receives a promise from Bulk Corp. that it will be paid $100 for repair work just completed that day.
    c. EG Corp. sells 100 shares of capital stock on the open market for $1,000 cash.
    d. RXG Company receives a loan from the State Bank in the amount of $5,000.

22. Earnings per share (EPS) is determined by which of the following computations?
    a. Total revenues divided by the number of shares of common stock outstanding
    b. Net income divided by the number of shares of common stock outstanding
    c. Pretax income divided by the number of shares of common stock outstanding
    d. Total revenues divided by Owners' Equity

23. AFG reported earnings per share of $15.50 and the number of shares of capital stock outstanding is 8,000. The income tax rate is 45%. Net income must have been:
    a. $ 516
    b. $ 3,600
    c. $ 17,778
    d. $ 55,800
    e. $124,000

24. During June, the Maple Restaurant had revenues of $3,000 and expenses of $1,800. The owner withdrew $600 cash from the business during the month. If owners' equity on June 30 was $8,600, owners' equity on June 1 must have been:
    a. $10,400.
    b. $ 9,800.
    c. $ 9,200.
    d. $ 8,000.
    e. some other answer.

25. Ten years ago the X Company bought a tract of land for $100,000 and built a factory on it. This past year a land appraiser determined that the value of the land was now $200,000 because of increasing land values. On X Company's balance sheet the land should be listed at:
    a. $100,000.
    b. $150,000.
    c. $200,000.
    d. an amount not determinable from the information given.

26. The accounting records of Cactus Farms show the following balances at 6-31-19E:

Cash	$100
Equipment	1,000
Accounts Receivable	300
Accounts Payable	200
Notes Payable	200
Retained Earnings	600
Capital Stock	700
Net Income	400
Expenses	1,100

Total assets as of 6-31-19E are:
a. $1,000.
b. $1,400.
c. $1,800.
d. $2,000.

27. Which of the following best describes the purpose of the balance sheet?
a. summarize revenues and expenses for the accounting period
b. report the inflows and outflows of cash
c. balance current period revenues with those of the previous period
d. report assets, liabilities and owners' equity as of a specific date

28. What effect do revenues and expenses eventually have on Owners' Equity?

	Revenues	Expenses
a.	increase	increase
b.	increase	decrease
c.	decrease	decrease
d.	decrease	increase

29. Which of the following is **not** an asset?
a. Inventory
b. Accounts Receivable
c. Revenue
d. Cash

30. The balance sheet differs from the other financial statements in that:
a. it is the most important statement to the investor.
b. it is prepared more frequently.
c. it is dated as of a specific point in time.
d. its purpose is to show where cash came from during the period, and how the cash was used.

31. The ABC Company recently purchased a warehouse for cash in which it intends to store inventory. On ABC's financial statements this warehouse should be reported as:
a. an expense.
b. an asset.
c. a revenue.
d. contributed capital.

32. Sub Company reported revenues of $10,000, expenses of $3,000, and dividends paid of $2,000 for the most recent accounting period. If Sub Company has 1,000 shares of stock outstanding, what is Sub's earnings per share for the period?
a. $10
b. $7
c. $5
d. $2

33. Which financial statement(s) report(s) the financial position of the firm at a specific point in time?
a. the balance sheet, income statement, and statement of changes in financial position
b. the balance sheet and income statement
c. the income statement only
d. the balance sheet only

34. Wasteful Corporation is preparing the income statement for the month ending December 31, 19B. The following transactions occurred during December.

Dec. 10   Paid off an account payable arising the purchase of supplies used in Nov. 19B.....$1,200.

Dec. 22   Paid rent of $400 for January of 19C.

Dec. 31   Purchased goods to be held in inventory for future sale....$50

What are total expenses for the month ended December 31, 19B?
a. $ -0-
b. $1,200
c. $1,600
d. $1,650

CHAPTER ONE: ANNOTATED SOLUTIONS

1. a	7. a	13. a	19. a	25. a	31. b
2. c	8. b	14. d	20. a	26. b	32. b
3. c	9. d	15. a	21. b	27. d	33. d
4. c	10. c	16. b	22. b	28. b	34. a
5. b	11. b	17. c	23. e	29. c	
6. a	12. a	18. d	24. d	30. c	

> *The correct answer and the percentage of students answering the question correctly (when it was used on an introductory accounting examination) are shown in parentheses at the beginning of each annotated solution that follows.*

1. (a,90) Only the owners of a corporation enjoy the privilege of limited liability. Limited liability means that the maximum amount an owner can lose is the amount of his/her investment. Under both the proprietorship and partnership forms of organization, the owners have unlimited liability. That is, their personal assets may be attached in order to pay off the debts of the business.

2. (c,79) Unlimited liability is **not** an advantage (and relates only to partnerships and proprietorships anyway).

3. (c,71) Corporate profits are first taxed when earned by the corporation, and then a second time when stockholders receive them as dividends.

4. (c,82) This question is a straightforward application of the entity concept.

5. (b,26) The primary purpose of accounting is to provide information that is useful in making economic decisions. Responses a, c and d are all activities that contribute to the primary goal of making information useful for decision-making.

6. (a,77) In 1494, Paciolo wrote the first book regarding the basic accounting model that is still used today. It described a system developed by Italian merchants.

7. (a,88) GAAP means Generally Accepted Accounting Principles. The other suggested answers are nonsense.

8. (b,75) While responses a, c, d, and e may be good ideas, there is currently no procedure in place to implement them. Assurance to users that financial statements are fairly presented currently comes as a result of an audit performed by an independent CPA.

9. (d,80) The process of verifying financial information and expressing an opinion as to the fairness of the resulting financial statements is called auditing.

10. (c,82) The basic goal of an audit is to determine if the financial statements present fairly the firm's financial position. Usually, only a sample of transactions are examined. The auditor should report illegal activities to management but need not contact legal authorities. Preparation of tax returns is not part of auditing.

11. (b,44) CPA services fall into three broad categories: (1) auditing, (2) tax assistance, and (3) management advisory services (MAS). Preparation of tax returns, then, is part of the tax assistance category and not part of MAS. Responses a,c, and d are common MAS activities.

12. (a,76) The primary purpose of the audit (attest) function is to assure the dependability of the financial statements. This process lends credibility to the financial statements. Response b describes an MAS function and response d describes cost accounting. Response c is incorrect because management submits (and takes responsibility for) any required reports to the SEC.

13. (a,73) The FASB took over the APB's standard-setting function in 1973 and continues to do it currently.

14. (d,76) The Financial Accounting Standards Board (FASB) is currently the private sector organization that develops accounting standards and principles. Prior to the FASB, this function was provided by the Accounting Principles Board (APB).

15. (a,64) The five important groups predominating the development of financial accounting concepts and practices are the (1) AICPA, (2) FASB, (3) SEC, (4) the American Accounting Association, and (5) the FEI. The Government Accounting Office, then, is not one of those five.

16. (b,69) The description in this question is of the American Institute of Certified Public Accountants. The SEC is a government regulatory agency; the FASB is the standard setting body established in 1973; and the AAA is the national organization of accounting educators.

17. (c,79) The balance sheet is dated as of a specific day which causes responses a and b to be incorrect. Response d is incorrect because a statement of assets, liabilities, and owners' equity would be a balance sheet.

18. (d,44) An expense occurs when goods or services are consumed or used up. That is, no expense occurs upon purchase of an asset (item a); repaying a loan decreases liabilities (item b); and item c is an expense of the month of November. In item d we must be making the reasonable assumption that the gasoline was used up shortly after purchase.

19. (a,85) The only financial statement that is dated as of a specific point in time is the balance sheet. (Also, a ledger is not a financial statement.)

20. (a,73) Under the revenue principle, revenue should be recognized when it is earned. Usually this is deemed to have occurred when the sale is made. Under rare circumstances, revenue may be recognized at the other points listed as alternative answers. The question asked, though, for the point at which revenue is **commonly** recognized.

21. (b,57) Revenue is to be recognized in the period it is earned. Only response b meets this test. The revenue in response a will be earned during the months of February, March and April. Responses c and d do not involve revenue at all since goods have not been sold nor have services been rendered.

22. (b,94) By definition.

23. (e,73) Earnings per share = net income/number of shares outstanding. $15.50 = X / 8000 shares; X = $124,000. The tax rate is irrelevant to this question since EPS is computed on **after-tax** income.

24. (d,55) Revenue minus expense = net income ($3,000 - $1,800 = $1,200). Net income increases owners' equity while owner withdrawals ($600) decrease it. Let X = June 1 owners' equity. (X + net income - withdrawals = June 30 owners' equity.) So, X + $1,200 - $600 = $8,600; and X = $8,000.

25. (a,78) According to the cost principle, the land will continue to be recorded at $100,000 until sold. (Land is not depreciated because we assume it does not "wear out" like machinery does.)

26. (b,80) The asset accounts here are cash ($100), accounts receivable ($300), and equipment ($1,000) for a total of $1,400.

27. (d,94) By definition.

28. (b,90) By definition, revenues increase equity and expenses decrease it.

29. (c,62) Inventory, accounts receivable, and cash are all assets. Revenue is **not** an asset, but is earned when there has been an inflow of assets as a result of goods sold or services rendered.

30. (c,86) Only response c has any truth to it.

31. (b,77) The warehouse is a resource owned by the entity which means it is an asset.

32. (b,48) Earnings per share is equal to net income divided by the number of shares of stock outstanding. In this problem, net income is $7,000 (revenues of $10,000 minus expenses of $3,000) and the number of shares outstanding is 1,000. Therefore, $7,000 divided by 1,000 shares equals earnings per share of $7.

33. (d,86) By definition, only the balance sheet reports the financial position of a firm at a specific point in time. Both the income statement and the statement of changes in financial position report information for a **period** of time.

34. (a,54) Expenses are recognized when goods or services are consumed (or used up) during the period. In this problem, no goods or services were consumed during December of 19B. The supplies were consumed in November; the rental services will be consumed during January of 19C; and the goods held in inventory have not been consumed (or used up) either.

CHAPTER TWO:
THE FUNDAMENTAL ACCOUNTING
MODEL AND TRANSACTION ANALYSIS

1. "Oil Can Charlie" mortgaged his gas station to obtain operating capital for the business. The bank loaned the gas station $20,000. Concerning the gas station, which of the following increased as a result of this loan?
   a. revenues
   b. expenses
   c. equity
   d. liabilities

2. During an accounting period total assets decreased by $4 while stockholders' equity increased by $7. The change in total liabilities during this period was a(n):
   a. $ 3 increase.
   b. $ 3 decrease.
   c. $11 increase.
   d. $11 decrease.

3. During the year, the Jameson Co. had revenues of $75 and expenses of $40. Total liabilities at year end amounted to $105 and at the start of the year total stockholders' equity was $45. What are the total assets at year end?
   a. $225
   b. $185
   c. $150
   d. $145
   e. $140

4. The Fillmore Co. purchased a new delivery truck by making a cash down payment and signing a note for the balance. How will assets, liabilities, and stockholder's equity be affected by this transaction?

	Assets	Liabilities	Equity
a.	decreased	increased	no change
b.	increased	increased	no change
c.	increased	decreased	increased
d.	no change	increased	decreased
e.	no change	decreased	increased

5. Guido started a business by contributing $3,000 cash and a truck valued at $5,000. The company then purchased equipment by making a $3,000 down payment (which accounted for half its purchase price) and financed the other half by signing a note with the bank. After the above transactions, Guido's company balance sheet is composed of:

	Assets	Liabilities	Equity
a.	$ 8,000	$ 0	$ 8,000
b.	$ 8,000	$3,000	$ 5,000
c.	$11,000	$ 0	$11,000
d.	$11,000	$3,000	$ 8,000

6. Doe Corporation had the following transactions during the month of January.

   --Owners started the company by investing $100,000 in cash in exchange for capital stock.
   --Purchased $50,000 of equipment by making a $20,000 cash down payment and signed a 90-day note payable for the balance.
   --Purchased land for $5,000, signing a note payable for full amount.
   --Earned $15,000 of revenue, (of which $10,000 was received in cash with the balance on accounts receivable).

   What are total assets for the Doe Corporation at the end of January?
   a. $140,000
   b. $145,000
   c. $150,000
   d. $170,000

7. A debit is used to record:
   a. decreases in liabilities, increases in assets and decreases in owners' equity.
   b. increases in liabilities, increases in assets, and decreases in owners' equity.
   c. decreases in assets, decreases in liabilities and decreases in owners' equity.
   d. increases in assets, increases in revenues, and decreases in liabilities.

8. Ajax reports these account balances. Determine retained earnings.

Accounts Payable	$ 20
Land	10
Notes Payable	8
Equipment	120
Cash	40
Accounts Receivable	30
Investments	80
Inventory	36
Bonds Payable	100
Supplies Inventory	4
Common Stock	110
Buildings	100
Interest Payable	2
Retained Earnings	?

    a. $180
    b. $290
    c. $310
    d. $390

9. Connie's Company began the year with assets of $100, and liabilities of $20. During the year, the company earned $50 of net income. At year-end, assets were $180 and the liabilities were $40; no dividends had been paid. During the year, Connie must have:
    a. withdrawn an extra $20.
    b. invested an extra $10.
    c. borrowed an extra $20.
    d. withdrawn an extra $10.

10. Tyler Corporation accounts have the following balances at year end. (All accounts have their normal type of balance.)

Advertising Revenue	$62
Salaries & Wages Expense	22
Depreciation Expense	15
Prepaid Insurance	10
Insurance Expense	5
Interest Revenue	3
Interest Expense	2
Accumulated Depreciation	30

The net income (or loss) for the period is:
    a. ($9).
    b. ($6).
    c. $11.
    d. $21.
    e. $31.

11. Revenue and expense accounts can be thought of as subdivisions of:
    a. asset accounts.
    b. liability accounts.
    c. owners' equity accounts.
    d. contra accounts.

12. The components of the fundamental accounting model are affected by transactions. The equality of this model is maintained by:
    a. recording revenue increases as debits.
    b. recording expense increases as credits.
    c. recording liability increases as credits.
    d. adjusting the trial balance for any difference between debit and credit totals.

13. If a transaction causes an asset account to increase, which of the following related effects may also occur?
    a. A decrease of an equal amount in a liability account.
    b. An increase of equal amount in another asset account.
    c. A decrease of equal amount in an owner's equity account.
    d. An increase of equal amount in a revenue account.

14. Generally accepted accounting principles require recognition of revenues when earned and recognition of expenses when incurred. This is known as:
    a. the entity concept.
    b. the unit of measure concept.
    c. accrual basis accounting.
    d. a qualitative characteristic of accounting.
    e. the cost principle.

15. Recognizing revenues when earned and expenses when incurred is a statement of what concept?
    a. cost basis
    b. accrual basis
    c. cash basis
    d. tax basis

16. Accrual basis accounting:
    a. is optional for companies reporting to the public.
    b. is not acceptable under GAAP.
    c. is inherent in the definitions used in the text for revenues and expenses.
    d. refers to recognizing transactions when cash is received and disbursed.

17. Given that retained earnings on December 31, 19B was $10 and the following information, determine what retained earnings must have been on January 1, 19A.

Year	Net Income	Dividends
19A	$5	$3
19B	$4	$3

    a. $ 1
    b. $ 3
    c. $ 7
    d. $13

18. Service revenue earned for the month of July by Action Inc. is as follows: collected in cash, $5,000; and uncollected at July 31, $1,500. The entry to record service revenue for the month will include a:
    a. credit to Accounts Payable of $1,500.
    b. debit to Service Revenue of $6,500.
    c. debit to Accounts Receivable of $1,500.
    d. credit to Cash of $5,000.

19. Which of the following transactions results in a **debit** to an expense account in 19C for Orange Company?
    a. On December 31, 19C, Orange Company borrowed $10,000 from the local bank on a one-year note at 12% interest.
    b. On January 1, 19C, Orange Company paid $750 on accounts payable.
    c. Orange Company declared and paid cash dividends of $1,000 to stockholders on October 1, 19C.
    d. On July 1, 19C, Orange Company paid $95 to repair a delivery van.

20. On July 1, 19A, three persons invested $100 each to form Prosper Company. Each person received 10 shares of $10 par value capital stock. Summarized financial data for 19A and 19B follow.

	19A	19B
Revenues	$15	$40
Expenses	8	22
Dividends	6	12

    Retained earnings balances at the end of 19A and 19B should be:
    a. $101 and $107.
    b. $ 7 and $ 18.
    c. $ 1 and $ 6.
    d. $ 1 and $ 7.

21. The collection of an account receivable in the amount of $1,500 was recorded by a debit to cash and a credit to accounts payable. If the error is not corrected, the balance sheet will show an:
    a. overstatement of total liabilities.
    b. understatement of total assets.
    c. understatement of total liabilities.
    d. overstatement of total stockholders' equity.

22. Interest of $100 is due on a note payable. Writing a check in payment of the **interest** due has what effect on the accounting records?
    a. Cash is decreased, interest expense is increased.
    b. Cash is decreased, notes payable is decreased.
    c. Only the cash account is affected, i.e. a decrease of $100.
    d. Cash is increased, interest revenue is increased.

23. Which of the following transactions would **decrease** total assets?
    a. Purchase of equipment for cash.
    b. Paid cash dividends to stockholders.
    c. Paid an account payable.
    d. b and c above.
    e. a, b, and c above.

24. The issuance of capital stock:
    a. decreases current assets.
    b. increases owners' equity.
    c. decreases contributed capital.
    d. increases retained earnings.

25. During 19X3, the Tempe Chemical Company had the following sales:

Cash sales	$150,000
Credit sales	$200,000

    Collections from customers during 19X3 amounted to $100,000 from the credit sales of 19X2 and $80,000 from the credit sales of 19X1. The total revenue that should be recognized in 19X3 using the accrual basis is:
    a. $150,000.
    b. $250,000.
    c. $300,000.
    d. $330,000.
    e. $350,000.

26. Company A borrowed $5,000 cash from the bank and signed an agreement to repay the amount plus 8% interest. The transaction is recorded by:
    a. Dr. Notes Receivable $5,000; Cr. Cash $5,000.
    b. Dr. Cash $5,000; Cr. Notes Receivable $5,000.
    c. Dr. Cash $5,000 and Interest Expense $400; Cr. Notes Payable $5,400.
    d. Dr. Cash $5,000; Cr. Notes Payable $5,000.

27. Stockholders invested $40,000 in cash into Company A. This transaction is recorded by Company A as a debit to:
    a. Capital Stock and a credit to Cash.
    b. Cash and a credit to Revenue of Company A.
    c. Cash and a credit to Capital Stock.
    d. Revenue of Company A and a credit to Dividends.

28. The normal balances of Prepaid Insurance and Insurance Expense are:
    a. debits.
    b. credits.
    c. debit and credit, respectively.
    d. credit and debit, respectively.

29. A social service agency earned $180,000 of revenue during April. Of this amount, 2/3 was on credit and will be collected over the next three months. The correct journal entry to record these facts is:

    a.
Cash	60,000	
Accounts Payable	120,000	
Fee Revenue		180,000

    b.
Cash	180,000	
Fee Revenue		180,000

    c.
Cash	60,000	
Accounts Receivable	120,000	
Fee Revenue		180,000

    d.
Fee Revenue	60,000	
Cash		60,000

30. Dotson Company's bookkeeper is recording a recent transaction in the journal. So far, a liability account has been increased. To complete the journal entry, which one of the following might properly be done?
    a. increase a revenue account
    b. decrease a contra account to revenue
    c. decrease an expense
    d. decrease an asset
    e. increase a contra account to equity

31. Depreciation for the year is being recognized on a building. Which combination of the following entries would be made to record this event?

	Debit entry to Depreciation Expense	Credit entry to Building
a.	Yes	Yes
b.	Yes	No
c.	No	Yes
d.	No	No

CHAPTER TWO: ANNOTATED SOLUTIONS

1. d	6. c	11. c	16. c	21. a	26. d	31. b
2. d	7. a	12. c	17. c	22. a	27. c	
3. b	8. a	13. d	18. c	23. d	28. a	
4. b	9. b	14. c	19. d	24. b	29. c	
5. d	10. d	15. b	20. d	25. e	30. e	

The correct answer and the percentage of students answering the question correctly (when it was used on an introductory accounting examination) are shown in parentheses at the beginning of each annotated solution that follows.

---

1. (d,88) When the business obtained the loan, assets increased by $20,000 as did liabilities.

2. (d,56) Remember that assets = liabilities + equity and that the balance is always maintained. If the left side (assets) is decreased by $4, and one of the parts on the right side (equity) increases by $7, the other part of the right side (liabilities) must decrease by $11. In this way, both sides show a net decrease of $4.

3. (b,64) Assets = Liabilities + Owners' Equity. At year end, owners' equity equals the beginning balance of owners' equity + net income for the year ($45 + $35 = $80). Therefore, assets = $105 + $80 = $185.

4. (b,75) This transaction will cause a net increase in assets (cost of truck - cash down payment) and an increase in liabilities caused by the note. There is no effect on equity since no equity accounts are involved in the journal entry.

5. (d,71) Guido's balance sheet will include assets of $11,000 (truck at $5,000 + equipment at $6,000), liabilities of $3,000 (the note payable to the bank), and equity of $8,000 (the difference between assets and liabilities).

6. (c,52) Included in total assets are the Equipment ($50,000), A/R ($5,000), Land ($5,000), and Cash of $90,000 (total of $150,000). The Cash account balance is determined as follows: add $100,000 cash investment by owners, deduct $20,000 used to purchase equipment and add $10,000 of revenue collected in cash ($100,000 - 20,000 + 10,000 = $90,000).

7. (a,89) By definition.

8. (a,45) Assets = liabilities + equity. Assets (cash + investments + land + equipment + accounts receivable + inventory + supplies inventory + buildings) = $420. Liabilities (accounts payable + notes payable + bonds payable + interest payable) = $130. Equity, then, equals $290 ($420 - $130). If common stock = $110, retained earnings must = $180 ($290 - $110).

9. (b,23) At the beginning of the year, owners' equity = $80 ($100 assets - $20 liabilities). At year-end, owners' equity = $140 ($180 assets - $40 liabilities). The $60 increase in owners' equity must consist of the $50 net income plus a $10 investment by Connie.

10. (d,57) Revenue - Expense = Net Income. The revenue accounts are advertising revenue and interest revenue. The expenses are salaries and wages, depreciation, insurance and interest. Therefore, ($62 + $3) - ($22 + $15 + $5 + $2) = $21. Prepaid insurance and accumulated depreciation appear on the balance sheet, not on the income statement.

11. (c,81) Revenues increase equity and expenses decrease it. Those accounts, then, can be thought of as subdivisions of owners' equity.

12. (c,70) Only response c is a proper statement. Response d is nonsense because if the trial balance doesn't balance, the error must be found.

13. (d,73) Debits are used to increase assets. The correct answer, therefore, will involve a credit.

14. (c,91) The statement in this question is a straightforward description of accrual basis accounting.

15. (b,89) Under the accrual basis of accounting, revenues are recognized when earned and expenses are recognized when incurred.

16. (c,55) Accrual accounting is **not** optional but is required by GAAP. The definitions of revenue and expense require that they be recognized when they occur rather than waiting until the related cash changes hands. To recognize revenues and expenses only when the cash is received or disbursed would be to use "cash basis" accounting.

17. (c,43) To solve this problem you must work backwards from 12/31/19B to 1/1/19A. In other words, start with ending Retained Earnings ($10) and then **subtract** cumulative net income ($9) and **add** cumulative dividends ($6). $10 - $9 + $6 = $7.

18. (c,74) The complete entry would be: debit cash $5,000, debit accounts receivable $1,500; credit service revenue $6,500.

19. (d,76) Responses a and c do not involve expenses at all. Response b involves an expense that has been previously recognized. Only response d involves an event in which an expense should be recognized in the current period.

20. (d,32) Net income for 19A is $7 of which $6 was paid out in dividends leaving retained earnings of $1. During 19B, net income was $18 of which $12 was paid out in dividends. This left $6 to be added to the previous $1 balance in retained earnings for a total of $7 at year-end 19B.

21. (a,71) The error described in this question is that a liability account was increased when an asset account should have been decreased. As a result, both liabilities and assets will be overstated. Given the possible answers listed, only response a can be correct. Stockholders' equity was not affected.

22. (a,55) The question asks only about the **interest** on the note, not the note itself. An expense is recognized and cash is disbursed.

23. (d,43) The purchase of equipment for cash leaves total assets the same. In selections b and c, an asset (cash) is being used to pay off a liability (Accounts Payable and Dividends Payable).

24. (b,81) The journal entry to record the sale of stock is: dr. Cash, cr. Capital Stock. Since capital stock is an equity account, and credit entries increase equity accounts, owners' equity has been increased.

25. (e,63) Revenue is recognized when the sales transaction takes place. Therefore, for 19X3, revenue that should be recognized is $350,000 (cash sales + credit sales). Whether the cash has been collected or not does not affect whether revenue has been earned.

26. (d,74) At the date of the transaction, no record of interest expense should be made since no interest expense has yet been incurred. Company A (the borrower) would credit Notes Payable, **not** Notes Receivable.

27. (c,91) Assets (such as cash) are increased with debits and equity accounts (such as capital stock) are increased with credits.

28. (a,61) The Prepaid Insurance account is an asset account while the Insurance Expense account is an expense account. Both types of accounts are increased with debits and (except in very rare circumstances) have debit balances.

29. (c,95) This transaction should be recorded with a debit to Cash (for 1/3 of $180,000); a debit to Accounts Receivable (for 2/3 of $180,000) and a credit to Fee Revenue for the total of $180,000.

30. (e,49) This problem describes a transaction that has already been partially recorded using a credit (a liability account was increased). To complete the entry, a debit is needed. Of the options given, only the increase of a contra account to equity would require a debit.

31. (b,68) Depreciation expense is recorded with a debit to Depreciation Expense and a credit to Accumulated Depreciation. The specific asset account (Building in this problem) is **not** credited.

CHAPTER THREE: THE ACCOUNTING INFORMATION PROCESSING CYCLE

1. Financial statements are designed to meet the needs of:
   a. investors.
   b. managers.
   c. employees.
   d. a wide range of decision makers.

2. Journal entries are customarily listed in:
   a. chronological order.
   b. numerical order.
   c. financial statement order.
   d. account number order.

3. A trial balance:
   a. guarantees that all transactions were accounted for correctly.
   b. provides a check on the equality of debits and credits.
   c. is usually prepared before the ledger is posted.
   d. is prepared before transactions are entered into the journal.

4. Which of the following statements is **false**?
   a. The trial balance is usually prepared from the journal.
   b. The ledger is the book of final entry.
   c. Financial statements can be prepared from the trial balance.
   d. Posting involves the transfer of entries from the journal to ledger.

5. The term "posting" is best defined as:
   a. the recording of business transactions in the journal.
   b. the process of transferring the debits and credits from the journal to the proper ledger accounts.
   c. the adding of the debit and credit columns on a worksheet.
   d. using the chart of account numbers when recording business transactions in the journal.

6. A trial balance in which total debits equal total credits proves:
   a. that the posting from the ledger to the trial balance was done correctly.
   b. that the recording of all transactions in the journal was done correctly.
   c. the equality of debits and credits.
   d. that no transaction was omitted from the accounting records.

7. Upon comparison of the 19X1 and 19X2 balance sheets for the Winston Company it was found that total assets increased in 19X2 by $40,000 and total liabilities increased by $55,000. Assuming that no additional capital stock was sold and no dividends were paid during 19X2, the income statement should show:
   a. net income of $40,000.
   b. net income of $15,000.
   c. net loss of $15,000.
   d. net loss of $55,000.

8. Collectively, all the accounts of a company are contained in a record known as a:
   a. ledger.
   b. journal.
   c. financial statement.
   d. worksheet.

9. Which of the following errors would cause the totals of a trial balance to be out of balance?
   a. A collection of a $500 account receivable journalized by a debit of $500 to Accounts Receivable and a credit of $500 to Cash.
   b. A collection of a $500 account receivable journalized by a debit of $50 to Cash and a credit of $50 to Accounts Receivable.
   c. A payment of a $329 account payable journalized by a debit of $239 to Accounts Payable and a credit of $239 to Notes Payable.
   d. none of the above

10. Journalizing consists of:
    a. entering debits and credits in the appropriate ledger accounts.
    b. recording the economic effects of a transaction in chronological order.
    c. analyzing a transaction to determine its effect on assets and liabilities.
    d. listing account balances to show debits and credits are equal.

11. Preparation of the trial balance would be likely to detect which of the following errors?
    a. Recording the collection of an account receivable by crediting Cash and debiting Accounts Receivable.
    b. Failing to record an accrued expense at year end.
    c. Recording the same transaction twice.
    d. Recording the payment of a $54 liability by crediting Cash $45 and debiting Accounts Payable $45.
    e. None of these errors are likely to be detected by preparing a trial balance.

12. The Journal is useful because it:
    a. provides a listing of each transaction in account order sequence.
    b. provides financial data in a convenient form for preparing financial statements.
    c. is a handy storage area for the source documents.
    d. provides a single place to record the dual economic effects of each transaction.

13. The accounting record where complete transactions are listed in chronological order is called the:
    a. journal
    b. ledger
    c. worksheet
    d. balance sheet
    e. trial balance

14. The purchase of a building for cash:
    a. increases current assets.
    b. increases operational assets.
    c. increases total assets.
    d. decreases total assets.

15. Which of the following phases of the accounting cycle occurs after preparation of the trial balance?
    a. recording of transactions in the book of original entry
    b. preparation of the financial statements
    c. determination of the economic effect of each transaction on the entity
    d. posting of journal entries to the appropriate ledger accounts

16. The Byrd Company purchased a truck for $10,000 on July 1, 19A. The truck has a four year life and no residual value. The depreciation expense for **19B** is what amount (if the straight-line method is used)?
    a. $1,250.
    b. $2,500.
    c. $3,750.
    d. $5,000.

17. On July 1, 19A, Bosco Company purchased equipment for $1,000. It is expected to last for five years. At **December 31, 19D,** the book value (or carrying value) will be:
    a. $750.
    b. $700.
    c. $500.
    d. $300.
    e. $250.

18. Which of the following statements regarding extraordinary items is **not** true?
    a. Extraordinary items are included as part of income from operations.
    b. Extraordinary items are unusual in nature.
    c. Extraordinary items are infrequent in nature.
    d. Extraordinary items are shown net of income tax effects.

19. Information on the financial statements is subclassified in order to:
    a. increase the length of financial statements.
    b. serve the needs of a specific group of users.
    c. enhance the understandability and usefulness of data.
    d. aggregate the data.

20. The financial statements of Alquist Co. contain the following selected accounts.

Capital Stock	$300
Inventories	50
Accounts Payable	150
Automobiles & Trucks	500
Cash	250
Patents	100
Long-Term Liabilities	200
Retained Earnings	250

Working capital amounts to:
a. $300.
b. $200.
c. $150.
d. $100.

21. Calculate total current assets from the following amounts.

Short-term liabilities	$10
Inventory	15
Long-term liabilities	20
Store equipment	30
Cash	5
Accumulated Depreciation	5
Short-term savings account	20
Notes Receivable, short-term	5

a. $15
b. $30
c. $40
d. $45

22. A corporation with 1,000 shares of capital stock outstanding had net income of $3,500 after an extraordinary item of $9,000 (net of tax). How would earnings per share appear on the income statement?

	Income Before *Extraordinary Item*	*Net Income*
a.	$ 3.50	$9.00
b.	$ 9.00	$3.50
c.	$12.50	$9.00
d.	$12.50	$3.50

23. Current assets:
a. **must** be consumed or realized in cash within one year.
b. are arranged on the balance sheet in order of decreasing liquidity.
c. are similar to operational assets in that they have fairly long lives.
d. include both short-term and long-term amounts.

24. The two major subclassifications usually found in the stockholders' equity section of the balance sheet are:
a. Contributed Capital and Retained Earnings.
b. Retained Earnings and Dividends Paid.
c. Contributed Capital and Dividends Paid.
d. Dividends Paid and Net Income.
e. Dividends Received and Dividends Paid.

25. The average time period between the purchase of merchandise and the conversion of this merchandise back into cash is called the:
a. span of control.
b. operating cycle.
c. working capital conversion period.
d. fiscal year.

26. Poli Company carried a vacant lot on its books at its cost of $40,000. Recently, the land was condemned by the state government because of a planned freeway. Poli received $60,000 as full payment from the state. Assume this event is properly classified as an extraordinary item, and that Poli's average tax rate is 30%. What is the after-tax amount of this extraordinary gain?
a. $26,000
b. $20,000
c. $14,000
d. $ 6,000
e. zero

27. Minnesota Company owns a patent with a 7 year remaining life. It should be classified on the balance sheet as a(n):
a. intangible asset.
b. deferred charge.
c. operational asset.
d. prepaid expense.

28. The Lynn Corp. purchased a delivery van on July 1, 19A for $4,500. The van has a four year life and a $500 residual value. The book value at **December 31, 19B** is: (assume straight-line method)
    a. $ 500.
    b. $1,500.
    c. $3,000.
    d. $4,000.
    e. $2,500.

29. In order for a gain or loss to be properly classified as **extraordinary**, it must be:
    a. unusual in nature.
    b. infrequent in occurrence.
    c. unusual and infrequent.
    d. unusual, infrequent, and deferred.

30. The operating cycle is:
    a. always less than one year.
    b. often used for differentiating between intangible and fixed assets.
    c. defined as being one year in length.
    d. sometimes less than a year and sometimes longer than a year.

31. Gross margin on sales is computed as:
    a. net income divided by net sales.
    b. net sales minus operating expenses.
    c. net sales minus cost of goods sold.
    d. net sales minus net income.

32. Which of the following tests must be met before a special event or transaction can be classified on the income statement as an extraordinary item?

	Unusual in Nature	Infrequent in Occurence
a.	Yes	Yes
b.	Yes	No
c.	No	Yes
d.	No	No

33. Which of the following is **not** true about the accounting cycle?
    a. The first step in the cycle is to collect raw data.
    b. Transaction analysis determines the economic effect of an event on assets, liabilities, and equity.
    c. The trial balance provides a check on the equality of debits and credits at a particular point in time.
    d. The ledger is the book of original entry.

CHAPTER THREE:
ANNOTATED SOLUTIONS

1. d	6. c	11. e	16. b	21. d	26. c	31. c
2. a	7. c	12. d	17. d	22. d	27. a	32. a
3. b	8. a	13. a	18. a	23. b	28. c	33. d
4. a	9. d	14. b	19. c	24. a	29. c	
5. b	10. b	15. b	20. c	25. b	30. d	

> *The correct answer and the percentage of students answering the question correctly (when it was used on an introductory accounting examination) are shown in parentheses at the beginning of each annotated solution that follows.*

1. (d,51) Accountants prepare what are called "general purpose" financial statements. That is, they are designed to meet the needs of a wide range of users.

2. (a,84) It is an important requirement to record the economic data of each transaction as the economic events occur (chronologically).

3. (b,95) Per the accounting cycle, responses c and d are incorrect. Although a trial balance does provide a check on the equality of the debits and credits, it does not guarantee that all transactions are accounted for; or accounted for correctly.

4. (a,35) The trial balance is prepared from data in the ledger. Per the accounting cycle, responses b, c, and d are true.

5. (b,86) This question is a straightforward definition of the term "posting." Responses a, c, and d are all procedures performed in the accounting cycle, but they have nothing to do with posting.

6. (c,56) The equality of the debits and credits is the only proven item. It is still possible that a transaction was recorded or posted incorrectly or omitted altogether.

7. (c,47) Assets = Liabilities + Owners' Equity. The income statement should show a net loss of $15,000 which corresponds to the decrease in owners' equity of $15,000. Therefore, Assets (+$40,000) = Liabilities (+$55,000) + Owners' Equity (-$15,000).

8. (a,64) By definition.

9. (d,58) For responses a, b, and c, the individual accounts on the trial balance would have incorrect amounts, but the trial balance itself would still balance. Total debits would equal total credits.

10. (b,83) This is a straightforward description of journalizing. Response a describes posting; c must be done **before** journalizing, and d describes a trial balance.

11. (e,62) Typically, the only errors that will be detected by preparing a trial balance are those in which the amount of the debit entry is different than the amount of the credit entry (i.e. where debits don't equal credits). In response a, it is the accounts that are in error, not the amounts. In response b, no entry was made at all. In response c, debits still equal credits; and in response d, the amount is wrong but the debit still equals the credit.

12. (d,58) Response d is a good description of the journal. The other responses are nonsense.

13. (a,87) By definition.

14. (b,74) Operational assets are increased, current assets (cash) are decreased, and total assets remain the same.

15. (b,51) Response b is the best answer because **all** financial statements are prepared **after** the trial balance. Response d is partially correct, though, in that adjusting journal entries and closing journal entries are posted after the trial balance is prepared. Routine journal entries, however, are posted before a trial balance is prepared so this cannot be the best answer.

16. (b,74) Since there is no residual value, merely divide the $10,000 cost by the 4 year life and obtain a $2,500 annual depreciation expense. (Note that the question requires depreciation expense for 19B and not for 19A. 19A's depreciation would be for only 1/2 a year since the asset was purchased at midyear.)

17. (d,58) Book value = original cost - accumulated depreciation. With an expected life of five years, the annual depreciation expense would be $200. Accumulated depreciation, then, after 3 1/2 years would be $700 ($200 x 3 1/2 = $700). Original cost ($1,000) minus accumulated depreciation ($700) = $300.

18. (a,79) By definition, extraordinary items must be both unusual and infrequent. They are reported separately on the income statement net of income tax effects. Response "a," therefore, is false.

19. (c,83) Response c yields the only responsible rationale for subclassifications on financial statements. There is no need to try to increase the length of financial statements as they are often long and complicated as is. Accountants prepare general purpose financial statements instead of ones for specific groups. To subclassify information is to **disaggregate** the data.

20. (c,75) Working capital = current assets (cash $250 + inventories $50) minus current liabilities (accounts payable $150) = $150.

21. (d,54) The following are current assets: cash ($5), short-term savings account ($20), inventory ($15), and short-term notes receivable ($5), for a total of $45.

22. (d,67) Net income after the extraordinary item (EI) is the same as net income (NI). Therefore, NI per share is $3,500/1000 shares = $3.50. If NI **after** a $9,000 extraordinary item is $3,500, the EI must have been a loss. This means that NI before the EI must have been $12,500. (Alternatively, of course, NI before EI could have been a negative $5,500 and the EI a gain of $9,000. The related EPS for this situation, however, was not offered as a possible answer.)

23. (b,58) Responses c and d are nonsensical since they include items that are noncurrent. Response a is very close to being correct but is not true if the operating cycle is longer than one year. Current assets are customarily arranged in order of decreasing liquidity.

24. (a,78) The Dividends Paid account is closed (during the closing process) to Retained Earnings and does not appear in Owners' Equity on the balance sheet or in any other financial statement. This makes all responses except the first one incorrect. Further, net income does not appear on the balance sheet but on the income statement.

25. (b,74) The statement in this question is a straightforward description of the operating cycle.

26. (c,78) The pre-tax gain of $20,000 ($60,000 cost - $40,000 received) will be taxed at 30% resulting in $6,000 of taxes to be paid. The $20,000 gain minus the $6,000 tax obligation yields a $14,000 after-tax gain.

27. (a,71) Assets without physical substance and having a long-term life are classified as intangible assets. Many such assets result from a grant of rights by government (e.g. copyrights and patents).

28. (c,58) The depreciation expense is $1,000 per year. One and one-half years have passed so Accumulated Depreciation = $1,500. Cost ($4,500) - Accumulated Depreciation ($1,500) = Book Value ($3,000).

29. (c,65) According to APB #30, an item of gain or loss must be **both** unusual and infrequent to be classified as an extraordinary item.

30. (d,57) The operating cycle is the period of time between expenditure of cash to acquire inventory and the receipt of cash from selling that inventory. For most businesses, the operating cycle is much shorter than one year. For other businesses, however, the operating cycle may be many years in length (e.g. a distiller of whiskey)

31. (c,79) By definition, net sales minus cost of goods sold equals gross margin.

32. (a,95) By definition, an extraordinary item must be **both** unusual in nature and infrequent in occurence.

33. (d,78) The best answer here is response d since it is the journal (not ledger) which is the book of original entry. (One might argue that response b is also false since transaction analysis might also involve evaluating the effect(s) on revenue or expense. Technically, however, revenues and expenses increase and decrease equity, so response b is actually a correct statement.)

CHAPTER FOUR: CONCEPTUAL FRAMEWORK OF ACCOUNTING AND ADJUSTING ENTRIES

PART A: Conceptual Framework of Accounting

1. The **qualitative characteristic of reliability** holds that:
   a. financial statement information must be unbiased, accurate, and verifiable.
   b. estimates must never be used in revenue recognition.
   c. all expenses incurred in earning revenues should be identified, or matched with the revenues earned during the period.
   d. a proper "cutoff" of revenues and expenses must be accomplished each accounting period.

2. Which of the following is **not** a qualitative characteristic of financial information as discussed in your text?
   a. comparability
   b. relevance
   c. completeness
   d. reliability

3. Costs incurred in generating revenue must be expensed in the same accounting period in which the related revenue is realized. This is an example of which fundamental accounting principle?
   a. cost principle
   b. revenue principle
   c. continuity principle
   d. matching principle

4. In the determination of income it is important to identify all of the expenses associated with the revenue earned. Which basic principle of accounting deals with this issue?
   a. matching
   b. consistency
   c. revenue
   d. time-period

5. The cost principle of accounting:
   a. states that assets should be measured on the basis of the total cost incurred in acquisition.
   b. states that a society's monetary unit is to be used as the measurement device.
   c. requires that financial data be reported for relatively short periods of time; months, quarters, years.
   d. requires precise definition of the specific entity for which monetary or financial data are to be collected.

6. The accounting principle or assumption that divides the life of the entity into periods of equal length for reporting purposes is the:
   a. entity principle.
   b. time-period assumption.
   c. matching principle.
   d. unit-of-measure assumption.

7. The matching principle focuses on:
   a. assets and liabilities.
   b. revenue and expenses.
   c. assets and expenses.
   d. revenue and liabilities.

8. The time-period assumption:
   a. requires the selection of annual or monthly cut-off dates, but not both.
   b. effects the income statement but not the balance sheet.
   c. divides the life of a business into short time spans.
   d. establishes the balance sheet as covering a specific period of time.

9. The underlying principle that makes adjusting entries necessary is the:
   a. matching principle.
   b. objectivity principle.
   c. cost principle.
   d. consistency principle.

10. The matching principle means that:
    a. expenses are recorded in the same period as the revenues to which they are related.
    b. debits are matched with credits in each journal entry so that the entry balances.
    c. debits equal credits.
    d. liabilities are matched against the assets that will be used to liquidate them.

11. Under the revenue principle, revenue is realized when:
    a. cash is received for future services.
    b. the expense in generating the revenue has been paid.
    c. services are rendered or ownership to goods sold is transferred.
    d. cash is received for past services.

12. An accrued expense is an expense that has been:
    a. paid at the end of the period but not yet incurred.
    b. incurred but not paid at the end of the period.
    c. incurred and paid at the end of the period.
    d. capitalized by the end of the period.

13. The failure to record an accrued revenue will have what effects on the following classifications?

	Revenue	Assets	Liabilities
a.	Understate	Understate	None
b.	Understate	None	Understate
c.	Overstate	Overstate	None
d.	Overstate	None	Overstate

14. On June 1, 19X2, a three-year insurance policy was purchased and Prepaid Insurance was debited for the entire amount. The insurance policy expires on **June 1, 19X5.** An adjusting entry on December 31, 19X2 will apportion the amount between the:
    a. future periods only.
    b. past and current period.
    c. current and future periods.
    d. past, current and future periods.

15. The accrual of revenues will:
    a. increase liabilities.
    b. increase cash.
    c. increase owners' equity and assets.
    d. decrease assets.

16. Adjusting entries are made in order to satisfy the:
    a. consistency principle.
    b. objectivity principle.
    c. matching principle.
    d. materiality principle.
    e. adjustment principle.

17. Rentall Corp. made the following adjusting entries on 12-31-19A.

    Entry #1: Rent Revenue   XXX
                  Rent Collected in Advance   XXX

    Entry #2: Wages Expense   XXX
                  Wages Payable   XXX

    These entries are necessary because which of the following exist?

	Entry #1	Entry #2
a.	accrued revenue	deferred expense
b.	accrued revenue	accrued expense
c.	deferred revenue	deferred expense
d.	deferred revenue	accrued expense

18. On 1-1-19B the Ultra Safe Company paid $100 for a five year insurance policy. The company should report which of the following sets of account balances on its **December 31, 19D** financial statements?

	Balance Sheet	Income Statement
a.	Prepaid Insurance $100;	Insurance Expense $100
b.	Prepaid Insurance $ 60;	Insurance Expense $ 20
c.	Prepaid Insurance $ 40;	Insurance Expense $ 20
d.	Prepaid Insurance $ 40;	Insurance Expense $ 60

19. Unearned revenue is:
    a. unrecorded and uncollected.
    b. unrecorded and collected.
    c. recorded and uncollected.
    d. recorded and collected.

20. Which of the following transactions would **not** require an adjusting entry at the end of the accounting period (December 31, 19C) which is a Tuesday?
    a. The company borrowed $10,000 from the bank on June 1, 19C. Interest and principal on this note are due June 1, 19D.
    b. The company pays it employees every Friday for wages earned since the previous Friday.
    c. The company purchased a one-year insurance policy on January 1, 19C and debited Prepaid Insurance.
    d. The company paid two months rent in advance on November 1, 19C and debited Rent Expense.

PART B: Adjusting Entries Illustrated

21. On August 1, 19A, Slum Lord Apartments received $2,400 for 6 months advance rent from one of the tenants. If the $2,400 was journalized as revenue when received, the year-end adjusting entry for this transaction would be:
    a. Rent Revenue   400
           Rent Received in Advance   400
    b. Cash   400
           Rent Revenue   400
    c. Rent Rec'd in Advance   2,000
           Rent Revenue   2,000
    d. Rent Received in Advance 400
           Rent Revenue   400
    e. Cash   2,400
           Rent Revenue   2,400

22. How should rental fees collected one month in advance be reported in the financial statements?
    a. income statement--as revenue in the month collected
    b. balance sheet-- as a current liability
    c. balance sheet--as a separate item in stockholders' equity
    d. income statement--as an expense

23. On September 1, 19X6, Ray Company received $4,200 in advance from a tenant for 10 months rent. At that time, Ray Co. credited Deferred Revenue for the entire $4,200. The necessary adjusting entry at December 31, 19X6 would be:
    a. dr. Deferred Revenue $1,680; cr. Rent Revenue $1,680.
    b. dr. Rent Revenue $2,000; cr. Deferred Revenue $2,000.
    c. dr. Deferred Revenue $2,520; cr. Rent Revenue $2,250.
    d. dr. Cash $1,680; cr. Deferred Revenue $1,680.

24. Chappy Company requires its customers to pay for their orders one month before it will be shipped to them. Chappy should credit what account to record receipt of the advanced payment?
    a. an accrual
    b. an asset
    c. a liability
    d. retained earnings

25. On December 31, 19A, ABC collected $1,200 rent in advance from a tenant. This amount was to cover rent for all of 19B. At December 31, 19A, ABC properly recorded this transaction. At the end of **19B**, which of the following adjusting entries is be necessary? (Assume reversing entries are **not** used.)
    a. debit Cash and credit Rent Revenue
    b. debit Rent Revenue and credit Rent Collected in Advance
    c. debit Rent Expense and credit Cash
    d. debit Rent Collected in Advance and credit Rent Revenue

26. On March 31, 19A, Highly Bizarre Company purchased a one-year insurance policy for $1,200 and recorded it with a debit to Prepaid Insurance. The adjusting entry at December 31, 19A would include a:
    a. debit to Insurance Expense of $1,000.
    b. credit to Prepaid Insurance of $900.
    c. debit to Insurance Expense of $300.
    d. credit to Prepaid Insurance of $300.

27. Floorspace, Inc. collected one year of rent in advance on August 1, 19A. The entry made at that date was:

Cash $24,000
    Rent Collected in Advance $24,000

At year end (12-31-19A), what adjusting entry should be made?

	Rent Collected in Advance	*Rent Revenue*
a.	debit $10,000	credit $10,000
b.	debit $14,000	credit $14,000
c.	credit $10,000	debit $10,000
d.	credit $14,000	debit $14,000

28. Kane Company rents out apartments for $300 per month. A tenant paid $900 on June 1, 19C and Kane Company recorded the receipt with a $900 debit to Cash, a credit to Rent Revenue of $300 and a credit to Rent Received in Advance of $600. On June 30, 19C (the end of Kane's accounting period), Kane Company should prepare:
  a. an adjusting entry debiting Rent Collected in Advance.
  b. an adjusting entry crediting Rent Revenue.
  c. an adjusting entry crediting Rent Collected in Advance.
  d. an adjusting entry debiting Rent Revenue.
  e. no adjusting entry.

29. Poor Tenant Company rented office space from the Rich Landlord Corporation on November 1, 19B. The rent was for six months and Poor Tenant made the following entry:

Rent Expense   600
    Cash   600

The adjusting entry on December 31, 19B should include a:
  a. debit to Rent Expense of $400.
  b. credit to Rent Expense of $200.
  c. debit to Prepaid Rent of $200.
  d. debit to Prepaid Rent of $400.
  e. credit to Prepaid Rent of $400.

30. On 8-1-19C, Bancorp invested $1,000 in a 12%, 6 month note receivable. The total amount of interest will be received by Bancorp on 1-31-19D. Which of the following statements is **true** assuming that Bancorp has a December 31 accounting year-end?
  a. No interest revenue should be recognized in 19C because the money will not be received until 19D.
  b. Interest revenue of $50 should be recognized in 19C.
  c. Interest revenue of $120 should be recognized at 12-31-19C through an adjusting entry.
  d. Interest revenue of $120 should be recognized at 8-1-19C since the amount is measurable and the collection date is fixed.

31. Given the following information, determine the appropriate adjusting entry at year-end 19C.

Beginning supplies inventory	$800
Supplies on hand 12/31/19C	$400
Purchase of supplies during 19C	$300

	Debit Supplies Expense	*Credit Supplies Inventory*
a.	$400	$400
b.	$1,100	$1,100
c.	$500	$500
d.	$700	$700

32. Company Z purchased machinery two years ago on January 1, for $6,600. It will be used for 3 years and sold for $600. To record depreciation in the current year, the adjusting entry is:
  a. Depreciation Expense   2,000
        Accumulated Depreciation   2,000
  b. Depreciation Expense   2,200
        Accumulated Depreciation   2,200
  c. Depreciation Expense   600
        Accumulated Depreciation   600
  d. Accumulated Depreciation 2,000
        Depreciation Expense   2,000
  e. Depreciation Expense   2,000
        Machinery   2,000

33. Determine the cash payments made for insurance premiums from the following information.

<u>Prepaid Insurance:</u>
Balance, beginning of the period $220
Balance, end of the period $195

Assume that $475 of insurance expired during the period and that all insurance premiums are paid in cash.
a. $475
b. $195
c. $695
d. $450

34. The Arson Company purchased a two-year fire insurance policy on July 1, 19C. The $5,000 policy was recorded with a debit to Prepaid Insurance. On June 30, 19D (end of the annual accounting period) what adjusting entry is required?

a. Prepaid Insurance   2,500
    Insurance Expense   2,500
b. Insurance Expense   2,500
    Prepaid Insurance   2,500
c. Insurance Expense   1,250
    Prepaid Insurance   1,250
d. Insurance Expense   2,500
    Cash   2,500

35. On January 1, 19C, Speedo Company purchased a company car. It got a terrific deal on the car, paying only $10,000 (while the market value was $30,000). The estimated useful life of the car is 5 years, with no salvage value. The depreciation expense on the car for 19C is:
a. $ 2,000.
b. $ 6,000.
c. $10,000.
d. $30,000.

36. Melanie Company recorded the purchase of a two-year insurance policy with a debit to Insurance Expense. The necessary adjusting entry at the end of the accounting period would include a:
a. debit to insurance expense.
b. credit to prepaid insurance.
c. debit to prepaid insurance.
d. credit to cash.

37. The records of Gizmo, Inc. show the following information for the most recent fiscal year.

Supplies Inventory, beg. balance $5,000
Supplies purchased during the year $17,500
Supplies Inventory, ending balance $4,900

What is the correct amount of Supplies Expense for the year?
a. $ 7,600
b. $17,400
c. $17,600
d. $27,400

38. The Risky Shift Company purchased a one-year insurance policy on July 1, 19A and made the following journal entry:

Insurance Expense   1,200
  Cash   1,200

A second one-year policy was purchased on September 1, 19A and recorded as follows:

Prepaid Insurance   600
  Cash   600

The adjusting entry on December 31, 19A should include a **net** debit or credit to Insurance Expense of:
a. $200 credit
b. $200 debit
c. $400 credit
d. $400 debit
e. $600 credit

39. At December 31, 19D, the Santiago Company made the following adjusting entry:

Prepaid Insurance   500
  Insurance Expense   500

Assume the purchase price of the insurance policy was $1,200 and that it was originally debited to Insurance Expense. If it is a one-year policy, on what date was the policy purchased?
a. January 1, 19D
b. June 1, 19D
c. August 1, 19D
d. August 31, 19D

40. On October 1, 19A, Rodriguez Inc. borrowed $10,000 from a local bank on a 12 month note at 15% interest. The principal plus interest is due October 1, 19B. What adjusting entry will Rodriguez need to make at December 31, 19A?

   a. Interest Expense   375
         Interest Payable   375

   b. Interest Expense   250
         Interest Payable   250

   c. Interest Payable   375
         Interest Expense   375

   d. Interest Payable   250
         Interest Expense   250

41. The Country Surfboard Company has four employees working 8 hours per day Monday through Friday shaping and glassing surfboards at $10 per hour. They receive their wages each Friday for that week's work. If the end of the accounting period occurs on a Wednesday, the adjusting entry to record accrued wages would include a:
   a. debit to wages expense of $320.
   b. credit to wages payable of $640.
   c. credit to wages expense of $960.
   d. credit to wages payable of $960.

42. On April 1, 19A, Baldwin Corporation borrowed $50,000 cash from a local bank on a one-year, 12% note. The following correct entry was made.

   Cash   50,000
     Note Payable   50,000

What adjusting entry, if any, would be necessary on December 31, 19A if the interest and principal are due April 1, 19B?
   a. dr. Interest Expense $1,500; cr. Interest Payable $1,500
   b. dr. Interest Expense $4,500; cr. Cash $4,500
   c. dr. Interest Expense $4,500; cr. Interest Payable $4,500
   d. No adjusting entry would be necessary.

43. An adjusting entry:
   a. always involves two income statement accounts.
   b. always involves two balance sheet accounts.
   c. always involves a balance sheet account and an income statement account.
   d. usually involves a balance sheet account and an income statement account, but could involve two income statement accounts.
   e. could involve two balance sheet accounts, two income statement accounts, or a balance sheet account and an income statement account.

44. Recording the same payment of a liability twice would have which one of the following effects?
   a. understatement of assets, liabilities, and owners' equity
   b. no effect on net income, owners' equity, and total assets
   c. understatement of total assets and total liabilities and no effect on net income and owners' equity
   d. some other combination of effects

45. If an adjusting entry is made which increases an asset account, which of the following statements is **true**?
   a. A revenue account must have increased.
   b. An expense account must have decreased.
   c. A liability account might have increased.
   d. A revenue account might have increased.

46. When Careless Company recorded its adjusting entries at year-end, it inadvertently omitted an entry to reduce a deferred expense. As a result:
   a. assets will be understated and expenses will be understated.
   b. assets will be overstated and income will be overstated.
   c. liabilities will be understated and expenses will be understated.
   d. liabilities will be understated and expenses will be overstated.

47. After preparing the unadjusted trial balance at year end, the Controller for Harry Hardtop Used Cars discovered the following additional information.

> (1) A 12%, $100 Note Payable was signed two months ago. Principal and interest are due one year from the date of the note. (The note had been properly recorded when signed, but no interest has been recognized to date.)

> (2) Service revenues collected and recorded as revenue during the period included $20 collected for services to be performed in the **next** accounting period.

The adjustments required by the above information will have what effect, if any, on the following?

	Assets	*Liabilities*	*Net Income*
a.	up $100	up $122	down $ 22
b.	no change	up $ 18	down $ 18
c.	no change	up $ 2	down $ 2
d.	no change	up $ 22	down $ 22

48. Failure to record an accrued expense at year end will cause:
    a. assets to be overstated.
    b. liabilities to be understated.
    c. assets to be understated.
    d. owners' equity to be understated.
    e. the balance sheet not to balance.

49. On December 31, 19A, the balance sheet of Tree Top Airlines indicated a balance in the Prepaid Insurance account of $5,000. During 19B, Tree Top purchased an additional $2,500 of insurance. If the proper balance in the Prepaid Insurance account on December 31, 19B is $3,500, what is Tree Top's insurance expense for 19A?
    a. $7,500
    b. $5,000
    c. $4,000
    d. $2,500

CHAPTER FOUR: ANNOTATED SOLUTIONS

1. a	8. c	15. c	22. b	29. d	36. c	43. c
2. c	9. a	16. c	23. a	30. b	37. c	44. c
3. d	10. a	17. d	24. c	31. a,d	38. c	45. d
4. a	11. c	18. c	25. d	32. a	39. b	46. b
5. a	12. b	19. d	26. b	33. d	40. a	47. d
6. b	13. a	20. d	27. a	34. b	41. d	48. b
7. b	14. c	21. a	28. e	35. a	42. c	49. c

> *The correct answer and the percentage of students answering the question correctly (when it was used on an introductory accounting examination) are shown in parentheses at the beginning of each annotated solution that follows.*

1. (a,89) By definition.

2. (c,29) Responses a,b, and d are qualitative characteristics discussed in the text. While completeness may be desirable, financial statements cannot be expected to include **all** possible information.

3. (d,79) By definition of the matching principle.

4. (a,71) This is a straightforward description of the matching principle at work.

5. (a,80) Response a is a straightforward definition of the cost principle. Response b describes the unit-of-measure assumption, c describes the time-period assumption, and d has to do with the entity principle.

6. (b,72) By definition.

7. (b,85) Since the matching principle requires that the expenses of a period be matched against the related revenues of the period, only response b can be correct.

8. (c,51) The time-period assumption is that the life of the business entity can be divided up into short timespans. Because of a desire to have information about enterprise activities over relatively short periods (i.e. one year or less), adjusting entries become necessary when an event spans more than one period.

9. (a,91) It is the desire to match revenues with their related expenses which causes the need for period-end adjustments.

10. (a,79) Under the matching principle, the revenues of a period are first determined and then the expenses incurred in generating those revenues are matched against them on the income statement.

11. (c,79) The revenue principle states that revenue should be recognized when it is earned. Revenue is considered to be earned when the goods involved are sold or when the services involved are rendered.

12. (b,73) An accrued expense arises when either goods or services have been consumed but (as of the end of the period) have not been given accounting recognition in the books or paid for.

13. (a,66) Revenue is accrued with a debit to Accounts Receivable and a credit to Revenue. Failure to do so makes both accounts too small.

14. (c,45) According to the matching principle, expenses paid in advance of the use of the services or goods must be deferred to the periods in which such services or goods will be used. At 12/31/X2, part of the insurance policy has been used up and part is carried forward to be used in future periods.

15. (c,59) The adjusting entry that accrues a revenue is recorded by a debit to a receivable (asset) and a credit to revenue (an equity account).

16. (c,84) Adjusting entries are used to get the proper amount of revenue and expense recognized in the proper accounting period. This is part of the matching process where revenues are first identified with a period and then the related expenses are recognized.

17. (d,62) In entry #1, a revenue is being reduced and a liability established. This means revenue is being deferred to a later period. In entry #2, an expense is being recognized (accrued) and a liability is being set up.

18. (c,31) A five-year policy was purchased for $100 ($20 per year). Be sure to note that from 1-1-19B until 12-31-19D is **three** years. The balance sheet, then, should show two years insurance remaining ($40) while the income statement should show one year of expense ($20).

19. (d,52) "Unearned Revenue" has been collected in advance and recorded as a liability.

20. (d,44) Responses a, b, and c would all need adjusting entries as of the last day of the period. The situation in response d, however, does not need any adjusting entry since the entire amount paid in advance will have become expense by the end of December (i.e. two months of rental services will have been consumed by then).

21. (a,50) One month's rent is yet to be earned. Therefore, $400 (1/6 of $2,400) must be removed from the Rent Revenue account and credited to Rent Received in Advance.

22. (b,74) Since they have been collected in advance of being earned, the landlord has a liability to the tenant. Liabilities are reported on the balance sheet.

23. (a,70) On December 31, 19X6, 4/10 of the revenue (4 months out of 10) has been earned. Therefore, a debit to Deferred Revenue and a credit to Rent Revenue for $1,680 (4/10 of $4,200) is required.

24. (c,75) Chappy Company has a liability (obligation) since they must either ship goods in the future or refund their customer's money.

25. (d,60) At December 31, 19A the $1,200 should have been credited to Rent Collected in Advance (a liability account) since none of it is earned in 19A. By the end of 19B, the $1,200 has been earned and must be transferred from the liability account to Rent Revenue.

26. (b,91) The monthly insurance cost is $100. At December 31, 19A, nine months of insurance must be debited to insurance expense and removed from the prepaid insurance account.

27. (a,61) Upon collection, all $24,000 was credited to a liability account. At year end, the portion that has been earned must be removed from the liability account and credited to the Rent Revenue account. Response a does this.

28. (e,54) When Kane Company received the rent money in advance, Rent Revenue was credited with one month's rent and two month's rent was credited to a liability account. One month later (the end of the period) one month of revenue has been earned and two months remain unearned. The related accounts are already properly stated and no adjusting entry is needed.

29. (d,55) When paid, the entire $600 was debited to expense. At year end, only $200 ($100 per month) has been used up. The other $400 must be removed from Rent Expense and debited to Prepaid Rent.

30. (b,26) Interest is accruing on this note at the rate of $10 per month ($1,000 x 12% = $120 per year/12 months = $10 per month). From 8-1-19C to 12-31-19C is five months. Hence, $50 of revenue should be recognized for 19C.

31. (a or d,70) If the purchase of supplies during 19C was originally debited to expense, response a is correct. If the supplies were originally debited to an asset account, response d is correct.

32. (a,80) Annual depreciation expense is computed as "cost - residual value/estimated life (or $6,600 - $600/3 years = $2,000). The related adjusting journal entry is always a debit to Depreciation Expense and a credit to Accumulated Depreciation.

33. (d,43) The balance in prepaid insurance decreased during the year (from $220 to $195...a decrease of $25). This means that the amount of insurance used up ($475) was $25 more than the amount of new insurance coverage that that was purchased during the year. $475 - $25 = $450.

34. (b,83) By June 30, 19D, one-half of the insurance policy ($2,500) has been used up and must be removed from the Prepaid Insurance account (with a credit) and debited to Insurance Expense.

35. (a,85) The cost principle mandates that the car would be recorded in the books at the amount paid for it and that depreciation would be computed on that amount also. The annual depreciation expense would be computed as "cost - residual value/life" or $10,000/5 years = $2,000.

36. (c,59) If the entire amount of an insurance policy is debited to expense at the time of purchase, the unexpired amount (as of the end of the year) must be removed from the expense account and set up in an asset account. The necessary adjusting entry would be to debit Prepaid Insurance and credit Insurance Expense.

37. (c,82) The supplies inventory account decreased by $100 during the year. This means that all supplies purchased during the year ($17,500) were used up plus another $100 from the beginning inventory was used.

38. (c,32) Insurance expense for the year is $800; composed of $600 for the first policy (1/2 year x $1,200/year) and $200 for the second policy (1/3 year x $600/year). Since the current balance in Insurance Expense is $1,200, a $400 credit is necessary.

39. (b,23) The balance in Insurance Expense is $700 ($1,200 - $500) and this expense correlates to the amount of time that has passed. Therefore, $700/$1,200 x 12 months = 7 months. The date of June 1 is 7 months from the year end.

40. (a,65) Rodriguez must debit interest expense and credit interest payable for $375 ($10,000 x 15% x 1/4 year).

41. (d,38) As of the end of the period (Wednesday) the employees are each owed $10 per hour for 8 hours for 3 days. $10 x 8 hours x 3 days x 4 employees = $960. The entry to accrue this is a debit to Wages Expense and a credit to Wages Payable.

42. (c,63) Interest expense must be debited and interest payable must be credited for nine months interest ($50,000 x 12% x 9/12 = $4,500). Note that no cash is due to be paid until April 1, 19B.

43. (c,36) Adjusting entries are used to accrue and defer revenues and expenses. In each case there is a balance sheet account affected and an income statement account affected. (This question presumes that entries made to correct errors are not properly called "adjusting entries." They might be called "correcting entries" instead.)

44. (c,28) When a liability is paid, an asset is decreased as well as a liability. Recording this event twice, then, would result in both being understated. Income and owners' equity are not affected since expense or revenue accounts are not involved.

45. (d,35) An entry that increases an asset requires a debit to do so; therefore, the other part of the entry must involve a credit. All four possible answers involve credits, but neither response a nor response b can be correct because they contain the word **must**. Response c cannot be correct since the entry would then include two balance sheet accounts and no income statement account. Response d is the only possible answer.

46. (b,47) Deferred expense accounts are asset accounts such as Prepaid Insurance or Prepaid Rent. If one was not properly reduced at year-end the result would be that the asset was overstated and the related expense account (insurance expense or rent expense) would be understated. This would cause net income to be overstated.

47. (d,59) Adjustment #1 would debit interest expense and credit interest payable (a liability) for $2. Adjustment #2 would debit service revenue and credit revenue received in advance (a liability) for $20. The total increase in liabilities, then, is $22. Net income is decreased by the $20 reduction in a revenue account and the $2 increase in an expense account. Assets are not affected.

48. (b,41) An accrued expense is recorded by debiting an expense account and crediting a liability account. When this is not done, liabilities (and expenses) are understated.

49. (c,90) The beginning balance was $5,000 and an additional $2,500 was purchased during the year making $7,500 of insurance coverage available. If $3,500 is still unused at year-end, $4,000 must have been consumed ($7,500 - $4,000 = $3,500).

CHAPTER FIVE: INFORMATION PROCESSING IN AN ACCOUNTING SYSTEM

1. Listed below are six different phases of the information processing cycle at the end of the accounting period.

   1. Prepare financial statements
   2. Close temporary accounts
   3. Prepare a post-closing trial balance
   4. Prepare a worksheet.
   5. Record adjusting entries

   Which one of the following sequences of the end-of-period process is correct?
   a. 5,4,2,1,3
   b. 4,5,2,1,3
   c. 4,1,2,5,3
   d. 5,2,1,4,3
   e. 4,1,5,2,3

2. Which of the following shows selected phases of the accounting cycle in the correct chronological order?
   a. data collection, closing entries, preparation of financial statements
   b. posting, journalizing, worksheet preparation
   c. transaction analysis, preparation of financial statements, journalizing adjusting entries
   d. preparation of worksheet, transaction analysis, closing entries

3. The closing process has which of the following objectives?
   a. To reverse out the effects of certain adjusting entries made at the end of the previous period.
   b. To establish a zero balance in the revenue and expense accounts to start the new accounting period.
   c. To transfer net income (or loss) to retained earnings.
   d. Both a and b above
   e. Both b and c above

4. Following are selected elements of the accounting cycle.

   A. Worksheet
   B. Journalize Adjusting Entries
   C. Journalizing
   D. Financial Statements
   E. Posting to Accounts
   F. Journalize Closing Entries

   What is the most appropriate order of these steps?
   a. C E B F D A
   b. E C A B F D
   c. C E A D B F
   d. C D B E A F
   e. C E A B D F

5. Which one of the following is **not** found on the end-of-period worksheet?
   a. adjusting entry information
   b. unadjusted trial balance
   c. financial statement information
   d. information for closing entries
   e. journal entries

6. The 19C year end balance sheet reported retained earnings of $30,000 while the accompanying income statement reported $22,000 net income. During 19C, $5,000 cash dividends were paid. The amount of retained earnings on the 19B balance sheet must have been:
   a. $ 3,000.
   b. $17,000.
   c. $47,000.
   d. $13,000.

7. Revenue and expense accounts are often called:
   a. permanent accounts.
   b. real accounts.
   c. temporary accounts.
   d. deferred accounts.

8. The process of journalizing and posting adjusting entries is performed:
   a. at the end of the accounting period.
   b. for use in quarterly as well as annual statements.
   c. throughout the annual accounting period.
   d. to reduce temporary account balances to zero.

9. Permanent accounts are distinguished by which of the following?
   a. Only a portion of the account is closed by closing entries.
   b. Reversing entries have no effect upon the balances.
   c. No adjustments are necessary at the end of the period because a balance always exists.
   d. Balances are brought forward to the subsequent accounting period.

10. Select the true statements that relate to the **closing** of temporary accounts at the end of the account period.

    1. Balances in the revenue and expense accounts are transferred to the retained earnings account via Income Summary.
    2. The closing of the Dividends Paid account increases the amount of expenses in determining net income (or loss).
    3. Income Summary is a permanent account used to facilitate the closing procedure.

    a. Statement #1 only
    b. Statement #2 only
    c. Statements #1 and #3
    d. Statements #1 and #2
    e. Statement #3 only

11. Which of the following accounts should be closed at the end of the accounting period?
    a. Income Tax Payable
    b. Sales Commissions Receivable
    c. Rent Revenue Collected in Advance
    d. Accumulated Depreciation
    e. None of the above should be closed.

12. Assume the following adjusted trial balance accounts and amounts:

Cash	$10 dr.
Wages Payable	10 cr.
Machines	50 dr.
Revenue	80 cr.
Accounts Payable	20 cr.
Unearned Revenue	30 cr.
Wages Expense	30 dr.
Other Expenses	40 dr.

    One necessary closing entry would require that Income Summary be:
    a. debited, $110.
    b. credited, $120.
    c. credited, $70.
    d. credited, $110.
    e. credited, $80.

13. Following are amounts from an adjusted trial balance. In the closing process, what amount will be closed to Retained Earnings from Income Summary?

Assets	$25
Liabilities	$10
Capital Stock	5
Interest Expense	10
Sales Revenue	50
Rent Expense	10
Retained Earnings	5
Dividends Paid	15
Wages Expense	10

    a. $10
    b. $20
    c. $30
    d. $45
    e. $ 5

14. McMinnville Company had net income of $20,000 for the year. The closing entry to record the net income is:

a. Cash	20,000	
Capital Stock		20,000
b. Income Summary	20,000	
Retained Earnings		20,000
c. Income Summary	20,000	
Capital Stock		20,000
d. Cash	20,000	
Retained Earnings		20,000
e. Net Income	20,000	
Retained Earnings		20,000

USE THE FOLLOWING INFORMATION FOR THE NEXT TWO QUESTIONS.

Year end account balances are as follows: (Each account has its normal debit or credit balance).

Dividends Paid	$10
Sales	12
Depreciation Expense	4
Commissions Earned	7
Administrative Expense	5
Revenue Collected in Advance	2
Selling Expense	1
Retained Earnings	40

15. Just before closing the Income Summary account, its balance would be:
    a. $ 9 cr.
    b. $10 cr.
    c. $11 cr.
    d. $ 1 cr.

16. After all closing entries are made, the ending balance in Retained Earnings should be:
    a. $39.
    b. $41.
    c. $49.
    d. $51.

17. Which of the following accounts is **not** closed at the end of the period?
    a. Depreciation Expense
    b. Dividends Paid
    c. Accumulated Depreciation
    d. Interest Revenue
    e. Income Summary

18. Jaspo Company's just completed worksheet reveals net income of $700 for the period. Which of the following closing entries will be necessary?

a.	Net Income	700	
	Retained Earnings		700
b.	Cash	700	
	Net Income		700
c.	Income Summary	700	
	Retained Earnings		700
d.	Revenue	700	
	Net Income		700

19. Which of the following statements provides the best description of the purpose of closing entries?
    a. To facilitate posting and taking a trial balance.
    b. To reduce the balances of revenue and expense accounts to zero so they may be used to accumulate information of the next period.
    c. To determine the amount of net income or loss for the period.
    d. To complete the record of various transactions which are begun in one accounting period and concluded in a later period.

20. Which set of entries would be made during the closing process at the end of an accounting period in which there was a profit?
    a. dr. expense accounts and income summary; cr. retained earnings
    b. cr. expense accounts and retained earnings; dr. revenue accounts
    c. cr. revenue accounts and income summary; dr. expense accounts
    d. dr. income summary and retained earnings; cr. expense accounts
    e. No closing entries are necessary when there is a profit.

21. Revenue and expense accounts are called temporary accounts because
    a. data are collected in them for the current accounting period only.
    b. account balances are adjusted for inflation.
    c. their balances are carried forward from accounting period to accounting period.
    d. they are not as important as the asset, liability, and equity accounts (which are permanent).

22. Which of the following accounts **must** be credited during the closing process when there has been a net loss for the period?
    a. accounts receivable
    b. income summary
    c. retained earnings
    d. dividends payable

23. ABS Corp. had net income during 19E. A careless employee made the following incorrect entry to close the Income Summary account.

Income Summary   XXX
    Accumulated Depreciation   XXX

How will this erroneous entry affect the basic accounting equation?
a. owners' equity will be overstated and assets will be understated
b. owners' equity will be understated and assets will be overstated
c. owners' equity will be overstated and expenses will be understated
d. owners' equity will be understated and assets will be understated

24. Which of the following is **not** a correct closing entry?

a. Income Summary   XXX
        Supplies Expense   XXX

b. Sales Revenue   XXX
        Income Summary   XXX

c. Retained Earnings   XXX
        Dividends Paid   XXX

d. Income Summary   XXX
        Prepaid Insurance   XXX

25. Which of the following is **not** one of the functions performed by closing entries?
a. transfer revenue and expense account balances to retained earnings
b. record an economic event that has occurred during the accounting period, but which has not yet been recorded
c. zero out the Dividends Paid account
d. reduce all temporary account balances to zero

26. Which one of the following accounts will **not** have a zero balance after all closing entries have been made at year end?
a. wages expense
b. service revenue
c. insurance expense
d. accumulated depreciation

27. The following accounts represent an adjusted trial balance of a company at the end of its first year of operations. What will be the ending balance in retained earnings if all closing entries are properly journalized and posted?

Cash	$ 4
Sales Revenue	30
Account Receivable	5
Rent Revenue	8
Accounts Payable	10
Depreciation Expense	5
Trucks	6
Dividends Paid	2
Capital Stock	5
Repair Expense	8
Salaries Expense	23

a. $ 0
b. $ 2
c. $36
d. $38

28. The Bucko Company ledger had the following balances after adjusting entries.

Cash	$500
Accounts Payable	150
Dividends Paid	550
Capital Stock	200
Retained Earnings	0
Revenues	800
Expenses	100

Which is the entry necessary to close the revenue and expense accounts?

a. Revenues   800
        Expenses   100
        Income Summary   700
    Income Summary   700
        Retained Earnings   700
b. Revenues   800
        Expenses   100
        Capital Stock   700
c. Expenses   100
    Income Summary   700
        Revenues   800
d. Income Summary   700
        Retained Earnings   700

29. When preparing the closing entries at the end of the accounting cycle, which accounts are closed?
   a. all of them
   b. only revenue and expense accounts
   c. all temporary accounts
   d. all real accounts

30. A company's adjusted trial balance included the following accounts and balances prior to closing:

Cash	$ 1,000
Sales	15,000
Inventory	500
Dividends Paid	1,000
Accounts Payable	2,000
Expenses	12,000
Retained Earnings	4,000

   What will be the balance in the retained earnings account after all closing entries are made and posted?
   a. $3,000
   b. $6,000
   c. $7,000
   d. $8,000

31. Which of the following financial documents proves the equality of debits and credits in the ledger after the books have been closed?
   a. income statement
   b. post-closing trial balance
   c. adjusted trial balance
   d. balance sheet
   e. statement of changes in financial position

32. Revenue and expense accounts at the beginning of the accounting period should have a balance of:
   a. a net amount equal to the retained earnings balance at the end of the prior period.
   b. zero.
   c. the cumulative amount of revenue and expense since the company's beginning.
   d. a net amount exceeding contributed capital.

33. Kumen Company's worksheet year-end on December 31, 19D showed the following amounts related to Sales Revenue.

   (1) in the credit column of the Unadjusted Trial Balance: $400,000
   (2) in the credit column of the Adjustments: $50,000
   (3) in the credit column of the Adjusted Trial Balance: $450,000

   What is the proper balance in the Sales account on January 1, 19E after all closing entries for 19D have been posted but before any entries reflecting 19E sales activity have been recorded?
   a. $450,000
   b. $400,000
   c. $350,000
   d. $0

34. The summarized data for Jaslyn Company at December 31, 19B are listed below:

   Capital Stock (4,000 shares, par value $15) = $60,000
   Retained Earnings at December 31, 19B (after closing) = $40,000
   Total Revenues earned during 19B = $70,000
   Total Expenses incurred during 19B = $50,000
   Total Dividends declared and paid during 19B = $10,000

   Total stockholders' equity at **December 31, 19B** (after closing) is:
   a. $ 20,000.
   b. $ 40,000.
   c. $ 60,000.
   d. $ 80,000.
   e. $100,000.

35. Last year Khalsa Corp.'s books showed revenues of $150,000 and total expenses of $78,000. The CPA firm auditing Khalsa's year-end financial reports has notified them of several items not showing on the books;

　　1) depreciation expense for the year was $5,000;
　　2) an insurance payment of $4,000 for a 4 year policy (of which only one year has expired) was expensed in full; and
　　3) income taxes at a rate of 30% had not been computed.

Khalsa's corrected net income was:
a. $49,000.
b. $50,400.
c. $51,800.
d. $70,000.
e. $74,000.

USE THE FOLLOWING INFORMATION FOR THE NEXT THREE QUESTIONS.

Students, Inc. was incorporated on June 1, l9A. During June, the following transactions occurred:

　　-- 100,000 shares of common stock were issued for cash at $5 per share.
　　-- Students, Inc. purchased a company car on June 30, 19A for $30,000. The company paid 10% down and borrowed the balance from a local bank.
　　-- Students, Inc. sold 300,000 gadgets at $10 each. 40% of these sales were for cash and the rest were on account.
　　-- Students, Inc. incurred the following expenses: Materials, $1,800,000; Wages, $600,000; Other operating expenses, $100,000. 30% of these expenses were paid in June, 19A.

Assume there were no taxes or other transactions for Students, Inc. during the month of June, 19A.

36. The cash balance on the June 30, 19A balance sheet is:
a. $450,000.
b. $447,000.
c. $947,000.
d. $950,000.

37. Total liabilities on the June 30, 19A balance sheet are:
a. $ 750,000.
b. $1,777,000.
c. $2,500,000.
d. $2,530,000.

38. Retained earnings on the June 30, 19A balance sheet :
a. $ 450,000.
b. $ 500,000.
c. $1,000,000.
d. not determinable from the information given.

39. Which of the following statements **best** describes reversing entries?
a. They reverse the effects of closing entries.
b. They **must** be used if a company prepares interim financial statements.
c. They are prepared **before** the related adjusting entries are journalized.
d. They are an optional procedure in the accounting cycle.

40. Dividends are:
a. expensed when **paid**.
b. expensed when **incurred**.
c. never expensed.
d. extraordinary items.
e. a reduction of earnings per share.

41. The worksheet is:
a. a required financial statement.
b. prepared before adjusting entries are entered in the journal.
c. usually not used when interim financial statements are prepared.
d. an optional financial statement that is often distributed to users along with the balance sheet and income statement.

CHAPTER FIVE: ANNOTATED SOLUTIONS

1. e	8. a	15. a	22. b	29. c	36. c
2. c	9. d	16. a	23. d	30. b	37. b
3. e	10. a	17. c	24. d	31. b	38. b
4. c	11. e	18. c	25. b	32. b	39. d
5. e	12. e	19. b	26. d	33. d	40. c
6. d	13. b	20. b	27. a	34. e	41. b
7. c	14. b	21. a	28. a	35. a	

> *The correct answer and the percentage of students answering the question correctly (when it was used on an introductory accounting examination) are shown in parentheses at the beginning of each annotated solution that follows.*

1. (e,45) Information processing at the end of the accounting cycle begins with the worksheet (#4). After completion, the actual financial statements can be prepared (#1). After this the adjusting entries are recorded in the journal (#5), the closing entries are journalized and posted (#2), and finally, a post- closing trial balance is prepared (#3).

2. (c,71) By definition of the steps in the accounting cycle.

3. (e,83) Response a describes reversing entries, not the closing process. Both b and c are correct statements.

4. (c,50) Per the accounting cycle, journalizing and posting of adjusting and closing entries typically occurs **after** the financial statements have been prepared.

5. (e,68) Journal entries are found only in the journal.

6. (d,46) The beginning balance of retained earnings for 19C (which is the same as the ending balance of 19B) + net income for the year - dividends = ending balance of retained earnings for 19C. Therefore, X + $22,000 - $5,000 = $30,000; X = $13,000.

7. (c,89) Temporary accounts (also called nominal accounts) are ones that are closed out to a zero balance at the end of the accounting period. Revenue and expense accounts are the most common examples of temporary accounts. Other examples would be Dividends Paid and Income Summary.

8. (a,49) According to the accounting cycle, adjusting entries are journalized and posted at the end of the accounting period just prior to closing.

9. (d,76) Permanent accounts are those that are **not** closed out to a zero balance at the end of the accounting period. As such, permanent accounts usually have balances that are brought forward to the next period.

10. (a,55) Statement #2 is false because dividends are **not** an expense. Statement #3 is false because Income Summary is a temporary account. Only statement #1, therefore, is correct.

11. (e,64) Only temporary (nominal) accounts are closed at the end of the accounting period. All the selections given are permanent (real) accounts.

12. (e,23) There is only one revenue account and it has a balance of $80. During the closing process this balance must be transferred to Income Summary. The journal entry will be a debit to Revenue ($80) and a credit to Income Summary ($80). (Note that Unearned Revenue is a **liability** account.)

13. (b,37) The amount closed from Income Summary to Retained Earnings is equal to net income. Revenue ($50) minus expenses (Wages, $10; Interest, $10; Rent, $10) is $20.

14. (b,67) Net income is the balance in income summary after all revenue and expense accounts have been closed thereto. Income summary is then closed to retained earnings.

15. (a,32) The debits to income summary include depreciation, administrative, and selling expenses ($4 + $5 + $1 = $10). The credits (total of $19) are sales ($12) and commissions earned ($7). Income summary, then, has a net credit balance of $9.

16. (a,37) Ending retained earnings = beginning balance + net income - dividends; or retained earnings = $40 + $9 - $10 = $39.

17. (c,69) Accumulated depreciation is a contra-account to an asset (or permanent) account. It is not closed unless the related asset is sold or otherwise disposed of.

18. (c,65) Response c must be correct since all the other answers have an entry to a "net income" account. There is no such account. Also, response c is the proper entry to close income summary when there is a $700 profit.

19. (b,86) Response b is a straightforward description of why closing entries are necessary.

20. (b,43) It takes a credit entry to close an expense account; a debit entry to close a revenue account. When there is a profit, income summary will have a credit balance; hence, income summary must be debited and retained earnings must be credited.

21. (a,88) By definition.

22. (b,61) When there has been a loss, Income Summary will have debit balance after all revenue and expense accounts have been closed to it. A credit entry, then, is necessary to close Income Summary.

23. (d,38) The debit to Income Summary was correct, but the credit should have been to Retained Earnings. Since retained earnings was not credited (increased), equity is understated. Since accumulated depreciation was credited (increased) in error, this contra-account to an asset is overstated which makes total assets understated.

24. (d,61) Response d is not a closing entry since asset accounts (such as Prepaid Insurance) are not closed.

25. (b,68) Each response (except b) describes a proper function of closing entries. Response b describes a routine journal entry (or perhaps an adjusting entry), but not a closing one.

26. (d,93) Only permanent accounts have non-zero balances after closing entries. Accumulated depreciation is a permanent account.

27. (a,45) The key to this question is to ignore all balance sheet accounts since they are not closed at the end of the period. Merely net the revenue accounts (credits of $8 + $30) against the expense accounts (debits of $5 + $8 + $23). This yields a balance of $2. Since the Dividends account ($2) is closed with a debit to Retained Earnings, the net effect is to leave R.E. with a balance of zero.

28. (a,75) In the closing process all revenue and expense accounts are first closed to Income Summary (the revenue accounts are debited to close them, and the expense accounts are credited). The next step is to close the balance in Income Summary to Retained Earnings.

29. (c,89) All temporary accounts are closed at the end of the accounting period. Response b is incorrect because while revenue and expense accounts are temporary accounts there are other temporary accounts besides them (such as Dividends Paid).

30. (b,57) In this problem you must determine what effect the closing process has on the Retained Earnings (RE) account. Remember that net income will increase RE while dividends will decrease it. From the data given, net income will be $3,000 (Sales - Expenses) and dividends are $1,000. To beginning RE of $4,000, then, add $3,000 and subtract $1,000 for an ending RE balance of $6,000.

31. (b,53) This is the defined purpose of a **post-closing** trial balance.

32. (b,93) Closing entries are prepared at the end of every accounting period to close all temporary accounts out to a zero balance. Since revenue and expense accounts are temporary accounts, they will all have zero balances at the beginning of the next period.

33. (d,75) After the posting of all closing entries for 19D, the Sales account should have a zero balance.

34. (e,57) At 12/31/19B, total stockholders' equity consists of Capital Stock ($60,000) and Retained Earnings ($40,000). Revenue, expenses and dividends are already included in the ending balance of Retained Earnings.

35. (a,58) The $78,000 of expenses should be (1) increased by $5,000 (Depreciation Expense), and (2) decreased by $3,000 (only $1,000 of the insurance is expense) for a correct total expense of $80,000. $150,000 of Revenue - $80,000 of expense = $70,000 Pretax Income. After 30% taxes ($21,000), net income = $49,000.

36. (c,58) Since this is a new company, the year-end cash balance will be the difference between cash inflow during the year and cash outflow. Cash inflows were $1,700,000 ($500,000 from sale of stock + $1,200,000 cash collected from the sale of gadgets). Cash outflows were $753,000 ($3,000 down payment on the company car + $750,000 paid out for expenses. $1,700,000 minus $753,000 = $947,000.

37. (b,51) There are two liabilities at year-end; $27,000 owed on the company car ($30,000 less 10% down payment) and $1,750,000 owed for expenses incurred during June (total expenses of $2,500,000 x 70%). $27,000 plus $1,750,000 = $1,777,000.

38. (b,45) Net income for the year was $500,000 (revenues of $3,000,000 minus expenses of $2,500,000). Since this is a new company there was no beginning balance in Retained Earnings; further, no dividends were paid. Retained Earnings at the end of the first year, then, is equal to net income of the first year.

39. (d,53) Reversing entries are not mandatory. They are helpful, but an accounting system could function without them. All the other responses are nonsense.

40. (c,42) Dividends are **not** an expense...ever! They are a distribution of profits. They have no effect on the amount of earnings per share but are a distribution of it. EPS is neither increased nor decreased by the declaration or payment of dividends.

41. (b,71) When a worksheet is used, it is prepared **before** adjusting entries are entered into the journal. This is because the adjusting entries are first identified while preparing the worksheet.

CHAPTER SIX: ACCOUNTING FOR SALES REVENUE AND COST OF GOODS SOLD

PART A: Accounting for Sales Revenue

1. Gross Margin is the difference between:
   a. sales revenue and cost of goods sold.
   b. gross sales and sales discounts and returns.
   c. sales revenue and operating expenses.
   d. sales revenue and all expenses except income tax.

2. The Old Oak Company's records reflect the following balances as of December 31, 19C. Determine the cost of goods sold.

Beginning Inventory	$ 8,000
Sales Returns	2,000
Purchases	16,000
Freight-In	1,000
Ending Inventory	6,000
Freight-Out	3,000
Sales	40,000
Purchase Returns	2,000

   a. $20,000
   b. $18,000
   c. $17,000
   d. $15,000
   e. $14,000

3. A credit sale is made for $500 and the terms are 2/10,n/30. What is the **theoretically preferable** journal entry?
   a. Accounts Receivable   510
         Sales Revenue   510
   b. Accounts Receivable   490
         Sales Discount   10
         Sales Revenue   500
   c. Accounts Receivable   490
         Sales Revenue   490
   d. Accounts Receivable   500
         Sales Discounts   10
         Sales Revenue   490

4. Cartier sold a diamond to Tiffany for $10,000 with a 40% trade discount and terms of 2/10,n/30. As expected, Tiffany paid for it 9 days later. The **preferred** entry on Cartier's books at the time of sale is:

   a. Accounts Receivable   10,000
         Sales Revenue   10,000

   b. Accounts Receivable   5,880
         Sales Revenue   5,880

   c. Sales Revenue   6,000
         Accounts Receivable   6,000

   d. Sales Revenue   5,880
         Accounts Receivable   5,880

   e. Accounts Receivable   6,000
         Sales Revenue   6,000

5. Which of the following statements is **true** concerning accounting for sales discounts?
   a. They are part of the calculation of Cost of Goods Sold.
   b. Under the materiality principle, sales discounts should only be given accounting recognition if they are 2% or greater.
   c. The related account receivable should be recorded at the full purchase price.
   d. The net method is conceptually preferable to the gross method.

6. Assume goods are sold at a gross price of $200 with credit terms of 2/10,n/30. The conceptually preferable entry to record this event includes a credit to the Sales Revenue account of:
   a. $196.
   b. $198.
   c. $200.
   d. $202.
   e. $204.

7. Many different types of discounts are used. One type is merely used by a vendor for quoting sales prices; the amount after the discount is the actual sales price. The type of discount described here is a:
a. trade discount.
b. five finger discount.
c. sales discount.
d. cash discount.

8. In using the allowance method in accounting for bad debt expense, the underlying accounting concept is the:
a. cost principle.
b. revenue principle.
c. consistency principle.
d. matching principle.
e. objectivity principle.

9. Macadamia Nuts Co. had net credit sales of $450,000 for 19A. The allowance for doubtful accounts showed a $1,000 debit balance before a 1% bad debt loss rate was applied. What is the balance found in the allowance account after recording the bad debt expense?
a. $4,500 debit
b. $3,500 credit
c. $5,500 debit
d. $4,500 credit
e. $3,500 debit

10. Small Risk, Inc. reports the following data for 19C.

Beginning Accounts Receivable	$12
Ending Accounts Receivable	17
Beginning Allowance for Doubtful Accounts	2
Ending Allowance for Doubtful Accounts	5
Credit Sales for the Year	30

What is the net realizable value of accounts receivable at year end?
a. $13
b. $12
c. $10
d. $ 9
e. $ 8

11. The "Allowance for Doubtful Accounts" represents:
a. the total of actual credit losses for the period plus the estimated losses for the next operating cycle.
b. a contra-asset account designed to reduce receivables to estimated realizable value.
c. the total of uncollectible accounts for the current period.
d. cash which has been segregated to make up for anticipated credit losses.

12. Trimble Toys uses the allowance method of accounting for bad debts. On April 1, 19X4, an account (which arose in 19X2) was determined to be worthless. The proper journal entry to be made at April 1, 19X4, would include a debit to:
a. allowance for doubtful accounts.
b. accounts receivable.
c. inventory.
d. bad debt expense.

13. Sunbelt Tools uses the allowance method to account for bad debt expense. If a customer's account was determined to be uncollectible, Sunbelt Tools would write off this account with which of the following entries?
a. dr. Bad Debt Expense; cr. Accounts. Receivable
b. dr. Bad Debt Expense; cr. Allowance for Doubtful Accounts
c. dr. Allowance for Doubtful Accounts; cr. Accounts Receivable
d. dr. Allowance for Doubtful Accounts; cr. Bad Debt Expense

14. Writing off an uncollectible account using the allowance method:
a. is a procedure used to arrive at the net realizable value of accounts receivable.
b. eliminates a specifically identifiable bad debt from accounts receivable.
c. satisfies the matching principle by debiting an expense account and crediting accounts receivable.
d. recognizes an expense for the amount of a receivable determined to be uncollectible.

15. Dave Hansen, who had been buying items from the Thrifty Drug Store on credit, said he could not pay any of his debts and declared bankruptcy. Consequently, Thrifty Drug Store, which uses the allowance method of accounting for bad debts will make which of the following entries?

    a. dr. Allowance for Doubtful Accounts; cr. Accounts Receivable
    b. dr. Accounts Receivable; cr. Allowance for Doubtful Accounts
    c. dr. Allowance for Doubtful Accounts; cr. Bad Debt Expense
    d. dr. Bad Debt Expense; cr. Allowance for Doubtful Accounts

16. Assume a company uses the allowance method to account for bad debts. The entry to write off as uncollectible a specific account receivable would:
    a. increase expenses.
    b. decrease total assets.
    c. have no effect on total assets or expenses.
    d. decrease net sales revenue.

17. Bad debt expense is reported on the:
    a. income statement under "gains and losses."
    b. balance sheet as a reduction of accounts receivable.
    c. income statement as an operating expense.
    d. income statement as a deduction from sales to arrive at net sales.

18. The following data are selected from the Income Statement.

Gross Sales	$1,000
Cost of Goods Sold	600
Sales Returns	140
Bad Debt Expense	50
Allowance for Doubtful Accounts	40

    Net sales must have been:
    a. $260.
    b. $400.
    c. $860.
    d. $920

19. At year end, Alabama Irrigation estimated that 2% of its net credit sales would not be collectible. Before any entry has been made to account for this fact, selected accounts had the following balances.

Allowance for Bad Debts (debit balance)	$5,000
Sales (all on credit)	2,100,000
Sales Returns and Allowances	100,000

    The adjusting entry required by the above information is:

    a. Bad Debt Expense   40,000
           Allowance for Bad Debts   40,000
    b. Bad Debt Expense   45,000
           Allowance for Bad Debts   45,000
    c. Bad Debt Expense   42,000
           Allowance for Bad Debts   42,000
    d. Allow. for Bad Debts   40,000
           Bad Debt Expense   40,000
    e. Allow. for Bad Debts   37,000
           Bad Debt Expense   37,000

20. Bush is unhappy with the quality of goods purchased from Tree. If this dispute is resolved by Tree granting a sales allowance, which one of the following combinations of events will occur?

	Goods are Kept By the Buyer	*A Discount is Allowed by the Seller*
a.	Yes	Yes
b.	No	Yes
c.	Yes	No
d.	No	No

PART B: Accounting for Cost of Goods Sold

21. The difference between net sales and cost of goods sold is called:
    a. operating profit.
    b. net income.
    c. gross margin.
    d. income from operations.

22. Tami's Chamis has the following information available.

Beginning Inventory	$ 8,000
Sales	35,000
Net Purchases	20,000
Ending Inventory	15,000

What is the amount of Tami's cost of goods sold?
a. $43,000
b. $28,000
c. $27,000
d. $22,000
e. $13,000

USE THE FOLLOWING INFORMATION FOR THE NEXT TWO QUESTIONS.

The following are adjusted account balances for the Boston Tea Company at the end of 19B.

Sales	$80,000
Cost of Goods Sold	65,000
Beginning inventory	50,000
Purchases	40,000
Sales Returns and Allowances	2,000

23. The ending inventory for 19B is:
a. $13,000.
b. $15,000.
c. $25,000.
d. $35,000.

24. Gross profit as a percentage of net sales is approximately:
a. 16.7%.
b. 20.0%.
c. 33.3%.
d. 66.7%.

25. The Cost of Goods Available for Sale during the year was $90,000 and the Sales Revenue for the year was $120,000. If the gross margin ratio was 60%, the ending inventory must have been:
a. $18,000.
b. $36,000.
c. $42,000.
d. $48,000

26. Based on the following information, what is cost of goods sold?

Purchases	$108,000
Transportation-In	2,000
Purchase Returns	1,000
Beginning Inventory	10,000
Ending Inventory	6,000
Bad Debt Expense	5,000

a. $109,000
b. $110,000
c. $119,000
d. $107,000
e. $113,000

27. For the year 19B, ABC Corporation had gross sales of $100, sales returns and allowances of $20, a gross margin on sales of 30%, and anticipated losses from bad debts of $10. What was cost of goods sold for 19B?
a. $49
b. $56
c. $63
d. $70

28. Tempe Time Company reported net income before income taxes of $30,000, sales of $200,000 and administrative expenses of $60,000. The cost of sales and gross margin must have been what amounts?

	Cost of Sales	Gross Margin
a.	$ 90,000	$ 90,000
b.	$110,000	$ 90,000
c.	$140,000	$ 90,000
d.	$140,000	$ 90,000
e.	$140,000	$ 90,000

29. Under the periodic inventory system, the Purchases account is used to record:
a. only cash purchases of merchandise inventory.
b. only purchases of merchandise inventory on account.
c. purchases of any asset acquired by the business.
d. all merchandise inventory acquired for resale.
e. cost of merchandise sold.

30. Which of the following is characteristic of a **perpetual** inventory system?
    a. minimal record maintenance, no need to perform physical counts and delayed recording of cost of goods sold
    b. detailed inventory record maintenance and immediate recording of cost of goods sold
    c. the physical count is the only data needed to determine the cost of goods sold
    d. the inventory record is useless for interim reports

31. Inventory shrinkage may best be discovered by utilizing:
    a. the cost principle.
    b. a periodic inventory system.
    c. a perpetual inventory system.
    d. the revenue principle.

32. In comparing the periodic and perpetual inventory systems, which of the following statements is **true**?
    a. The periodic system results in better inventory control.
    b. Closing entries are more complex under the perpetual system.
    c. Inventory shrinkage is more easily identified under a perpetual system.
    d. The periodic inventory system is more costly to operate.
    e. A physical inventory count should not be made when the perpetual system is used.

33. Under the perpetual method of accounting for inventory, the sale of goods would result in which journal entry below?

    a. Cost of Goods Sold
          Goods Available for Sale

    b. Goods Available for Sale
          Cost of Goods Sold

    c. Cost of Goods Sold
          Inventory

    d. Cost of Goods Sold
          Purchases

34. Phoenix Fertilizer uses a periodic inventory system. At 1-1-19D, inventory was $100. At 12-31-19D, the amount of inventory on hand was $50 and the accounting records showed the following balances:

Accounts Receivable	$ 60
Accounts Payable	30
Purchases	400
Purchase Discounts	8
Sales	700
Expenses	150

    Gross Margin for 19D must have been:
    a. $108.
    b. $258.
    c. $300.
    d. $442.

35. When an item that cost $40 is sold for $60 under the perpetual inventory system, two entries must be made. The first is:

    Accounts Receivable (or Cash) 60
        Sales Revenue   60

    Which additional entry is also necessary?
    a. dr. inventory $40; cr. cost of goods sold $40
    b. dr. cost of goods sold $40; cr. purchases $40
    c. dr. purchases $40; cr. inventory $40
    d. dr. cost of goods sold $40; cr. inventory $40
    e. no second entry is necessary under the perpetual system

36. Which of the following sets of accounts would be found in the trial balance of a company using the **perpetual** inventory system?
    a. purchase returns & allowances, cost of goods sold, inventory, transportation- in
    b. inventory, sales returns & allowances, cost of goods sold, cash
    c. sales returns & allowances, purchases, freight-in, inventory
    d. cost of goods sold, inventory, purchases, sales discounts

37. Inventory items having an invoice price of $100 were purchased on credit by Ann, subject to credit terms of 2/10, n/30. When Ann recorded this transaction, she debited Purchases for $98. Which combination of inventory system and recording method does Ann use?

	Inventory System	Recording Method
a.	periodic	gross
b.	periodic	net
c.	perpetual	gross
d.	perpetual	net

38. A firm using the periodic inventory system returned $50 worth of goods to its supplier because they were defective. The firm's entry to record this return would include a credit to:
a. cash.
b. inventory.
c. purchases.
d. purchase returns.

39. Wally's Clock Works uses a **perpetual** inventory system. A recently completed physical count showed that $50,000 of goods were on hand. At the time of the physical count, the ledger balances of selected accounts were as follows:

Cash	$10,000
Inventory	50,000
Cost of Goods Sold	200,000

Which entry (if any), is necessary to record the effects of the physical count?
a. Inventory   50,000
       Cash   50,000
b. Inventory   50,000
       Cost of Goods Sold   50,000
c. Income Summary   50,000
       Inventory   50,000
d. Cost of Goods Sold 50,000
       Inventory   50,000
e. No entry is necessary.

40. When the **perpetual** inventory system is used, which combination of the following two accounts are closed at the end of the period to the Income Summary account?

	Cost of Goods Sold	Purchases
a.	Yes	Yes
b.	Yes	No
c.	No	Yes
d.	Yes	No

41. Assume a firm uses the periodic inventory system and is making closing entries at year end. Which combination of entries below will be made to **Income Summary** for the ending Merchandise Inventory amount and in closing the Purchases account balance, respectively?

	Merchandise Inventory	Purchases
a.	debit	debit
b.	debit	credit
c.	credit	debit
d.	credit	credit

42. Which of the following closing entries would be used with a **periodic** inventory system?

1.	Income Summary	xx	
	Purchases		xx
2.	Income Summary	xx	
	Inventory (beginning)		xx
3.	Purchase Ret. & Allow.	xx	
	Income Summary		xx
4.	Inventory (ending)	xx	
	Income Summary		xx

a. entry #3 only
b. entries #1, #2, and #3 only
c. entries #1, #2, and #4 only
d. entries #2 and #4 only
e. all four of the entries

43. Which of the two inventory systems requires a journal entry be made when inventory shrinkage is discovered?

	Periodic	Perpetual
a.	Yes	Yes
b.	Yes	No
c.	No	Yes
d.	No	No

44. The necessary adjusting entries at the end of the accounting period related to recognition of bad debt expense and physical inventory counts are best described as being specifically made necessary by the:
   a. full disclosure principle.
   b. unit of measure concept.
   c. separate entity assumption.
   d. matching principle.

45. Which of the following computations would yield cost of goods available for sale?
   a. ending inventory + purchases
   b. ending inventory + cost of goods sold
   c. beginning inventory + ending inventory - cost of goods sold
   d. beginning inventory + purchases + freight in - cost of goods sold

46. I.B. Crazy purchased inventory of $1,000 on terms of 2/10,n/30. The purchase was recorded using the "net method." Crazy then paid for the items **after** the discount period had expired. In recording the payment, the accountant must:
   a. debit Accounts Payable for $1,000.
   b. credit Cash for $980.
   c. credit Purchase Discounts Lost for $20.
   d. debit Accounts Payable for $980.

47. The Talking Parrot Pet Store uses a periodic inventory system. During 19X4, the firm properly recorded all purchases and had an accurate count of ending inventory. The ending inventory for 19X3, however, had been understated. What effect, if any, would this have on Cost of Goods Sold and Net Income in 19X4?
   a. none
   b. CGS understated; NI understated
   c. CGS overstated; NI understated
   d. CGS overstated; NI overstated
   e. CGS understated; NI overstated

48. Determine ending inventory from the following data.

Purchases	$1,000
Purchase Returns	50
Sales	2,000
Transportation-In	100
Beginning Inventory	100
Gross Margin	900

   a. $50
   b. $150
   c. $250
   d. $450

49. Stefano Company uses a periodic inventory system and is preparing closing entries. Those entries will include which of the following?
   a. credit to Purchase Returns
   b. debit to Transportation-In
   c. credit to Cost of Goods Sold
   d. credit to Purchases

CHAPTER SIX: ANNOTATED SOLUTIONS

1. a	8. d	15. a	22. e	29. d	36. b	43. c
2. c	9. b	16. c	23. c	30. b	37. b	44. d
3. c	10. b	17. c	24. a	31. c	38. d	45. b
4. b	11. b	18. c	25. c	32. c	39. e	46. d
5. d	12. a	19. a	26. e	33. c	40. b	47. e
6. a	13. c	20. a	27. b	34. b	41. c	48. a
7. a	14. b	21. c	28. b	35. d	42. e	49. d

> *The correct answer and the percentage of students answering the question correctly (when it was used on an introductory accounting examination) are shown in parentheses at the beginning of each annotated solution that follows.*

1. (a,86) By definition, gross margin is the difference between sales revenue and the cost of goods sold.

2. (c,20) Cost of goods sold = beginning inventory + net purchases - ending inventory. Also, net purchases = purchases + freight in - purchase returns and allowances. Therefore, in this problem, cost of goods sold = $8,000 + $15,000 ($16,000 + $1,000 - $2,000) - $6,000 = $17,000.

3. (c,66) Conceptually, the sale and receivable should be recorded at the amount expected to be collected (i.e. 98% of $500).

4. (b,47) The invoice price after the 40% trade discount is $6,000. From this amount, the 2% discount ($120) is deducted. Preferably, the sale should be recorded on Cartier's books at the amount that is expected to be collected ($6,000 - $120 = $5,880). As usual, Accounts Receivable should be debited and Sales Revenue credited.

5. (d,71) Response a would involve purchase (not sales) discounts. Response b is nonsense. Responses c and d require you to distinguish between the gross method and net method of recording sales. Your author points out that the net method is conceptually preferable.

6. (a,75) Conceptually, this transaction should be recorded at the net amount that is expected to be received from the customer. Since a 2% discount has been offered for prompt payment, $196 is expected to be collected (98% x $200). The debit and credit must be for identical amounts.

7. (a,52) A trade discount is a method sometimes used by sellers for quoting prices; the amount after the trade discount is the actual sales price. For example, a wholesaler might use trade discounts when quoting prices to a retailer.

8. (d,54) The most relevant concept is the matching concept since the allowance method results in the bad debt expense being recorded in the same period as the related revenue that causes the expense.

9. (b,48) When recording bad debt expense, a credit of $4,500 (1% x $450,000) is credited to the allowance account. When this is netted against the $1,000 pre-existing debit balance, the account is left with a $3,500 credit balance.

10. (b,56) Net realizable value of accounts receivable is the gross amount owed by customers minus the balance in the allowance for doubtful accounts. Ending accounts receivable ($17) minus the ending allowance for doubtful accounts ($5) = $12.

11. (b,61) The Allowance for Doubtful Accounts represents the amount that is **not** expected to be collected in the normal course of business. It is a contra- account that is deducted from the gross accounts receivable.

12. (a,47) Under the allowance method, the entry to write off an uncollectible account is: debit Allowance for Doubtful Accounts, credit Accounts Receivable.

13. (c,44) Under the allowance method, the write-off entry is always a debit to Allowance for Doubtful Accounts and a credit to Accounts Receivable.

14. (b,35) This question asks about the write-off of an uncollectible account. Only response b describes what happens when this action is taken (i.e. a specific account is removed from accounts receivable). Responses a and c describe the process or effect of the adjusting entry that sets up the allowance for bad debts.

15. (a,48) The allowance account must be reduced (with a debit) as must the Accounts Receivable account (with a credit).

16. (c,34) When the allowance method is being used, the write-off entry reduces both an asset (accounts receivable) and its contra-account (allowance for doubtful accounts) by an equal amount. The result is that the net value of the asset is not changed. No expense account is involved in the write-off.

17. (c,38) Bad debt expense is an operating expense caused by extending credit to customers who do not pay.

18. (c,40) Net sales is the difference between Gross Sales ($1,000) and Sales Returns and Allowances ($140) for an answer of $860.

19. (a,50) In this problem, bad debt expense is calculated as the "rate" times "net credit sales" (or 2% times $2,000,000 = $40,000). Expenses are recorded with debits.

20. (a,63) By definition, a sales allowance means that the seller grants an additional discount to the buyer and that the buyer keeps the goods.

21. (c,94) By definition, when cost of goods sold is subtracted from net sales the resulting amount is called gross margin.

22. (e,87) Cost of goods sold = beginning inventory + net purchases - ending inventory. Therefore, cost of goods sold = $8,000 + $20,000 - $15,000 = $13,000.

23. (c,88) Cost of goods sold = beginning inventory + net purchases - ending inventory (or $65,000 = $50,000 + $40,000 - X; X = $25,000).

24. (a,54) Gross profit = net sales - cost of goods sold (or $78,000 - $65,000 = $13,000). $13,000 (gross profit) divided by $78,000 (net sales) = 16.7%.

25. (c,21) Use the CGS formula (CGS = BI + NP - EI) to solve this problem. Further, remember that Cost of Goods Available = BI + NP. If the gross margin ratio is 60%, then gross margin was $72,000 (60% x $120,000) and CGS was therefore $48,000. Substituting known amounts into the CGS formula yields the following: $48,000 = $90,000 - X. X, then, = $42,000.

26. (e,63) Cost of goods sold = beginning inventory + net purchases - ending inventory. Also, net purchases = purchases + transportation in - purchase returns and allowances. Therefore, cost of goods sold = $10,000 + ($108,000 + $2,000 - $1,000) - $6,000 = $113,000.

27. (b,46) Remember that the gross margin percentage is always a portion of net sales and that if gross margin is 30% of net sales, CGS must be 70% of net sales. In this problem, net sales are $80 (gross sales of $100 - sales returns of $20). Cost of goods sold, then, is 70% of $80 (or $56).

28. (b,71) Sales - cost of goods sold = gross profit; and gross profit - administrative expenses = net income before taxes. Therefore, gross profit = administrative expenses + income before taxes ($60,000 + $30,000) = $90,000. Cost of goods sold = sales - gross profit ($200,000 - $90,000) = $110,000.

29. (d,65) Both cash and credit acquisitions of merchandise are debited to Purchases. Acquisitions of non-merchandise assets do **not** go in Purchases, nor does any record of merchandise sold.

30. (b,91) Under the perpetual system (1) much record maintenance is required, (2) the physical count and inventory record must be reconciled to obtain cost of goods sold, and (3) inventory values for the interim reports are taken directly from the inventory record.

31. (c,83) Responses a, d, and e are unrelated to the issue. Under the perpetual system, shrinkage is the difference between the physical count and the inventory account balance. Under the periodic system, any shrinkage is "buried" in cost of goods sold.

32. (c,71) Under the perpetual system, there is a "perpetual" inventory balance kept in the ledger plus a physical count is taken at the end of the period. Any difference between these amounts may signal shrinkage. Under the periodic system, there is no ledger balance against which to compare the physical count.

33. (c,77) When a sale is made under the perpetual inventory system, cost of goods sold is debited and the inventory account is credited.

34. (b,72) Cost of goods sold = beginning inventory ($100) + purchases ($400) - purchase discounts ($8) - ending inventory ($50) = $442. Sales ($700) - cost of goods sold ($442) = gross margin ($258).

35. (d,77) A second entry is necessary under the perpetual system to bring the cost of goods sold account (debit) and the inventory account (credit) up to date.

36. (b,65) The accounts titled purchases, purchase returns and allowances, and transportation-in are used only under a periodic system.

37. (b,63) Debiting the Purchases account means that the periodic system is being used. (Under perpetual, acquisitions of inventory are debited to the Inventory account.) Recording the purchase at $98 (net of the $2 discount) means that the net method is being used.

38. (d,43) When a company uses the periodic inventory system, returns to suppliers of inventory previously purchased is credited to Purchase Returns.

39. (e,71) The ledger balance of inventory is correct as of the time of the physical count, so no adjustment is necessary.

40. (b,64) The Purchases account is **not** used with the perpetual system.

41. (c,46) Be sure that you have read this question **very** carefully. It asks about debits and credits to the **Income Summary** account. The entry involving the Merchandise Inventory account will include a debit to merchandise Inventory and a **credit** to Income Summary. The entry to close the Purchases account will have a **debit** to Income Summary and a credit to Purchases.

42. (e,67) Under the periodic system, entry #1 is used to close the Purchases account while entry #2 closes the beginning inventory balance. Entry #3 is used to close the Purchase Returns and Allowances account and entry #4 establishes the new ending inventory balance.

43. (c,57) Under the perpetual system, inventory shrinkage is detected when the end-of-period physical inventory count is less than the existing ledger balance for inventory. A journal entry is necessary to account for the loss (expense) and to reduce the inventory account balance to the amount actually on hand. Under the periodic system, the amount of inventory shrinkage is nearly impossible to determine. The ending inventory count is simply smaller than it would otherwise be which causes cost of goods sold for the period to be higher by the amount of any shrinkage.

44. (d,81) Adjusting entries are made necessary by the matching principle. That is, adjusting entries are prepared in order to make sure that the proper amounts of revenue and expense are recognized each period.

45. (b,30) All goods available for sale are (1) sold during the year or (2) in ending inventory.

46. (d,37) The account payable was recorded on the books at $980. When liquidated, the account must be debited for the same amount ($980).

47. (e,46) 19X4's beginning inventory was understated. By using the CGS formula (CGS = BI + P - EI), it can be determined that this causes CGS to be understated. If cost of goods sold is too small, this makes net income too large (overstated).

48. (a,73) First determine that CGS is $1,100 (sales of $2,000 minus gross margin of $900). Then, use the CGS formula. CGS ($1,100) = BI ($100) + Purchases ($1,000) - Purchase Returns ($50) + Transportation-In ($100) = Ending Inventory. Solving, EI must equal $50.

49. (d,63) Response c is nonsense since there is no cost of goods sold account under a periodic system. Responses a and b are incorrect since they are backwards. That is, Purchase Returns would be debited and Transportation-In would be credited when closing. Only response d is a correct closing entry.

CHAPTER SEVEN: COSTING METHODS FOR MEASURING INVENTORY AND COST OF GOODS SOLD

PART A: Measuring Ending Inventory and Cost of Goods Sold With a Periodic Inventory System

1. A company showed the following account balances at year-end.

Sales	$11,000
Cost of goods sold	5,000
Inventory	1,000
Expenses	2,000

   A physical inventory count revealed that the ending inventory balance should only be $800. What should be the net income of the company assuming all other balances are correct?
   a. $3,800
   b. $4,000
   c. $4,200
   d. $4,800

2. If errors in counting inventory cause beginning inventory to be understated by $7,000 and ending inventory to be understated by $3,000, the resulting net income figure will be:
   a. understated by $10,000.
   b. overstated by $10,000.
   c. understated by $4,000.
   d. overstated by $4,000.

3. Simple, Inc. uses the periodic method of inventory valuation. If the December 31, 19B ending inventory was overstated by $2,000, then:
   a. 19B's cost of goods sold would be overstated.
   b. 19C's gross margin would be overstated.
   c. 19C's net income would be understated.
   d. 19B's cost of goods available for sale would be overstated.

4. Goose Hollow Company uses the periodic inventory system and understated its 19A ending inventory. If no further errors were made, the retained earnings account at year-end **19B** will be:
   a. overstated.
   b. understated.
   c. correctly stated.
   d. the same as at the end of 19A.

5. Which of the following should be included in a company's ending inventory?
   a. goods purchased FOB destination and not yet arrived
   b. goods out on consignment
   c. goods sold FOB shipping point and in transit to buyer
   d. goods in on consignment

6. If Lars Company overstated its beginning inventory in Year 2, what effect will this have on net income and cost of goods sold for year 2, respectively, assuming that the purchases and ending inventory of year 2 are correctly stated?
   a. overstate; understate
   b. understate; overstate
   c. overstate; no effect
   d. no effect; understate

7. Goods in transit at the end of the accounting period that have been shipped "FOB Shipping Point" should be included in the ending inventory of:
   a. the seller.
   b. the buyer.
   c. both the seller and buyer.
   d. the freight company.

8. The Kahala Co. completed its physical inventory count at year end Dec. 31, 19A. The inventory totaled $100,000. During the audit, however, the independent CPA obtained the following information that is not reflected in the $100,000 amount.

   1. Goods in transit on Dec. 31, 19A from a supplier, with terms FOB shipping point, cost $2,000.
   2. On Dec. 31, 19A, a customer paid for goods and asked that they be delivered on Jan. 2, 19B. The $1,000 cost of the goods was included in the physical inventory taken by Kahala.

   What is the correct amount of inventory for Kahala Co at 12/31/19A?
   a. $103,000
   b. $101,000
   c. $ 99,000
   d. $ 97,000
   e. $ 95,000

9. DeSilva Company had 80 watches on hand at June 1, 19D, costing $45 each. Purchases and sales of watches during the month of June were as follows (assume a periodic system).

Date	Purchases	Sales
June 8	50 @ $50	
June 16		40 @ $90
June 19	60 @ $60	
June 25		100 @ $90

   The cost of inventory on hand at June 30, 19D, if FIFO is used is:
   a. $3,600.
   b. $3,000.
   c. $2,500.
   d. $2,250.

USE THE FOLLOWING INFORMATION FOR THE NEXT TWO QUESTIONS.

	Units	Unit Cost
Beginning inventory	5	$4
Purchase #1	4	3
Purchase #2	5	2
Purchase #3	6	3

Assume this firm uses the **periodic** method of accounting for inventory.

10. If 8 units were sold during the period and LIFO is used, what ending inventory amount should be found on the balance sheet?
    a. $38
    b. $31
    c. $29
    d. $22

11. Assume, instead, that 14 units remain in ending inventory and that FIFO was used. What amount is cost of goods sold?
    a. $42
    b. $37
    c. $23
    d. $18

USE THE FOLLOWING INFORMATION FOR THE NEXT TWO QUESTIONS

Sam's Hofbrau uses a periodic inventory system. The following information is given.

Jan. 1	Beginning Inventory 100 units @ $10 each
Feb. 6	Sold 50 units @ $25 each
Mar. 9	Purchased 500 units @ $11 each
Apr. 2	Purchased 300 units @ $13 each
Dec. 1	Sold 840 units @ $28 each
Dec. 5	Purchased 100 units @ $14 each

12. What is the cost of **ending inventory** on a FIFO basis?
    a. $1,540
    b. $1,530
    c. $1,450
    d. $1,110

13. What is the **cost of goods sold** on a weighted average cost basis?
    a. $17,221
    b. $14,982
    c. $11,800
    d. $10,680
    e. $10,502

USE THE FOLLOWING INFORMATION FOR THE NEXT TWO QUESTIONS. ALSO, ASSUME A PERIODIC INVENTORY SYSTEM IS USED.

Event	Units	Unit Cost
Purchase #1	2	$2
Purchase #2	3	3
Purchase #3	5	4

14. If FIFO is used and 6 units are sold, the ending inventory amount is:
    a. $10.
    b. $16.
    c. $17.
    d. $23.
    e. $33.

15. If LIFO is used and 3 units remain in ending inventory, the cost of goods sold is:
    a. $ 7.
    b. $12.
    c. $21.
    d. $26.
    e. $33.

USE THE FOLLOWING INFORMATION FOR THE NEXT TWO QUESTIONS.

At the end of the current accounting period, the inventory records of Value, Inc. showed the following transactions.

Beginning inventory	50 units @ $2
Purchase #1	50 units @ $3
Sale #1 (@ $5 per unit)	40 units
Purchase #2	30 units @ $4
Purchase #3	10 units @ $5
Sale #2 (@ $6 per unit)	20 units
Ending inventory	80 units

16. Compute the dollar amount of **ending inventory** using the weighted average inventory costing method (assume a periodic system).
    a. $140
    b. $180
    c. $240
    d. $280

17. Compute the dollar amount of **cost of goods sold** using the FIFO inventory costing method (assume a periodic system).
    a. $130
    b. $190
    c. $230
    d. $290

18. During a period of **declining** prices, which of the following inventory cost flow assumptions would **minimize** income taxes for a given period?
    a. FIFO
    b. LIFO
    c. Average Cost
    d. All result in the same amount of taxes.

19. The advocates of LIFO maintain that:
    a. current costs are matched with current selling prices.
    b. the lowest possible costs are always shown in ending inventory.
    c. the oldest inventory is relieved of its cost before the newer purchases.
    d. the highest possible costs are always shown in ending inventory.

20. Which of the following statements is **false**?
    a. In a period of decreasing prices, LIFO yields a higher net income than does FIFO.
    b. In a period of increasing prices, FIFO yields a higher ending inventory dollar amount than does LIFO.
    c. In a period of decreasing prices, FIFO yields a higher goods available for sale amount than does LIFO.
    d. In a period of increasing prices, LIFO yields a higher cost of goods sold amount than does FIFO.

21. Which of the following statements is **true**?
    a. When prices are rising, LIFO will show a higher income than FIFO.
    b. When prices are rising, LIFO will result in a higher ending inventory valuation than FIFO.
    c. When prices are declining, LIFO will show lower income than FIFO.
    d. When prices are declining, LIFO will result in a higher ending inventory valuation than FIFO.

22. Which of the following statements are true when unit costs are declining?

    1. LIFO will result in higher net income than will FIFO.
    2. Ending inventory under FIFO will be higher than under LIFO.
    3. Ending inventory under FIFO will be lower than under LIFO.

    a. Statements #1 and #2 are true.
    b. Statements #1 and #3 are true.
    c. Only statement #1 is true.
    d. Only statement #2 is true.
    e. Only statement #3 is true.

23. In periods of steadily rising prices, which of the the following inventory methods will always yield the highest ending inventory cost?
    a. weighted average
    b. LIFO
    c. FIFO
    d. cannot be determined from the information given

24. In a period of decreasing prices the inventory valuation method which yields the lowest gross margin on sales is:
    a. FIFO.
    b. LIFO.
    c. Weighted Average.
    d. impossible to determine.

25. The accounting principle that prevents companies from using the inventory valuation method that provides the most favorable net income each year is the:
    a. cost principle.
    b. continuity principle.
    c. economic utility principle.
    d. consistency principle.

PART B: Application of a Perpetual Inventory System and Selected Inventory Costing Problems

26. Noise and Abuse Record company uses a FIFO perpetual inventory system.

Type of Event	Number of Units	Unit Cost	Total Cost
Beginning inventory	100	$7	$700
Purchases:			
January 3	50	8	400
June 12	200	9	1,800
December 20	120	10	1,200
Goods available	470		$4,100

Sales during the year(in units):
January 6	40
June 18	220
December 24	60

Determine cost of goods sold and ending inventory, respectively.
    a. $2,630 and $1,470
    b. $1,470 and $2,630
    c. $2,870 and $1,230
    d. $2,630 and $1,480
    e. $2,460 and $1,640

27. Given the following information, compute **cost of goods sold** assuming a LIFO perpetual inventory is used.

Date	Event	Units	Unit Cost
1-1	Beginning Inventory	100	$5
3-1	Purchase #1	10	6
4-1	Sale	20	
6-1	Purchase #2	10	7
9-1	Purchase #3	10	8
12-1	Sale	25	

    a. $225
    b. $285
    c. $325
    d. $425

28. Assume the following information.

	Units	Total Cost	Total Sales
Inventory, May 1	30	$ 300	
Purchase, May 10	90	1,080	
Sale, May 15	40		$ 800
Purchase, May 25	20	280	
Sale, May 30	60		1,500

If a perpetual inventory system using LIFO is in effect, what are ending inventory and cost of goods sold, respectively?
a. $440 and $1,220
b. $520 and $1,140
c. $500 and $1,160
d. $474 and $1,186
e. $420 and $1,240

29. With reference to periodic and perpetual inventory systems, which statement is correct?
a. The perpetual system can result in better management control over inventory.
b. Under a perpetual system, the company doesn't ever take a physical inventory count.
c. The periodic system involves more paperwork so the use of the computer is almost a necessity in actual practice.
d. The periodic system requires use of the FIFO costing assumption.
e. Both systems yield the same valuations under the LIFO assumption, but yield different inventory valuations under the FIFO assumption.

USE THE FOLLOWING INFORMATION FOR THE NEXT THREE QUESTIONS.

Description	Units	Unit Cost	Total Cost
Beginning Inventory	20	$5	$100
Purchase #1	50	4	200
Sale #1	40		
Purchase #2	100	6	600
Sale #2	90		
			$900

Ending inventory via year-end physical count is 40 units.

30. If this company uses a **PERPETUAL SYSTEM** with the LIFO method, the debit to cost of goods sold for Sale #1would be in the amount of:
a. $540.
b. $420.
c. $200.
d. $180.
e. $160.

31. If this company uses a **PERIODIC SYSTEM** with the FIFO method, cost of goods sold for the entire year would be
a. $720.
b. $660.
c. $342
d. $240.
e. $180.

32. If this company uses a **PERIODIC SYSTEM** with the weighted average method, ending inventory would be closest to which of the following?
a. $740.
b. $688.
c. $212.
d. $160.
e. $120.

USE THE FOLLOWING INFORMATION FOR THE NEXT TWO QUESTIONS.

Sam's Pharmacy had the following purchases and sales of a medical product during the year.

Date
Jan. 1   Beginning Inventory 300 units @ $11 = $3,300
Apr. 4   Purchase 200 units @ $12 = $2,400
May 15 Sale 400 units
Aug. 8   Purchase 300 units @ $15 = $4,500
Oct. 3   Sale 300 units
Dec. 6   Purchase 100 units @ $15 = $1,500

33. What amount should be assigned to ending inventory under a **periodic** system if the weighted average method is used?
a. $2,200
b. $2,500
c. $2,600
d. $3,000

34. What amount should be assigned to ending inventory under a **perpetual** system if the LIFO method is used?
    a. $2,200
    b. $2,500
    c. $2,600
    d. $3,000

35. Massive, Inc., a multinational conglomerate wishes to estimate its inventory at the end of the first quarter of 19A. Given the following information, determine the estimated ending inventory.

Sales revenue	$200
Beginning inventory	30
Purchases	170
Gross margin on sales	40%

    a. $200
    b. $180
    c. $120
    d. $ 80
    e. $ 20

36. The Fredonia Company is destroyed by fire on 1-20-19A. The accounting records were saved and revealed the following.

Sales Revenue (to date this period)	$20
Beginning Inventory	6
Purchases (to date this period)	16

    Gross margin on sales has always been about 40%. If Fredonia's insurance company covers half the lost inventory, then Fredonia's loss from the fire will be:

    a. $ 4.
    b. $ 5.
    c. $ 8.
    d. $10.

37. The lower-of-cost-or-market basis of inventory valuation is based on which two accounting principles?
    a. cost and conservatism
    b. matching and revenue
    c. entity and materiality
    d. unit-of-measure and time-period

38. The Mauna Kea Macadamia Nut Company suffered a major fire on October 23, 19B. All merchandise was completely destroyed, but the accounting records kept in a fireproof cabinet were not damaged. Those accounting records provide the following information:

    Merchandise inventory, Jan. 1, 19B = $ 40,000
    Transactions through October 23, 19B:
      Purchases $120,000
      Sales $250,000

    The company has maintained a 60 percent gross margin on sales since it was started. Determine the amount of the inventory lost in the fire.
    a. $ 10,000
    b. $ 20,000
    c. $ 40,000
    d. $ 60,000
    e. $100,000

39. In August 19X6, the High Water Company experienced a large inventory loss. From partial records maintained elsewhere it is known that the company had a December 31, 19X5 ending inventory of $40,000. Further, suppliers report that total purchases during 19X6 were $150,000. If High Water Co. had an historical (and current) gross margin percentage of 25%, what is the dollar amount of the inventory loss?
    a. $112,000
    b. $ 47,500
    c. $ 30,000
    d. $ 37,500
    e. cannot be determined from the above information

40. Measuring inventories on a lower-of-cost-or-market basis (LCM) means:
    a. there has been a departure from the cost principle in favor of the conservatism principle.
    b. that if inventory at cost is lower than inventory at market, a loss should be recognized.
    c. that any resulting losses are recorded in the period the merchandise is sold.
    d. that FIFO inventory costs are affected but LIFO inventory costs are not.

41. Ron Tonkin Autos used one of its vehicles as a demonstrator during the current year. The normal selling price of the car is $9,280. Its original cost to the dealership was $8,300. Assume the estimated sales value of the vehicle in its existing condition is $7,900 and that estimated selling and disposal costs are $670. Assuming that net realizable value is to be used here, at what amount should this vehicle be included in ending inventory?
    a. $7,230
    b. $7,900
    c. $8,300
    d. $8,570
    e. $9,280

42. Inventories, under certain circumstances, may be valued at replacement cost (RC) or net realizable value (NRV). Which of the following statements regarding these concepts is **true**?
    a. Neither the RC nor NRV rule is applied to inventory items damaged during shipment.
    b. RC and NRV will result in the same inventory value.
    c. NRV is applied to damaged or shop-worn goods, while RC is applied to new goods where significant market declines have occurred.
    d. Valuation of inventories at RC and NRV will result in recognition of a loss at the time the related goods are sold.

43. Concerning LIFO and FIFO, which one of the following statements is true?
    a. When unit costs are declining, FIFO will result in higher net income and lower ending inventory.
    b. When unit costs are increasing, LIFO will result in higher net income and higher ending inventory.
    c. When unit costs are declining, FIFO will result in lower net income and lower ending inventory.
    d. When unit costs are increasing, FIFO will result in lower net income and higher ending inventory.

CHAPTER SEVEN: ANNOTATED SOLUTIONS

1. a	8. b	15. d	22. b	29. a	36. b	43. c
2. d	9. b	16. c	23. c	30. e	37. a	
3. c	10. a	17. a	24. a	31. b	38. d	
4. c	11. c	18. a	25. d	32. c	39. e	
5. b	12. b	19. a	26. a	33. c	40. a	
6. b	13. e	20. c	27. b	34. c	41. a	
7. b	14. b	21. d	28. e	35. d	42. c	

> *The correct answer and the percentage of students answering the question correctly (when it was used on an introductory accounting examination) are shown in parentheses at the beginning of each annotated solution that follows.*

Author's Note: The annotated solutions in this chapter make liberal use of certain common abbreviations such as:

- CGS = Cost of Goods Sold
- BI = Beginning Inventory
- NP = Net Purchases (i.e. Purchases + Transportation-In - Returns)
- EI = Ending Inventory

1. (a,26) Remember that CGS = BI + NP - EI. In this problem an error was made in ending inventory (EI). EI was overstated by $200 which makes cost of goods sold (CGS) understated by $200. The correct CGS, then, should be $5,200. Sales - CGS - expenses = net income or $11,000 - $5,200 - $2,000 = $3,800.

2. (d,34) First, determine the effect of these errors on cost of goods sold (CGS). The understatement of beginning inventory causes CGS to be $7,000 too small. The understatement of ending inventory causes CGS to be $3,000 too large. The net effect on CGS is that CGS is $4,000 to small. If CGS is $4,000 to small, net income is $4,000 to large.

3. (c,39) Use the cost of goods sold formula (CGS = BI + P - EI) and the income statement format (Sales - CGS = Gross Margin) to solve this problem. If 19B EI (in the CGS formula) is too large, the resulting CGS for 19B will be too small. Since EI of 19B becomes BI of 19C, 19C's CGS will be overstated which will make 19C's net income too small.

4. (c,15) The key to this question is the assumption that no further errors were made. Since the periodic system was used, the ending inventory of 19A would automatically become the beginning inventory of 19B. This beginning inventory is misstated, but it is not caused by a **new** error. It is merely the carry-over from the original error. In any event, a self-correcting error is involved and results in 19B's ending retained earnings being properly stated.

5. (b,72) Goods **out** on consignment have **not** been sold. They are, therefore, part of ending inventory.

6. (b,53) CGS will be overstated since Goods Available for Sale (BI + NP) is overstated. If CGS (or any other expense) is overstated, Net Income is understated.

7. (b,69) Title passes at the point named in the shipping terms (i.e. shipping point). The goods, therefore, belong to the buyer.

8. (b,64) Corrected Inventory Cost (of $101,000) = $100,000 (as computed originally) + $2,000 (FOB shipping point) - $1,000 (title has already passed).

9. (b,71) EI (in units) = BI + NP - Units Sold. Therefore, EI (units) = 80 + 110 - 140 = 50 units. Under FIFO, the EI consists of units that were purchased most recently. Therefore, EI (in dollars) = 50 units x $60 = $3,000.

10. (a,78) Under LIFO, the **oldest** 12 units remain (5 @ $4 + 4 @ $3 + 3 @ $2 = $38).

11. (c,60) Under FIFO, the 6 oldest units were **sold** (5 @ $4 + 1 @ $3 = $23).

12. (b,85) Of the 1,000 units available for sale, 110 remain in ending inventory. Under FIFO, the ending inventory is composed of the newest units. In this case, 100 @ $14 + 10 @ $13 = $1,530.

13. (e,54) First compute the weighted average cost. (100 @ $10 + 500 @ $11 + 300 @ $13 + 100 @ $14 / 1000 units = $11.80) The 890 units sold (50 + 840) times $11.80 = $10,502 cost of goods sold.

14. (b,80) Under FIFO, the 4 most recently acquired units will remain in ending inventory. Each of those units cost $4. 4 units x $4 = $16.

15. (d,59) Under LIFO, the 7 most recently acquired units would constitute cost of goods sold. That would include 5 units at $4 ($20) plus 2 units at $3 ($6). Total cost of goods sold = $26.

16. (c,61) First compute the weighted average cost per unit. (50 units @ $2 + 50 @ $3 + 30 @ $4 + 10 @ $5 / 140 units = $3) Ending inventory (80 units) times weighted average unit cost ($3) = $240.

17. (a,69) Under FIFO, the first 60 units available were the ones assumed sold. (There were 140 units available and 80 were left over.) Cost of the first 60 units was $130 (50 @ $2 + 10 @ $3).

18. (a,67) Minimum income taxes would occur when minimum net income was reported. When prices are declining, the higher inventory costs are the earlier ones. It is the FIFO method that results in the earlier inventory costs being charged to cost of goods sold. This minimizes net income and taxes.

19. (a,48) Under LIFO, the most recently acquired goods are matched (expensed) on the income statement with revenues of the current period. Responses b and d may or may not be true depending upon whether prices are increasing or decreasing. Response c describes FIFO.

20. (c,52) In a period of decreasing prices, FIFO would yield a lower **ending inventory** than LIFO. When this lower amount is carried forward into the next period as **beginning inventory** it will cause Cost of Goods Available for Sale to be lower than if LIFO were being used.

21. (d,58) LIFO will result in a higher inventory valuation because the ending inventory will be composed of the earliest purchases which were at higher prices. In contrast, FIFO results in an ending inventory composed of the latest purchases, which are at lower prices.

22. (b,51) When unit costs are declining, FIFO causes the newer (lower) costs to appear in the EI and the older (higher) costs to appear in CGS. Hence, statements #1 and #3 are true; #2 is false.

23. (c,74) When prices are rising, the newer (higher) costs are in ending inventory when the FIFO method is used.

24. (a,57) In a period of decreasing prices, the cost of the oldest goods are highest. FIFO releases these older (higher) costs to the income statement via cost of goods sold. This results in a low gross margin. LIFO would yield the highest gross margin. Weighted average would yield results in between FIFO and LIFO.

25. (d,90) According to the consistency principle, the same accounting methods and procedures should be used from period to period to assure that the data reported in the financial statements are reasonably comparable over time.

26. (a,83) CGS + EI = Cost of Goods Available for Sale ($4,100). CGS can be analyzed as follows: For the January 6 sale, CGS is 40 units @ $7/unit ($280); for the June 18 sale, CGS is 60 units @ $7/unit + 50 units @ $8/unit + 110 units @ $9/unit ($420 + $400 + $990 = $1,810); for the Dec. 24 sale, CGS is 60 units @ $9/unit ($540). Total CGS = $280 + $1,810 + $540 = $2,630. Cost of Goods Available - CGS = EI, so $4,100 - $2,630 = $1,470.

27. (b,72) For the sale on 4/1, the Cost of Goods Sold is:

		Units	Unit Cost	Total
3/1	Purchase	10	6	$ 60
1/1	Beginning balance	10	5	50
		20		$110

For the sale on 12/31, the Cost of Goods Sold is:

9/1	Purchase	10	8	$ 80
6/1	Purchase	10	7	70
1/1	Beginning balance	5	5	25
		25		$175

The total Cost of Goods Sold is $285 ($110 + $175).

28. (e,43) CGS for the 1st sale is $480 (40 units x $1,080/90) and is $760 for the 2nd sale [(20 x $280/20) + (40 x $1,080/90)]. Total CGS is $1,240. EI = Goods Available - CGS = $1,660 - $1,240 = $420.

29. (a,65) Perpetual provides a continuous record of what the inventory balance on hand is (or should be). At any time, a check can be made for shortages.

30. (e,76) All 40 units would be from purchase #1 (40 x $4 = $160).

31. (b,46) All units except for the last 40 acquired were sold. CGS = (20 x $5) + (50 x $4) + (60 x $6) = $660.

32. (c,57) Cost of Goods Available/# of units available = weighted average cost ($900/170 = $5.29). EI = $5.29 x 40 = $212.

33. (c,76) First compute the weighted average cost per unit. (300 @ $11 + 200 @ $12 + 300 @ $15 + 100 @ $15/900 units = $13 per unit) Ending inventory of 200 units x $13 per unit = $2,600.

34. (c,73) The ending inventory of 200 units is composed of 100 January 1 units (100 x $11 = $1,100) + 100 December 6 units (100 x $$15 = $1,500) for a total cost of $2,600.

35. (d,52) Sales - Gross Profit (Gross Margin % x Sales) = CGS. Therefore, $200 - (.40 x $200) = $120. Also, CGS = BI + NP - EI. Therefore, $120 (CGS) = $30 (BI) + $170 (NP) - X (EI); X = $80.

36. (b,43) Use your knowledge of the income statement format and the cost of goods sold formula. If sales were $20 and the gross margin percentage = 40%, then gross margin was $8. If gross margin = $8, then cost of goods sold equals $12. Using the CGS formula, $12 = $6 + $16 - ending inventory. Solving, ending inventory (the amount destroyed) = $10. Since the insurance company will cover half the loss, Fredonia's portion of the loss is only $5.

37. (a,52) The cost principle is involved since cost is one of the alternative valuations in LCM. The cost principle is violated under LCM, however, if replacement cost (market) is less than cost. This is an application of the conservatism principle in that the writedown (loss) is recognized immediately rather than waiting until the goods are sold.

38. (d,37) Use the gross margin method. CGS = Sales - gross margin (or $250,000 - [$250,000 x .60]) = $100,000. Further, CGS = BI + NP - EI. Substituting in known amounts, $100,000 = $40,000 + $120,000 - X. X = $60,000.

39. (e,47) Sales must be known to solve this problem (using the Gross Margin Method of Estimating Inventory). If sales were given as being $190,000, for example, the answer is b.

40. (a,58) Use of LCM is based on the conservatism principle. Response b would lead (if anywhere) to a gain. Response c is incorrect since such losses are recognized in the period in which they occur. Response d is nonsense.

41. (a,63) Net realizable value = estimated selling price ($7,900) - estimated selling and disposal costs ($670) = $7,230.

42. (c,57) Net Realizable Value is applied to damaged or shopworn goods when it is below cost and is the estimated amount to be received when the deteriorated goods are sold. By contrast, Replacement Cost is applied to new goods.

43. (c,61) FIFO results in the oldest costs flowing to the income statement as CGS and the newest costs flowing to the balance sheet as ending inventory. If unit costs are declining, the older and higher costs will go to the income statement and reduce net income. At the same time, the newer and lower costs go to the balance sheet for a lower ending inventory amount.

CHAPTER EIGHT: CASH, SHORT-TERM INVESTMENTS IN SECURITIES AND RECEIVABLES

PART A: Safeguarding and Reporting Cash

1. Which of the following is **not** an objective in the management of cash?
   a. Prevent loss from fraud or theft.
   b. Keep the various sources of cash at a minimum.
   c. Avoid large amounts of idle cash in checking accounts.
   d. Avoid cash shortages so that necessary payments can be made on time.
   e. Provide an accurate record of cash receipts, cash payments, and cash balances.

2. The concept of internal control refers to:
   a. audit procedures used to detect theft.
   b. policies of the Securities and Exchange Commission used to ensure that companies are not fraudulent.
   c. policies and procedures of an entity designed to safeguard assets.
   d. a method used to reconcile the bank statement.

3. Which **one** of the following is **not** an element of internal control?
   a. The person who receives cash should **not** have responsibility for it.
   b. Authorization of checks should be separated from the signing of checks.
   c. Significant disbursements should be made by check.
   d. Handling of cash should be separated from the accounting for it.

4. Which of the following items found on a bank reconciliation will require an adjusting entry?
   a. outstanding checks
   b. deposits in transit
   c. NSF checks
   d. error made by the bank

5. Which of the following is **not** a satisfactory internal control procedure?
   a. The person writing a check should be responsible for signing it.
   b. Have all cash receipts deposited daily intact.
   c. Make cash payments via prenumbered checks.
   d. Separate the handling of cash from the accounting for it.

USE THE FOLLOWING DATA FOR THE NEXT TWO QUESTIONS

August Bank Statement Information

Balance on 7/31/X9	$ 4,500
Checks cleared during August	16,500
NSF check	75
Service charge	25
Balance 8/31/X9	$4,900

August Cash Ledger Account Information

Beginning balance	$4,000
August deposits	17,000
August checks written	18,000

At August 31, outstanding checks were $5,300 and deposits in transit were $3,300.

6. The reconciled cash balance at 8/31/X9 will be:
   a. $4,900.
   b. $3,000.
   c. $2,900.
   d. cannot be determined from the above information

7. A necessary journal entry to record the NSF check would be:
   a. dr. Cash; cr. Accounts Receivable
   b. dr. Accounts Receivable; cr. Cash
   c. dr. Sales Returns and Allowances; cr. Accounts Receivable
   d. no entry is required

USE THE FOLLOWING INFORMATION FOR THE NEXT TWO QUESTIONS.

Given below is information about Mt. Hood's cash account and related bank statement at October 31. Assume there were no outstanding checks or deposits in transit at the end of the previous month.

Mt. Hood Company

Cash account balance at October 31	$50
October checks written	30
October deposits	40
Cash on hand	5
Bank Statement balance at Oct. 31	45
Deposits during October	25
Checks cleared during October	25
October service charges	5
NSF check	5
Proceeds of a note collected	20

8. What is the true cash balance that should be reported on the balance sheet at October 31?
   a. $45
   b. $50
   c. $55
   d. $60

9. Which of the following will require a journal entry at October 31?
   a. the outstanding checks
   b. the cash on hand
   c. the deposits in transit
   d. the service charges

10. The Cohen Company received its bank statement for the month of May. It showed an ending balance of $5,450. Considering the following information, what is the true cash balance for the month ending May 31?

Deposits in transit	$600
Outstanding checks	$300
Bank service charges	10
NSF check from customer	400

   a. $5,750
   b. $5,340
   c. $5,150
   d. $5,040

11. ABC Corp. received its checking account statement from Valley National Bank and discovered that a check from Mr. B (one of ABC's customers) had been returned because Mr. B did not have sufficient funds in his account. How should ABC Corp. record this event in its journal?
    a. No entry is needed because the bad debt expense has already been estimated for the year.
    b. Accounts receivable should be increased and the Allowance for Doubtful Accounts should also be increased.
    c. Sales Returns and Allowances should be increased and Accounts Receivable should be decreased.
    d. Accounts Receivable should be increased and Cash should be decreased.

12. Which of the following items will be **added** to the "Depositor's Books" side in preparing a bank reconciliation?
    a. payment of a note payable by the company
    b. NSF check from a customer
    c. deposits in transit at the beginning of the month
    d. collection by bank of company's note receivable

13. Which of the following items on the bank reconciliation requires journal entries to update the cash account?
    a. Only those items listed on the "Depositor's Books" side.
    b. Only those items listed on the "Bank Statement" side.
    c. Both those items listed on the "Depositor's Books" side and the "Bank Statement" side.
    d. None of the above is true; all reconciling differences will work out automatically when they clear the bank.

14. If the end of the month bank statement shows a balance of $35,000; there are outstanding checks of $5,000; deposits in transit of $3,000; cash on hand of $500; and the bank erroneously charged a $300 check to our account, the correct ending cash balance is:
   a. $37,800.
   b. $33,800.
   c. $33,200.
   d. $32,800.

15. Counterfeit Company just received the bank statement dated June 30, 19C, which indicated an ending balance of $15,750. Counterfeit's books show a balance in the cash account of $11,800 at June 30. The bookkeeper gives you this additional information.

Outstanding Checks @ June 30:	$5,625
Accounts Receivable @ June 30:	35,400
NSF Check Found In June's Bank Statement:	500
Deposits In Transit @ June 30:	2,050
Bank Service Charge For June :	25
Payroll Check #1999 For $100 Was Erroneously Recorded In Counterfeit's Books At:	$1,000

   What is Counterfeit's true cash balance at June 30, 19C?
   a. $10,375
   b. $12,175
   c. $13,175
   d. $19,325

PART B: Measuring and Reporting Short-Term Investments

16. Which combination of the following criteria must an investment meet in order to be listed on the balance sheet under current assets?

	Readily Marketable	Management Intends a Short Holding period
a.	Yes	Yes
b.	Yes	No
c.	No	Yes
d.	No	No

17. Company XX owned the following short-term equity investments at the end of the annual accounting period.

Investment	Cost	Market Value
A	$5,200	$5,000
B	4,000	4,000
C	6,100	6,200

   Short-term investments should be listed on the balance sheet at:
   a. $15,100.
   b. $15,200.
   c. $15,300.
   d. $15,400.

18. On December 1, DeKalb Corporation invested in the following short-term marketable securities. Also presented are the respective market values at December 31 (DeKalb's year-end).

Security	Cost	Market at Dec. 31
A Corp. Common Stock	$3	$ 5
B Corp. Common Stock	5	4
C Corp. Preferred Stock	4	1

   What amount is required in the Allowance to Reduce Short-Term Investments to Market account at December 31?
   a. $0
   b. $2
   c. $3
   d. $4
   e. $5

19. Cone Company acquired and held the following portfolio of marketable equity securities during 19D.

Security	Cost	Market
X	$ 100	$ 110
Y	200	220
Z	300	250

After all necessary adjusting entries have been prepared at 12-31-19D, what amount should appear in the account titled "Allowance for Decline in Market Value of Marketable Securities?"
a. $50 debit
b. $50 credit
c. $0
d. $20 debit
e. $20 credit

20. On July 1, 19A, XYZ Company purchased short-term investments totaling $50. Due to market fluctuations, the value of the portfolio had changed by Dec. 31, 19A, end of the accounting period. The portfolio is summarized below.

Equity Security	Acquisition Cost	Market at 12-31-19A
A	$20	$15
B	15	5
C	10	15
D	5	5

XYZ Company should make which of the following entries at 12-31-19A?
a. dr. Unrealized Loss on Short-Term Investments $10; cr. Allowance to Reduce Short-Term Investments to Market $10
b. dr. Allowance to Reduce Short-Term Investments to market $10; cr. Unrealized Loss on Short-Term Investments $10
c. dr. Unrealized Loss on Short-Term Investments $15; cr. Allowance to Reduce Short-Term Investments to Market $15
d. dr. Allowance to Reduce Short-Term Investments to market $15; cr. Unrealized Loss on Short-Term Investments $15

USE THE FOLLOWING INFORMATION FOR THE NEXT THREE QUESTIONS.

Equity Security	Cost at 1-1-19C	Market at 12-31-19C	Market at 12-31-19D
IBM	$ 600	$700	$ 700
Motorola	$1,200	$700	------
Honeywell	$1,000	$900	$1,000

21. At 12-31-19C, the balance in Allowance to Reduce Short-Term Investments to Market should be:
a. $ 500.
b. $ 600.
c. $2,300.
d. $2,800.

22. The Motorola stock was sold on 6-1-19D for $800. This transaction would have which one of the following effects?
a. an increase in current assets of $800
b. a decrease in current assets of $1200
c. a gain of $100
d. a loss of $400

23. The proper balance in Allowance to Reduce Short-Term Investments to Market at 12-31-19D (after the sale of Motorola stock on 6-1-19D) is:
a. $ 0.
b. $ 100.
c. $1,600.
d. $1,700.

24. Which of the following statements concerning short-term investments in equity securities is **false**?
a. If there is a drop in value, it is viewed as an unrealized loss that should be recognized in the period in which the drop occurred.
b. The cost includes the price paid plus all additional costs incurred to acquire the investment.
c. When the LCM rule is applied, the market value is determined on the portfolio amount rather than on an item-by-item basis.
d. In determining the gain or loss on sale of an individual security, consideration must be given to the balance in the allowance account.

25. Brown, Inc. has provided the following information regarding equity investments made during July of 19C:

Short-Term Investment	Acquisition Cost	Market Value at July 31, 19C
X Company	$ 8,000	$ 7,000
Y Company	12,000	14,000
Z Company	5,000	4,000

On August 10, 19C, Brown sold the Z company stock for $4,100. Assuming Brown prepares monthly financial statements, which set of entries below properly reflect the facts above?

a. July 31: dr. Unrealized Loss On Short-Term Investments 2,000; cr.Allowance To Reduce Short-term Investments 2,000

   Aug. 10: dr. Cash 4,100; cr. Gain On Sale Of Short-term Investment 100; cr. Short-term Investments 4,000

b. July 31: dr. Unrealized Loss On Short-Term Investments 2,000; cr. Allowance To Reduce Short-term Investments 2,000

   Aug. 10: dr. Cash 4,100; dr. Loss On Sale Of Short-term Investments 900; cr. Short-term Investments 5,000

c. July 31: No entry necessary.

   Aug. 10: dr. Cash 4,100; dr. Loss On Sale Of Short-term Investments 900; cr. Short-term Investments 5,000

d. July 31: No entry necessary.

   Aug. 10: dr. Cash 4,100; cr. Gain On Sale Of Short-term Investments 100; cr. Short-term Investments 4,000

26. A company's balance sheet at 12-31-19B included the following:

Short-term investment
   at LCM (cost = $30,000): $20,000

The market value of the investment at 12-31-19B is:
a. $30,000.
b. $20,000.
c. $10,000.
d. not determinable from the information given.

27. On 7-1-19A the Green Co. made the following short-term investments:

Company	Shares	Unit Price	Market Price at 12-31-19A
Red	10	$6	$4
Blue	10	8	9

The necessary adjusting entry on 12-31-19A will include a:
a. debit to Unrealized Loss of $20.
b. credit to Allowance to Reduce Short-Term Investments of $20.
c. debit to Unrealized Loss of $10.
d. debit to Allowance to Reduce Short-Term Investments of $10.

PART C: Measuring and Reporting Receivables

28. On June 1, 19A, the Down Home Farm Equipment Company sold Old McDonald a $100,000 tractor. Terms were 10% down with McDonald signing a note for the balance. McDonald made the cash down payment and signed a 10% note that was due in four months. On July 1, 19A, Down Home Company sold the McDonald note to a bank using a discount rate of 20%. The amount the bank paid for the note was:
a. $98,166.
b. $93,000.
c. $88,350.
d. $86,800.

29. Big Discount Grocery Store recently sold a parcel of land it had been holding as a potential building site for a second store. The buyer made a 25% down payment and signed a formal document containing an unconditional promise to pay the balance within 350 days plus interest at 12%. Which set of the following terms are appropriate to describe this event?

	Trade Receivable	Note Receivable	Short-Term
a.	Yes	Yes	No
b.	Yes	No	No
c.	No	Yes	No
d.	No	No	Yes
e.	No	Yes	Yes

30. Interest revenue on a 9%, 90-day Note Receivable, with a face value of $10,000, for **60 days** is equal to:
    a. $900.
    b. $225.
    c. $150.
    d. $ 15.

31. The Cabbage Patch Company received a note from one of its customers on March 1, 19A. The note was 90-days, 10%, and had a face value of $12,000. Thirty days later, Cabbage Patch discounted the note at a bank charging a 15% discount rate. Cash proceeds from the note were:
    a. $11,220.
    b. $11,839.
    c. $11,993.
    d. $12,000.
    e. $12,300.

32. Upon discounting a note receivable at the bank, the payee of the note might make which of the following journal entries?

    a. dr. Interest Expense and Notes Receivable Discounted; cr. Notes Receivable
    b. dr. Notes Receivable; cr. Interest Revenue and Cash
    c. dr. Interest Expense and Cash; cr. Notes Receivable
    d. dr. Cash; cr. Interest Revenue and Notes Payable

33. When a note receivable is discounted at a bank, the amount of money (interest) that the **bank** has earned when the note is paid at maturity is the difference between the:
    a. cash proceeds and face value.
    b. maturity value and face value.
    c. maturity value and cash proceeds.
    d. maturity value and bank discount.

34. Freddy discounted a $30,000, 60-day, 8% note on the day he received it. The bank had a discount rate of 6%. When recording the cash proceeds of the note on Freddy's books, which of the following would be included? (Assume a 360-day year.)
    a. revenue of $96
    b. expense of $96
    c. revenue of $100
    d. expense of $100

35. Nancy Tang Company sold a 12%, $5,000, 180-day note receivable to a local bank. Assuming that Nancy had held the note for 60 days before discounting it at 15%, how much would the bank pay for the note?
    a. $5,035
    b. $5,200
    c. $5,265
    d. $5,300

36. Which of the following statements is **false**?
    a. Short-term investments, both debt and equity, must be accounted for at the lower-of-cost-or-market.
    b. Factoring is the sale of accounts receivable to a financial institution.
    c. In a bank reconciliation, all additions and deductions from the cash balance per books must be recorded in the journal.
    d. Internal control refers to the policies and procedures of an entity designed primarily to safeguard assets.

37. Which of the following is **not** a constraint to accounting principles?
    a. materiality
    b. comparability
    c. conservatism
    d. cost benefit

38. XYZ Company made the following entry upon discounting a note receivable.

Cash	1,029
Notes Receivable	1,000
Interest Revenue	29

The bank at which the note was discounted held it for 2 months of its six month life, used a 12% discount rate, and earned $21 of revenue for providing its services. What was the maturity value of this note?
 a. $1,020
 b. $1,029
 c. $1,050
 d. $1,060

39. A $20,000, 12%, 120 day note receivable was sold to Shakey National Bank after 60 days at a discount rate of 18%. What were the cash proceeds of the note? (How much did the bank pay?)
 a. $19,982
 b. $20,000
 c. $20,176
 d. $20,384

40. Computer, Inc. sold a computer for $20,000. A 15%, 180 day promissory note was accepted from the customer. 60 days later, Computer sold the note to a bank where the discount rate was 18%. Assuming a 360-day year, how much cash did Computer, Inc. receive from the bank?
 a. $20,210
 b. $21,200
 c. $21,500
 d. $21,935

CHAPTER EIGHT: ANNOTATED SOLUTIONS

1. b	8. d	15. b	22. d	29. e	36. a
2. c	9. d	16. a	23. a	30. c	37. b
3. a	10. a	17. b	24. d	31. c	38. c
4. c	11. d	18. b	25. c	32. c	39. c
5. a	12. d	19. e	26. b	33. c	40. a
6. c	13. a	20. a	27. c	34. a	
7. b	14. b	21. a	28. c	35. a	

> *The correct answer and the percentage of students answering the question correctly (when it was used on an introductory accounting examination) are shown in parentheses at the beginning of each annotated solution that follows.*

1. (b,67) Preventing losses from fraud or theft, avoiding large amounts of **idle** cash, avoiding cash shortages and providing accurate records are all objectives of cash management. Minimization of **sources** of cash is not an objective. Those should most likely be maximized.

2. (c,87) By definition, internal control relates to those policies and procedures designed to safeguard assets. Thefts or fraud are usually caused by a lack of strong internal control procedures. Preparation of a bank reconciliation is an internal control procedure; but internal control is not a method of preparing a bank reconciliation.

3. (a,65) Response a is a ridiculous statement. **Of course** the person receiving cash must be held responsible for it.

4. (c,77) Only adjustments made to the "balance per books" side of the bank reconciliation require adjusting entries. Since (on the bank reconciliation) NSF checks are deducted from the balance per books, an adjusting entry must be made them. Outstanding checks, deposits in transit, and bank errors are adjustments to the "balance per bank" side and do not require adjusting entries.

5. (a,81) Usually, the responsibility for preparing checks is separated from the responsibility for signing them.

6. (c,63) Ending balance per books is $3,000 ($4,000 + $17,000 - $18,000). Both the service charge ($25) and the NSF check ($75) should be deducted from it to yield $2,900.

7. (b,76) When an NSF check is returned from the bank, a receivable should be established and the cash account decreased.

8. (d,53) The easiest way to solve this problem is to prepare a bank reconciliation on a piece of scratch paper. Starting with the "balance per books" of $50, add the proceeds of the note ($20) and deduct service charges ($5) and the NSF check ($5) for a true cash balance of $60. Alternatively, start with the "balance per bank" of $45 and add the deposit in transit ($40 - $25 = $15) and the cash on hand ($5); then deduct the outstanding checks ($30 - $35 = $5) for a balance of $60.

9. (d,76) All checks written, all deposits made, and the cash on hand are already included in the Oct. 31 cash balance. The only new information is the amount of the service charges and an entry must be made for that.

10. (a,38) The true cash balance can be computed as follows: Bank Balance + Deposits in Transit - Outstanding Checks. Therefore, $5,450 + $600 - $300 = $5,750. The NSF check and bank service charges are already included in the bank balance of $5,450.

11. (d,67) Since the bank has charged the NSF check back to ABC, ABC's cash account (in the ledger) needs to be reduced. Also, ABC will now attempt to collect from Mr. B so an account receivable needs to be established.

12. (d,55) Responses a and c have already been recorded in the depositor's books before the reconciliation is prepared, while the NSF check (response b) must be deducted.

13. (a,38) Journal entries are required for those items brought to the company's attention by the bank statement. All of these items (e.g. NSF checks, service charges, collections) appear on the "Depositor's Books" side of the bank reconciliation.

14. (b,55) Correct ending cash balance = Bank Statement Balance + Deposits in Transit - Outstanding Checks + Bank Error + Cash on Hand. Therefore, ending balance = $35,000 + $3,000 - $5,000 + $300 + $500 = $33,800.

15. (b,66) To the bank statement balance of $15,750 deduct outstanding checks ($5,625) and add deposits in transit ($2,050) for a true cash balance of $12,175. Alternatively, begin with the balance per books of $11,800 and deduct the NSF check ($500) and the service charge ($25); add the $900 effect of the error for a true cash balance of $12,715.

16. (a,71) To qualify as a short-term investment (a current asset), the investment must be readily marketable **and** a short-term holding period must be expected.

17. (b,57) The sum of the "market value" column ($15,200) is less than the sum of the "cost" column ($15,300). (Remember that the portfolio basis is used when applying lower-of-cost-or-market.)

18. (b,78) The required balance is the amount by which the cost equity securities ($12) exceeds the market value of the equity securities ($10) at the balance sheet date. The difference here is $2.

19. (e,57) Cost of the portfolio ($600) exceeds the market value of the portfolio ($580) by $20. That amount should appear in the allowance account. Since the allowance account is a contra-account to an asset, it should have a credit balance.

20. (a,62) Short-term investments should be valued at lower-of-cost-or-market (LCM) on a portfolio basis. Cost of the portfolio is $50 while its current market value is $40. A loss of $10 should be debited and a $10 credit entry made to the Allowance account.

21. (a,61) At 12-31-19C, the cost of the portfolio ($2,800) exceeds the market of the portfolio ($2,300) by $500. An allowance should be established in that amount.

22. (d,75) The sale of Motorola stock would involve a debit to Cash of $800, a debit to Loss on Sale of Short-Term Investments of $400, and a credit to Short-Term Investments of $1,200. NOTE: The sale of items from the portfolio does not involve the allowance account. The allowance account is used **only** at year end when the size of any necessary allowance is determined.

23. (a,44) At 12-31-19D there are only two securities remaining in the portfolio (IBM and Honeywell). Cost of the portfolio, then, is $1,600 ($600 + $1,000) while the market value is $1,700 ($700 + $1,000). Since market exceeds cost, no allowance is needed.

24. (d,64) The allowance account is a contra-account to the entire portfolio of investments and not to any individual security therein. Each security is still recorded at it's original cost even after the allowance account has been set up. When disposing of a security, therefore, the allowance account is not involved. Further, the allowance account is adjusted only at the end of the period.

25. (c,59) At July 31, 19C (end of the monthly accounting period) no entry is necessary because the market value of the portfolio is equal to the original cost. At August 10, 19C, there will be a $900 loss on sale of the investment since $4,100 was obtained in exchange for a security previously carried in the investment account at $5,000.

26. (b,82) When the lower-of-cost-or-market procedure (LCM) is used, the asset (or portfolio) is valued at the lesser of cost or market and the other amount is disclosed. In this problem, the higher amount is labeled as being cost ($30,000), so the lower amount must be market ($20,000).

27. (c,65) On a portfolio basis, the Fair Market Value of the short-term investments is $10 less than the cost and results in a debit to Unrealized Loss of $10.

28. (c,57) The maturity value of the note is $93,000 [$90,000 face value + interest of $3,000 ($90,000 x 10% x 4/12 year)]. The amount paid for the note is calculated as follows: Cash Proceeds = Maturity Value - (Maturity Value x Discount Rate x Time). In this case, $93,000 - ($93,000 x 20% x 3/12) = $88,350.

29. (e,67) The sale of land by a grocery store is **not** part of its regular business. Any resulting receivable, then, is a special receivable and **not** a trade receivable. The formal document that was signed was a note receivable and it is short-term because it is for less than one year.

30. (c,75) The interest revenue is calculated as follows: $10,000 x 9% x 60/360 = $150.

31. (c,55) Cash proceeds = Maturity Value - (Maturity Value x Discount Rate x Time). Maturity Value is the amount due at maturity (principal + interest = $12,300); Time is the number of days the bank holds the note divided by 360. Cash Proceeds, then, = $12,300 - ($12,300 x .15 x 60/360) = $11,993.

32. (c,65) When a note is discounted (sold) at a bank, the Notes Receivable account must be decreased and the Cash account increased. Only response c includes these entries. In addition, the debit to interest expense would occur if the bank's discount rate is greater than the rate of interest that the note pays.

33. (c,20) Maturity value is the amount the bank receives on the maturity date of the note. Cash proceeds is the amount the bank gave the discounter of the note. The difference between the two is the amount the bank earned for providing its services.

34. (a,34) The maturity value (MV) of this note is the principal ($30,000) plus interest ($400) at the due date. Cash Proceeds = MV - (MV x discount rate x time) or CP = $30,400 - ($30,400 x .06 x 1/6) = $30,096. The journal entry to record this discounting would be: dr. Cash $30,096; cr. Notes Receivable $30,000, and cr. Financing Revenue $96.

35. (a,57) The maturity value of the note is $5,300 ($5,000 face value plus $300 interest). The fee the bank wishes to charge for discounting the note is computed as follows: $5,300 x 15% x 1/3 year = $265. The amount the bank is willing to pay for the note, then, is $5,300 - $265 = $5,035.

36. (a,41) Only short-term equity securities must be accounted for at the lower-of-cost-or-market. While many companies also apply FASB #12 (LCM) to debt securities, there is no requirement that they do so.

37. (b,67) There are three constraints: (1) materiality, (2) conservatism, and (3) cost benefit. Comparability is a secondary qualitative characteristic of accounting information...not a constraint.

38. (c,59) The amount of cash remitted to the seller of the note ($1,029) plus the fee to be earned by the bank ($21) add up to the amount that the bank expects to collect on the maturity date of the note ($1,050).

39. (c,85) The formula for computing cash proceeds (CP) from a discounted note receivable is CP = Maturity Value - (Maturity Value x Discount Rate x Time). In this problem the maturity value is $20,800; the discount rate is 18%; and the time is 60 days. Substituting into the formula, CP = $20,800 - ($20,800 x .18 x 1/6) = $20,176.

40. (a,66) The cash proceeds = maturity value of the note - (maturity value of the note x discount rate x time bank will hold note). The maturity value is $21,500 (principal plus interest). Therefore, cash proceeds = $21,500 - ($21,500 x 18% x 1/3 year) = $20,210.

CHAPTER NINE: OPERATIONAL ASSETS – PROPERTY, PLANT AND EQUIPMENT; NATURAL RESOURCES; AND INTANGIBLES

PART A: Property, Plant, and Equipment, Including Depreciation

1. How many of the following accounts should be classified as **operational** assets?
   -- equipment   -- patents
   -- office supplies   -- mineral deposits
   -- land held as an investment
   a. one
   b. two
   c. three
   d. four
   e. five

2. Assume each of the following is owned by Bhagwan Enterprises. Which one could **not** be properly classified as a tangible operational asset?
   a. a new Rolls Royce automobile
   b. a trademark
   c. land containing a silver mine
   d. a warehouse

3. Golden Company purchased a new machine having an invoice price of $10,000. The terms of sale were 2/10, n/30. Other information relevant to this transaction follows.

   Transportation cost (paid by the seller) $100
   Installation cost (paid by Golden Company)   200
   Sales Tax   300

   At what amount should Golden Company record this new machine?
   a. $10,600
   b. $10,400
   c. $10,300
   d. $10,000
   e. $ 9,800

4. Which of the following are properly paired in describing the cost apportionment required by the matching principle?

   1. depreciation: intangible assets
   2. depletion: natural resources
   3. amortization: tangible non-natural resource assets

   a. Statement #1 only
   b. Statement #2 only
   c. Statement #3 only
   d. Statements #1 and #2 only
   e. Statements #2 and #3 only

5. Real estate fees incurred when purchasing buildings are treated on the financial statements as an:
   a. expense in the period in which the buildings are purchased.
   b. expense in the period when the fees are paid.
   c. extraordinary expense.
   d. asset.

6. Land and a building were acquired for $485,000. An appraisal showed the estimated values to be $175,000 for the land and $325,000 for the building. What amounts should be recorded in the accounting records for the land and building, respectively?

	Land	Building
a.	$175,000	$325,000
b.	$160,000	$325,000
c.	$175,000	$310,000
d.	$169,750	$315,250

7. The cost of sales tax when purchasing machinery for use in the factory is treated on the financial statements as a(n):
   a. current asset.
   b. tangible asset.
   c. intangible asset.
   d. expense in the period the asset is purchased.

8. Fumie Company made a basket purchase for $100,000. Land was appraised at $60,000 which was 40% of the fair value of the basket purchase. How much cost should be apportioned to the remaining purchased assets? Also, what was the sum of the appraised values for the purchased assets?

	Building Total	Appraised Value
a.	$40,000	$150,000
b.	$60,000	$250,000
c.	$40,000	$250,000
d.	$60,000	$150,000

9. Jones, Inc. purchased a warehouse and the land upon which it was located. The **basket purchase** price was $450,000. The land was appraised for $180,000 while the building was appraised for $360,000. In addition to these costs, $50,000 was paid for renovation and repair costs to get the warehouse ready for use. What account balances should Jones show in its ledger?
   a. Land $180,000; Warehouse $360,000
   b. Land $150,000; Warehouse $300,000
   c. Land $166,667; Warehouse $333,333
   d. Land $150,000; Warehouse $350,000

10. Alexander acquired a number of items for his ragtime band. He paid $1,500 total for a trombone, trumpet, and drum set. The fair market values of these items, respectively, were $500, $800, and $700. At what amount should the trombone be recorded on Alexander's books?
    a. $600
    b. $525
    c. $500
    d. $375
    e. $300

11. San Francisco Co. acquired land, buildings, and equipment at a lump sum amount of $400,000. Appraised values were as follows: land, $100,000; buildings, $150,000; and equipment, $250,000. The buildings should be recorded on the books at what amount?
    a. $ 80,000
    b. $120,000
    c. $150,000
    d. $200,000

12. The principal purpose for recording depreciation is to:
    a. provide a fund for financing replacement of depreciable assets.
    b. show conservative figures for financial statements.
    c. provide a deduction for income tax purposes.
    d. systematically allocate the asset's cost over its useful life.

USE THE FOLLOWING INFORMATION FOR THE NEXT THREE QUESTIONS.

A machine was purchased on January 2, 19A for $24,000. The machine had an estimated residual value of $3,000 and an estimated useful life of 5 years or 300,000 units.

13. 19A's depreciation expense, using the double-declining balance method is:
    a. $ 9,600.
    b. $ 7,000.
    c. $ 8,400.
    d. $16,000.
    e. $14,000.

14. 19A's depreciation expense, using sum-of-the-year's digits method is:
    a. $4,200.
    b. $7,000.
    c. $8,000.
    d. $9,600.

15. Assume that 70,000 units were produced in 19A. Depreciation expense, using the units-of-output method is:
    a. $4,200.
    b. $4,500.
    c. $4,900.
    d. $5,600.

16. Mrs. Coffee purchased a coffee grinder on January 1, 19A for $15. The estimated useful life was 3 years and the depreciation (based on the straight- line method) was $2 per year. The estimated residual value of the coffee grinder must have been:
    a. $9.
    b. $6.
    c. $5.
    d. $3.

17. Identify, respectively, (1) the depreciation method that initially ignores residual value and (2) the depreciation method in which depreciation expense is constant each year.
    a. sum-of-the-year's digits; double-declining balance
    b. productive output; straight-line
    c. sum-of-the-year's digits; straight-line
    d. double-declining balance; productive output
    e. double declining balance; straight-line

18. Which of the following depreciation methods **always** results in the most rapid decrease in an asset's book value?
    a. straight-line
    b. double-declining balance
    c. sum-of-the-year's digits
    d. could be either (b) or (c); it depends on estimated life of the asset

19. Assuming a useful life of three years, which of the following depreciation methods would **always** result in the least depreciation expense in the first year?
    a. straight-line
    b. sum-of-the-year's digits
    c. productive output method
    d. cannot be determined from the data given

20. State Company purchased a machine on January 1, 19A for $15,000. It had an expected life of five years and an estimated residual value of $3,000. Assuming that the sum-of-the-years' digits depreciation is used, determine book value **at Dec. 31, 19C**.
    a. $2,400
    b. $5,400
    c. $7,800
    d. $8,600

21. Given below is a partial depreciation schedule for an asset purchased for $10,000 on January 1, 19A. The asset was depreciated using the double- declining balance method.

Year-End	Book Value
19A	$6,000
19B	3,600
19C	2,160

The economic life of the asset must have been:
    a. 2.5 years
    b. 3 years
    c. 4 years
    d. 5 years

22. Scillio Bean, manager of the local mushroom farm, is a shady character who cares not for GAAP. Scillio cares only about incurring the lowest possible income tax expense during the current year. If Scillio could use any of the methods listed below, which method would he choose? (Assume a five year useful life and no residual value.)
    a. double-declining balance
    b. sum-of-the-years' digits
    c. 150% declining balance
    d. straight line

23. Marshall Company has just purchased a depreciable asset with a useful life of 6 years. The company will be choosing either the straight-line (SL) or sum-of-the-years' digits (SYD) method of depreciation. Which one of the following statements correctly describes what will happen under SL or SYD depreciation?
    a. SYD will result in a higher net income figure in the first year than will SL.
    b. Depreciation expense in the second year will be higher under SL than under SYD.
    c. Net income in the fifth year will be higher under SL than SYD.
    d. Depreciation expense will be lower in the sixth year under SYD than SL.

24. Assume a computer had a cost of $10,600, an estimated useful life of ten years, and a residual value of $600. Using the double declining balance method, what is the first year's depreciation?
    a. $2,120
    b. $2,000
    c. $1,060
    d. $1,000

25. On January 1, three years ago, Jansen Company acquired a fabricating machine for $15,000. Estimated useful life was 10 years and estimated residual value was $3,000. If double-declining balance depreciation has been used, what is the proper amount of depreciation expense for the **third** year?
    a. $1,500
    b. $1,536
    c. $1,920
    d. $3,000

26. Janada Company purchased a new piece of equipment on January 1, 19A for $45,000. It had an estimated life of four years and an estimated residual value of $5,000. Determine depreciation expense for the **second** year ending December 31, 19B using (1) sum-of-the-year's digits, and (2) double-declining balance.

	S-Y-D	D-D-B
a.	$16,000	$22,500
b.	$12,000	$11,250
c.	$13,500	$11,250
d.	$12,000	$ 8,437

27. Delgado Co. purchased a machine on January 1, 19X5 for $70,000. The machine has an estimated useful life of 5 years and a residual value of $5,000. The machine is being depreciated using the double-declining balance method. The accumulated depreciation account balance at **December 31, 19X6** should be:
    a. $16,800.
    b. $28,000.
    c. $41,800.
    d. $44,800.

28. An operational asset was being depreciated based on the following information.

Method	straight-line
Useful life	10 years
Acquisition cost	$12,000
Residual value	$ 2,000

    At the beginning of year 6, management decided that the residual value estimate should be reduced to $1,000. What is the proper amount of depreciation expense for year 6?
    a. $ 200
    b. $ 800
    c. $1,200
    d. $1,400

29. Conifer Tree Company purchased equipment for $1,000 on 1-1-19A. At that time, estimated useful life was 10 years and estimated residual value was $200. After three years of straight-line depreciation the estimated residual value was reduced to zero and the estimated useful life was reduced to four more years (until 12-31-19G). What will be the new annual depreciation expense for each of the next four years?
    a. $160
    b. $175
    c. $190
    d. $200

30. Assume the following:

Cost of machine	$43,000
Estimated useful life	8 years
Estimated residual value	$ 3,000
Accumulated depreciation through year 5 (assume straight-line)	$25,000

    During the sixth year, the estimates were revised to the following:

Revised estimated total useful life	7 years
Revised estimated residual value	$ 2,000

    Determine the accumulated depreciation account balance at the end of the sixth year.
    a. $ 8,000
    b. $33,000
    c. $34,500
    d. $36,000

PART B: Repairs and Maintenance, Natural Resources, and Intangible Assets

31. Extraordinary repairs are:
    a. capital expenditures.
    b. revenue expenditures.
    c. expensed currently in order to comply with the matching principle.
    d. reported on the income statement as extraordinary items.

32. The Big Cheese Sandwich Shoppe spent several thousand dollars on a capital expenditure to repair the roof. This amount should be recorded as an:
    a. expense.
    b. extraordinary item.
    c. asset.
    d. addition to capital.

33. Big Piney Lumber acquired a stand of timber for $3,100,000. It contains 10 million board feet and there is a $300,000 residual value. The firm estimates it will take about 5 years to harvest the timber. In the first year, 3 million board feet were harvested and sold. What is Big Piney's depletion expense for the first year?
    a. $930,000
    b. $840,000
    c. $620,000
    d. $560,000

34. Better Company acquired for cash the business of Old Company at a price of $70,000. The book value of Old company assets was $40,000 (there were no liabilities). Independent appraisers placed a fair market value of $60,000 on the Old Company assets. In recording this acquisition, Better Company should debit Goodwill in the amount of:
    a. $30,000.
    b. $20,000.
    c. $10,000.
    d. $ -0- .

35. The maximum period over which goodwill may be amortized is:
    a. 50 years.
    b. 40 years.
    c. 20 years.
    d. 17 years.

36. A difference between a deferred charge and a prepaid expense is that a deferred charge is:
    a. an expense to be paid and a prepaid expense has already been paid.
    b. a liability and a prepaid expense is an asset.
    c. a long-term asset and a prepaid expense is a short-term asset.
    d. a revenue and a prepaid expense is an expense.

37. The Nalani Tour Co. acquired a van for $10,000 on January 1, 19A. It had an estimated life of 4 years, a residual value of $2,000, and the company uses the sum-of-the-year's digits method of calculating depreciation at each year-end. If, on September 30, 19C, the Nalani Tour Co. sold the van for $6,000, which of the following should be recognized?
    a. $2,800 gain
    b. $1,200 loss
    c. $3,200 gain
    d. $1,600 gain

38. A delivery truck used by XYZ Company was destroyed by fire on April 1, 19X6. The accounting records provide the following information.

Depreciation method	straight-line
Acquisition date	January 1, 19X4
Estimated useful life	10 years
Acquisition cost	$12,000
Book value (12-31-X5)	$ 9,600
Accum. Deprec. (12-31-X5)	$ 2,400

What is the proper amount of depreciation expense for the year ending Dec. 31, 19X6?
    a. $ 300
    b. $ 150
    c. $1,200
    d. $1,400
    e. zero, because the truck was destroyed in 19X6.

39. Hector Company reports the following current information regarding an operational asset.

Cost	$5,000
Estimated residual value	1,000
Accumulated depreciation	3,000

If the asset is sold for $3,000, the amount of gain or loss would be a:
a. loss of $1,000.
b. gain of $1,000.
c. loss of $2,000.
d. gain of $2,000.

40. On January 1, 19X2, the Howe Company acquired a small office building for $8,000. It was depreciated using the straight-line method (on a 20 year estimated life with no residual value) and sold on December 31, 19X6 for $6,000. The journal entry to record the sale is:

a.
Cash	6,000	
Gain on Sale	2,000	
Building		8,000

b.
Cash	6,000	
Accum. Depreciation	2,000	
Building		8,000

c.
Cash	6,000	
Loss on Sale	2,000	
Building		8,000

d.
Building	8,000	
Cash		6,000
Accumulated Depreciation		2,000

41. Gidget's Gadgets sold an obsolete piece of equipment for $4,000. Original cost of the item had been $12,500 and its accumulated depreciation was $7,200. This transaction would result in a:
a. loss of $3,200.
b. loss of $1,300.
c. gain of $4,000.
d. loss of $8,500.

42. Which one of the following statements is **incorrect**?
a. Depreciation is the allocation of part of the prepaid cost of an asset.
b. When used to purchase an operational asset, non-cash consideration is valued at market value.
c. Repair costs incurred prior to the use of an operational asset should be debited to the asset account.
d. Each asset in a basket purchase should be recorded at its fair market value.
e. Revenue expenditures are expensed in the period incurred.

43. Which of the following is **false** about intangible assets?
a. They have no physical substance.
b. They have no real economic value.
c. They can be often be purchased or sold.
d. They are expensed through amortization over the life of the asset.

44. Which of the following is **not** an intangible asset?
a. patent
b. goodwill
c. leasehold improvement
d. franchise
e. natural gas

CHAPTER NINE: ANNOTATED SOLUTIONS

1. c	8. d	15. c	22. a	29. c	36. c	43. b
2. b	9. d	16. a	23. d	30. b	37. a	44. e
3. c	10. d	17. e	24. a	31. a	38. a	
4. b	11. b	18. b	25. c	32. c	39. b	
5. d	12. d	19. d	26. b	33. b	40. b	
6. d	13. a	20. b	27. d	34. c	41. b	
7. b	14. b	21. d	28. c	35. b	42. d	

> *The correct answer and the percentage of students answering the question correctly (when it was used on an introductory accounting examination) are shown in parentheses at the beginning of each annotated solution that follows.*

1. (c,34) Equipment, patents, and mineral deposits are all classified as operational assets. The land is properly classified as an investment (since it is not currently being used) and office supplies are current assets.

2. (b,91) A trademark in an intangible asset. (Assuming the Rolls Royce auto is used in operations of this business, it would be classified as a tangible operational asset.)

3. (c,57) The machine should be recorded net of the discount offered, ($9,800) regardless of whether it was taken. Also include the sales tax ($300) and installation costs ($200) since each is a necessary and proper expenditure to acquire the asset. Total = $10,300.

4. (b,76) Depreciation relates to tangible assets and amortization to intangible assets. Thus, only statement #2 is correct.

5. (d,45) Under the cost principle, all reasonable and necessary costs to acquire and place the operational asset in service should be debited to the asset account. Real estate fees would be considered necessary and reasonable.

6. (d,79) Individual items acquired in a basket purchase are recorded on the books according to the ratio of their fair market values. Fair values of the land and building total $500,000 ($175,000 + $375,000). Since the land accounts for 35% of the fair value of the "basket," 35% of the $485,000 actually spent should be allocated to cost of the land ($169,750). Similarly, 65% of $485,000 ($315,250) should be allocated to cost of the building.

7. (b,29) All costs necessary to acquire an asset and get it ready for intended use are part of the cost of the asset. Payment of sales tax is often a cost necessary to acquire an asset. The sales tax should be debited to the account of the asset acquired.

8. (d,56) If the land accounts for 40% of the appraised value of the basket purchase, 40% of the price paid (40% x $100,000 = $40,000) should be allocated to the land. This leaves 60% ($60,000) to be allocated to the other assets. To solve the second part of the problem, let "X" = the total appraised value of the assets purchased. We are told that 40% of "X" = $60,000. If .40X = $60,000, then X = $150,000.

9. (d,30) Relative market value of the assets is used to allocate the lump sum. The value allocated to the warehouse is determined by the following: ($360,000/($180,000 + $360,000)) x ($450,000) = $300,000. In addition, the $50,000 needed to get the warehouse ready for use is debited to the account as part of the acquisition cost ($300,000 + $50,000 = $350,000). The amount for land is computed as: ($180,000/($180,000 + $360,000)) x $450,000 = $150,000.

10. (d,54) The $1,500 is allocated to the three instruments in the ratio of each item's individual fair market value (FMV) to the total FMV of the group. FMV of the trombone is $500; total FMV is $2,000 ($500 + $800 + $700). $500/$2,000 = 25%; 25% of $1,500 is $375.

11. (b,74) Since the buildings account for 30% of the appraised value of all items purchased, they are to be assigned 30% of the actual amount paid (30% x $400,000 = $120,000).

12. (d,96) Response d is a straightforward description of why depreciation expense is recorded.

13. (a,65) Ignore salvage value under the double-declining method. The expense in any period is "twice the straight-line rate" (40%) times "book value" ($24,000). 40% x $24,000 = $9,600.

14. (b,68) Computed as: 5/15 x $21,000 = $7,000. (Remember to deduct residual value from original cost under this method.)

15. (c,70) Computed as: $21,000/300,000 units = $.07 per unit. $.07 x 70,000 units produced this period = $4,900. (Remember to deduct residual value from original cost under this method.)

16. (a,91) If the coffee grinder has a three year life and annual depreciation expense is $2, the total depreciation to be taken is $6. The original cost - $6 = $9 residual value.

17. (e,77) Under double-declining balance method, residual value is initially ignored when computing the depreciation expense. (Remember, though, that book value must **not** be allowed to fall below residual value.) Straight-line method yields equal depreciation expense each period.

18. (b,53) The double-declining balance method results in the most rapid decrease in book value since early year's depreciation is highest under this method. (NOTE: The units-of-production method **could** result in a more rapid decline than double-declining balance method, but that method was not an option in this question.)

19. (d,54) Because the productive output method is one of the alternatives, an answer cannot be determined from the information given. If relatively few units have been produced, this method results in very little depreciation. But the opposite is true if many units were produced.

20. (b,46) Notice that **three** years have passed since purchase. Original cost ($15,000) - accumulated depreciation to date (5/15 x $12,000 + 4/15 x $12,000 + 3/15 x $12,000 = $9,600) equals $5,400.

21. (d,53) In the first year, depreciation expense was $4,000 ($10,000 cost - $6,000 end-of-year-one book value). This represents a rate of 40% ($4,000/$10,000). The straight-line rate would be half the double-declining balance rate (20%). At 20% per year, an asset would be fully depreciated (using straight-line) in 5 years.

22. (a,71) Double-declining balance yields the **highest** first year depreciation expense which in turn results in the lowest first year net income and income tax expense.

23. (d,68) Under accelerated depreciation methods (such as SYD and double- declining balance), early years' depreciation is higher than straight- line but later years' depreciation is lower.

24. (a,67) Remember to ignore residual value here. First year depreciation would be $10,600 x 20% = $2,120.

25. (c,63) The double-declining balance rate is 20% (2 x 10%). This rate is multiplied times book value as an adjusting entry at each year-end. For years 1 and 2, respectively, depreciation expense is $3,000 and $2,400. This makes the book value at the end of year 3 = $9,600 ($15,000 cost minus $5,400 accumulated depreciation). Depreciation expense for year 3 is $1,920 (20% x $9,600).

26. (b,67) For sum-of-the-year's digits method, the depreciation expense in year 2 is computed as "cost minus residual value times 3/10" or $12,000 ($45,000 - $5,000 x 3/10). For DDB method, remember that residual value is ignored. Depreciation expense would be twice the straight-line rate times book value. In the first year, the expense is $22,500 (50% x $45,000); and for the second year $11,250 (50% x $22,500).

27. (d,38) Depreciation for 19X5 is $28,000 (.40 x $70,000), and for 19X6 it is $16,800 [.40 x ($70,000 - $28,000)]. Therefore, accumulated depreciation at December 31, 19X6 is $44,800 ($28,000 + $16,800).

28. (c,68) The new annual depreciation expense = (cost - accumulated depreciation - residual value)/remaining useful life. Therefore, the depreciation expense for year 6 is $1,200 ($12,000 - $5,000 - $1,000/5).

29. (c,71) Remember that when depreciation estimates are changed, there are no retroactive changes made to past financial statements. At the point of change, book value was $760 (cost of $1,000 - three years depreciation at $80 per year). If no residual value is now expected, this $760 must be allocated evenly over the coming 4 years. $760/4 = $190 per year.

30. (b,62) Remember that no retroactive changes are made if there are changes in estimates. The $25,000 already in accumulated depreciation remains there and the remaining depreciation to be taken is merely spread over the remaining years. As of the beginning of year 6, there is $16,000 yet to be depreciated ($43,000 cost - $25,000 accumulated depreciation to date - $2,000 new estimated residual value). This amount is to be spread evenly over only two more years (years 6 and 7). Half of the $16,000, then, is added to accumulated depreciation during year 6 for a year-end total of $33,000 ($25,000 + $8,000).

31. (a,62) Extraordinary repairs occur infrequently, involve relatively large amounts of money, and tend to increase the economic usefulness of the asset in the future. Examples would be major overhauls or the complete replacement of the roof on the factory. Since these expenditures will benefit more than one accounting period, they are capital expenditures. The term **extraordinary item** involves a completely different concept.

32. (c,48) The key to this question is the use of the term "capital expenditure". By definition, a capital expenditure is one that will benefit more than one accounting period. Accordingly, such an expenditure results in an asset being recorded on the books. Had the term "capital expenditure" not been used, the correct answer could have been either "expense" or "asset."

33. (b,71) The cost minus residual value ($3,100,000 - $300,000 = $2,800,000) must be spread over the 10 million board feet to obtain the "depletion cost per board foot" ($2,800,000 / 10,000,000 = $0.28 per board foot). $0.28 x 3,000,000 board feet harvested the first year = $840,000.

34. (c,52) Goodwill is computed as the difference between fair market value of specific assets acquired ($60,000) and the price paid ($70,000).

35. (b,43) Per APB Opinion #17, goodwill (or any other intangible asset) must be amortized over its economic life, not to exceed 40 years.

36. (c,25) A deferred charge, like a prepaid expense, represents an expenditure made to acquire goods and services to be used in generating future revenues. A deferred charge is a long-term prepayment whereas a prepaid expense represents a short-term prepayment.

37. (a,40) The amount of gain (loss) is the difference between the cash received and the book value of the van. Book value = cost - accumulated depreciation. At the date of sale, depreciation has been taken for 19A ($3,200), for 19B ($2,400) and for 3/4 of 19C ($1,200). Total accumulated depreciation, then, at September 30, 19C is $6,800 ($3,200 + $2,400 + $1,200). Cost - accumulated depreciation = $3,200 book value. Since it was sold for $6,000, the gain is $2,800.

38. (a,64) Depreciation expense = $12,000/10 year life = $1,200 per year. For the year in question, the asset should be depreciated only for the three months it was in use ($1,200 x 3/12 = $300).

39. (b,57) The gain (or loss) = cash received - book value. Cash received ($3,000) - book value ($2,000) = $1,000 gain. (Remember that book value = cost - accumulated depreciation.

40. (b,80) The building is being depreciated $400 per year ($8,000/20 = $400). On the date of sale, it is five (count 'em) years old so there is a $2,000 balance in Accumulated Depreciation. The correct journal entry, then, must include debits to Cash and Accumulated Depreciation and a credit to the Building account.

41. (b,88) At date of disposal the book value was $5,300 (cost of $12,500 - accumulated depreciation of $7,200). Since only $4,000 was received upon sale, a loss of $1,300 was incurred ($5,300 - $4,000).

42. (d,73) In a basket purchase, the sum of the fair market values (FMV) of the items acquired often exceeds the total price paid. The total actual purchase price is allocated to individual items in the ratio of each item's FMV as a percentage of the FMV of all items taken together. Each item is recorded, therefore, at less than it's specific FMV.

43. (b,78) Intangible assets are sometimes the most valuable assets a firm has.

44. (e,76) Natural gas is not an intangible asset but is a natural resource asset.

CHAPTER TEN: MEASURING AND REPORTING LIABILITIES

PART A: Measuring, Recording, and Reporting Liabilities

1. Fundamentally, liabilities are measured in accordance with the:
   a. revenue principle.
   b. matching principle.
   c. cost principle.
   d. materiality principle.

2. Implicit interest:
   a. is stated on the face of the note or loan document.
   b. exceeds the current prime rate charged by banks.
   c. is unstated and assumed to be included in the face amount of the note.
   d. is added to the face of the note when paid.

3. Current liabilities are defined as short-term obligations that will be paid within:
   a. one year.
   b. the current operating cycle.
   c. one year or the current operating cycle, whichever is shorter.
   d. one year or the current operating cycle, whichever is longer.

4. On March 1, Carla's Computer Store purchased $10,000 of inventory on sales terms of 2/10,n/30. On March 10, the invoice was paid in full. Assuming Carla records purchases using the net method, the journal entry to record payment on March 10 will include a:
   a. debit to Accounts Payable of $10,000.
   b. credit to Cash of $10,000.
   c. debit to Purchase Discounts of $200.
   d. credit to Purchase Discounts of $200.
   e. debit to Accounts Payable of $9,800.

5. JAS Company purchased inventory on account for $200. Balances in current assets and current liabilities were $5,000 and $2,500, respectively. The inventory purchase had which one of the following effects?
   a. decrease in the working capital ratio (current ratio)
   b. increase in the working capital ratio (current ratio)
   c. increase in working capital
   d. decrease in working capital

6. Sanders Co. received an 8%, $6,000 note on September 1, 19C. The principal and interest are due at the end of six months. If the accounting period ends on December 31, 19C, what amount of interest revenue should be recognized for 19C?
   a. $ 80
   b. $160
   c. $240
   d. $480

7. On December 31, 19B, Bartow Company received a tax bill for 19B property taxes which are due by March 31, 19C. To record this bill on the date received, Bartow should:
   a. debit Prepaid Taxes.
   b. debit Taxes Payable.
   c. debit Deferred Tax Expense.
   d. credit Taxes Payable.
   e. make no entry since the tax is due in 19C.

8. When a journal entry includes a credit to deferred income tax, which of the following conditions exists?
   a. The tax liability is overstated.
   b. The tax accrual exceeds the tax expense on the tax return.
   c. The tax expense on the tax return is excessive.
   d. The tax expense on the income statement exceeds the tax liability on the tax return.

9. At year-end, Tormey Company is preparing the entry to record its income tax expense and income tax liability. A debit to deferred income taxes means that:
   a. the tax liability exceeds the tax expense.
   b. net income exceeds total expenses.
   c. the tax expense exceeds the tax liability.
   d. the tax return does not balance.

10. For 19D, Garbo Company has a higher income tax expense (recorded on the income statement) than the amount of tax actually paid (according to the tax return). This difference should be:
    a. recorded as deferred taxes if it is a timing difference.
    b. recorded as deferred taxes if it is a permanent difference.
    c. recorded as deferred taxes if it is either a timing or permanent difference.
    d. not recorded, since only the income statement amount is correct.
    e. not recorded, since only the tax return amount is correct.

11. Recognition of deferred income taxes gives consideration to which of the following?
    a. materiality principle
    b. time value of money
    c. timing difference
    d. working capital

12. An entry will be made to the Deferred Income Tax account only when:
    a. expense and/or revenue items appear on the income statement and on the tax return in the same accounting period.
    b. expense and/or revenue items appear on either the income statement or on the income tax return but will never appear on both.
    c. expense and/or revenue items will appear on both the income statement and on the income tax return but in different periods.
    d. permanent differences arise between items shown on the income statement and the income tax return.

13. Deferred income taxes arise from:
    a. the existence of "permanent" differences.
    b. the issuance of capital stock at a price above par.
    c. differences in revenue or expense recognition between the IRS Code and GAAP.
    d. an inability to pay taxes in the current period coupled with a promise to make it up in a future period.

14. ABC Company purchased a machine which had a three-year life. ABC used straight-line depreciation for the income statement and a different method for the tax return. (You may assume that there are no other differences between the income statement and the tax return.) Which of the following statements, if any, correctly expresses the relationship of total income taxes payable to total income tax expense for the three years the machine is held?
    a. Total tax expense equals total taxes payable.
    b. Total tax expense is less than total taxes payable.
    c. Total tax expense is greater than total taxes payable.
    d. No formal statement may be made concerning the expected relationship of tax expense to taxes payable over the three year period.

15. On the date a non-interest bearing note is issued, which of the following is included in its face value?
    a. accrued interest.
    b. non-taxable interest.
    c. implicit interest.
    d. fully amortized interest.

16. On July 1, 19A, Bill Duncan, Inc. signed a $50,000 eight-year noninterest-bearing note payable to Trident Corp. Which of the following accounts will appear in the long-term liability section of Duncan's balance sheet for each of the next seven years?
    a. Discount on Notes Payable
    b. Deferred Taxes Payable
    c. Interest Expense Payable
    d. Accumulated Discount Payable

17. Potential obligations that will materialize only if certain events occur in the future are called:
    a. deferred liabilities.
    b. discounted liabilities.
    c. indefinite liabilities.
    d. contingent liabilities.

18. A contingent liability differs from other liabilities in that it:
    a. is for a fixed amount, but has an uncertain payment date.
    b. has a fixed payment date, but is for an uncertain (estimated) amount.
    c. is typically disclosed in the notes to the statements and not on the balance sheet itself.
    d. is usually disclosed with the long-term liabilities unless it will result in assets being paid out in the following period.

19. Cheat, Swindle and Scarf, P.C. has been notified by the IRS that its tax return has been audited and that additional taxes of $5,000 are due. They plan to hire a lawyer and contest the additional taxes. The $5,000 should be accounted for as:
    a. a contingent liability.
    b. an estimated liability.
    c. a prior period adjustment.
    d. deferred taxes.

20. Recording the same payment of a liability twice would have which of the following effects?
    a. understatement of assets, liabilities, and owners' equity
    b. no effect on net income, owners' equity, and total assets
    c. understatement of total assets and total liabilities and no effect on net income and owners' equity
    d. some other combination of effects

21. When a voucher system is being used, an approved voucher is required to disburse cash for which of the following categories of purchase?

	Purchase of Inventory	Purchase of Operating Assets
a.	Yes	Yes
b	Yes	No
c.	No	Yes
d.	No	No

PART B: Future Value and Present Value Concepts

22. Conceptually, the amount of a liability at any point in time is the:
    a. future value of the future outlays of assets required to pay the liability in full.
    b. present value of the future outlays of assets required to pay the liability in full.
    c. total future outlays of assets required to pay the liability in full.
    d. equivalent value of the future outlays of assets required to pay the liability in full.

NOTE: Interest factor tables for solving the present value and future value problems that follow can be found at the end of this chapter just prior to the solutions.

23. Mariana wishes to have $9,000 in her savings account four years from today. If the account pays 10% interest compounded annually, what single amount (rounded to the nearest dollar) must Mariana deposit today so that it would grow to the desired balance at the end of four years ?
    a. $ 1,939
    b. $ 2,839
    c. $ 5,913
    d. $ 6,147
    e. $13,177

24. A $10,000 debt must be paid off at the end of the fifth year. A single amount is to be deposited at 10% interest today to satisfy the debt. The total **interest** earned on the deposit over 5 years is:
    a. $3,791.
    b. $3,895.
    c. $6,105.
    d. $6,209.

25. In four years, Anne plans to take a trip to Europe and needs to have $4,000 at that time. In order to determine how much she must deposit in a savings account each week to provide the required amount of money for the trip she would use which of the following tables?
    a. future value of $1
    b. present value of $1
    c. future value of an annuity of $1
    d. present value of an annuity of $1

26. On each December 31, the Sly Stone Company plans to deposit $900 into a special fund. The fund will earn 12% interest which will be added to the fund balance at each year-end. The first deposit will be made Dec. 31, 19B. By December 31, 19D, the fund will have earned total **interest revenue** of:
    a. $701
    b. $337
    c. $324
    d. $229
    e. $108

27. On February 1, 19A, Carson Transportation Company acquired a new bus for $30,000. (Carson's fiscal year ends each January 31.) Carson made a $1,161 cash down payment and gave a 12% note payable in five equal annual installments. The payments are due each year on the last day of Carson's fiscal year. What will be the amount of each payment?
    a. $1,636
    b. $5,082
    c. $6,200
    d. $8,000
    e. $9,500

28. Eagle Feather Co. invested $8900 in a 3-year, 10% certificate of deposit. If the interest is compounded annually, what is the maturity value of this CD (rounded to the nearest dollar)?
    a. $13,031
    b. $11,846
    c. $11,570
    d. $10,736
    e. $ 8,066

29. Goldbaum, Inc. purchased sophisticated computer equipment by giving a 2-year noninterest-bearing note payable of $75,000. Assuming a 10% market rate of interest, at what amount should the computer equipment be recorded on Goldbaum's books (to the nearest dollar)?
    a. $35,714
    b. $37,500
    c. $43,215
    d. $61,980
    e. $75,000

30. What are the respective present values (discounted at 12%) of:

    (1) a receipt of $500 per year for ten years
    (2) a receipt of $10,000 in ten years

    a. $5,000; $10,000
    b. $2,825; $3220
    c. $3,106; $1,755
    d. $1,553; $5,650
    e. $1,755; $3,106

31. Roger Roy would like to retire in 10 years. He has already set up a savings account and will be receiving a pension. He would, however, like to have a little extra money so he and his wife will be able to do some traveling. He estimates that he can set aside $2,500 at the end of each of the next 10 years and that it will earn 11% interest. How much money will Roger Roy have in his travel account when he retires?
    a. $41,805
    b. $27,500
    c. $25,000
    d. $14,723
    e. $ 7,099

32. Assume Wilson performs services on January 1, 19A and in return will collect $1,000 on January 1, 19B and continue collecting $1,000 at the end of each year through 19K. What is the proper journal entry at January 1, 19A if 9% is the appropriate discount rate?

   a. Accounts Receivable   10,000
        Revenue   10,000
   b. Accounts Receivable   9,000
        Cash   1,000
        Revenue   10,000
   c. Accounts Receivable   6,418
        Revenue   6,418
   d. Accounts Receivable   10,000
        Revenue   4,050
        Deferred Interest   5,950

33. A specialized piece of equipment is to be purchased. The company, due to a cash shortage, cannot pay the $80,000 price all at once. The company plans to make equal payments at the end of each of the next three years. The amount of **interest** to be paid on the equipment (at 11%) is:
   a. $12,667.
   b. $18,212.
   c. $32,737.
   d. $96,214.

34. "Slick" Williams, an All-American basketball player, is negotiating a professional basketball contract. The team and "Slick"'s agent have agreed on the following alternative ways that "Slick" might collect his signing bonus.
     (1) $800,000 cash today.
     (2) $40,000 cash today plus $200,000 at the end of each of the next five years.
     (3) $0 today plus $2,400,000 at the end of ten years.
     (4) $0 today plus $105,000 at the end of each of the next 20 years.

At a 12% discount rate, which option has the greatest present value?
   a. Option #1
   b. Option #2
   c. Option #3
   d. Option #4

35. A company needs to establish a fund to pay off bonds maturing in the future. They wish to make six equal **annual** deposits to a bank that will pay the fund compound interest. In order to compute the size of the annual deposits to be made, we must divide the maturity value of the bonds by:
   a. a future value of an annuity of $1.
   b. a present value of an annuity of $1.
   c. a future value of $1.
   d. a present value of $1.
   e. six (for the six periods).

36. Being thrifty by nature, you deposit $5,000 into a savings account paying 8% interest compounded annually. High grade corporate bonds are yielding 10% interest. How much will be in your savings account at the end of seven years?
   a. $2,920
   b. $8,569
   c. $9,924
   d. $26,032

37. Small-Loss, Inc. is sold January 1, 19A. The sales contract requires three installments of $45,000 each at December 31, 19A, 19B, and 19C. Assuming a 12% discount rate, what is the present value of this sales contract?
   a. $151,848
   b. $135,000
   c. $108,081
   d. $ 63,221

38. Frank Duck and Associates purchased a new car on 1-1-19A at a cash price of $25,000. The purchase agreement calls for five equal annual payments beginning 12-31-19A. Each payment will include principal and interest on the unpaid balance at 10% per year. Using the following interest factors, determine the amount of the annual installment payment (rounded to the nearest dollar).
   a. $15,523
   b. $10,622
   c. $ 6,595
   d. $ 4,095

39. On January 1, 19D, Buck Slade, Inc. purchased a machine and gave in exchange a three-year, noninterest bearing note for $20,000. Assuming that the appropriate interest rate is 12%, what is the cost amount that should be recorded in the accounting records for this machine?
   a. $20,000
   b. $15,200
   c. $14,236
   d. $12,800

40. Mr. Miller inherited $1,000,000 which he promptly deposited in a bank account earning 10% interest. **Approximately** how much can Mr. Miller withdraw from savings each year for the next 20 years and exactly deplete the account with the 20th withdrawal?
   a. $112,000
   b. $117,000
   c. $127,000
   d. $139,000

41. Mrs. Jones really wants to buy a certain Mercedes auto that sells for $40,000. She has $2,100 in savings to use as the down payment and can arrange a five-year loan for the balance at 10% annual interest with equal payments at the end of each year. **Approximately** how much is each annual payment?
   a. $ 8,000
   b. $10,000
   c. $12,000
   d. $14,000

42. Mr. and Mrs. Togo are concerned about the cost of putting their 8 year old daughter through college someday. Therefore, they have decided to deposit $2,000 at the end of each year in a 10% savings account with annual compounding. **Approximately** how much will be in the Togo's savings account at the end of 10 years when the daughter starts college?
   a. $ 31,900
   b. $ 52,000
   c. $ 80,000
   d. $123,000

43. What single amount must be deposited today at 8% to pay off a $9,000 debt due at the end of seven years?
   a. $15,424
   b. $9,000
   c. $8,333
   d. $5,252
   e. $1,729

44. Wink Dinkerson wants to purchase a new Mercedes automobile. Due to a temporary cash shortage, however, he cannot pay the $60,000 price all at once. If he makes equal payments at the end of each of the next four years, what is the amount of each payment? (Assume a 10% interest rate.)
   a. $10,245
   b. $12,928
   c. $15,000
   d. $17,444
   e. $18,928

Periods/Rate	8%	9%	10%	11%	12%
Future Value of $1					
0	1.0000	1.0000	1.0000	1.0000	1.0000
1	1.0800	1.0900	1.1000	1.1100	1.1200
2	1.1664	1.1881	1.2100	1.2321	1.2544
3	1.2597	1.2950	1.3310	1.3676	1.4049
4	1.3605	1.4116	1.4641	1.5181	1.5735
5	1.4693	1.5386	1.6105	1.6851	1.7623
6	1.5869	1.6771	1.7716	1.8704	1.9738
7	1.7138	1.8280	1.9487	2.0762	2.2107
8	1.8509	1.9926	2.1436	2.3045	2.4760
9	1.9990	2.1719	2.3579	2.5580	2.7731
10	2.1589	2.3674	2.5937	2.8394	3.1058
20	4.6610	5.6044	6.7275	8.0623	9.6463
Present Value of $1					
1	0.9259	0.9174	0.9091	0.9009	0.8929
2	0.8573	0.8417	0.8264	0.8116	0.7972
3	0.7938	0.7722	0.7513	0.7312	0.7118
4	0.7350	0.7084	0.6830	0.6587	0.6355
5	0.6806	0.6499	0.6209	0.5935	0.5674
6	0.6302	0.5963	0.5645	0.5346	0.5066
7	0.5835	0.5470	0.5132	0.4817	0.4523
8	0.5403	0.5019	0.4665	0.4339	0.4039
9	0.5002	0.4604	0.4241	0.3909	0.3606
10	0.4632	0.4224	0.3855	0.3522	0.3220
20	0.2145	0.1784	0.1486	0.1240	0.1037
Future Value of an Annuity of $1					
1	1.0000	1.0000	1.0000	1.0000	1.0000
2	2.0800	2.0900	2.1000	2.1100	2.1200
3	3.2464	3.2781	3.3100	3.3421	3.3744
4	4.5061	4.5731	4.6410	4.7097	4.7793
5	5.8666	5.9847	6.1051	6.2278	6.3528
6	7.3359	7.5233	7.7156	7.9129	8.1152
7	8.9228	9.2004	9.4872	9.7833	10.0890
8	10.6366	11.0285	11.4359	11.8594	12.2997
9	12.4876	13.0210	13.5795	14.1640	14.7757
10	14.4866	15.1929	15.9374	16.7220	17.5487
20	45.7620	51.1601	57.2750	64.2028	72.0524
Present Value of an Annuity of $1					
1	0.9259	0.9174	0.9091	0.9009	0.8929
2	1.7833	1.7591	1.7355	1.7125	1.6901
3	2.5771	2.5313	2.4869	2.4437	2.4018
4	3.3121	3.2397	3.1699	3.1024	3.0373
5	3.9927	3.8897	3.7908	3.6959	3.6048
6	4.6229	4.4859	4.3553	4.2305	4.1114
7	5.2064	5.0330	4.8684	4.7122	4.5638
8	5.7466	5.5348	5.3349	5.1461	4.9676
9	6.2469	5.9952	5.7590	5.5370	5.3282
10	6.7101	6.4177	6.1446	5.8892	5.6502
20	9.8181	9.1285	8.5136	7.9633	7.4694
	8%	*9%*	*10%*	*11%*	*12%*

CHAPTER TEN: ANNOTATED SOLUTIONS

1. c	8. d	15. c	22. b	29. d	36. b	43. d
2. c	9. a	16. a	23. d	30. b	37. c	44. e
3. d	10. a	17. d	24. a	31. a	38. c	
4. e	11. c	18. c	25. c	32. c	39. c	
5. a	12. c	19. a	26. b	33. b	40. b	
6. b	13. c	20. c	27. d	34. a	41. b	
7. d	14. a	21. a	28. b	35. a	42. a	

> *The correct answer and the percentage of students answering the question correctly (when it was used on an introductory accounting examination) are shown in parentheses at the beginning of each annotated solution that follows.*

1. (c,48) The best answer (of those offered) is response c; the cost principle. That is, liabilities are stated at the amount currently necessary to liquidate them (i.e. what it would "cost" to liquidate them). A better answer would be that liabilities are measured in accordance with the concept of present value; that is, they should be stated at the present value of the future outlays necessary to liquidate them.

2. (c,73) The "implicit" is the opposite of the word "explicit." Whereas interest is usually explicitly stated (e.g. 8% or 13%), on a so-called non-interest bearing note the interest is implicit (not stated). Rather, it is included in the face amount of the note.

3. (d,80) By definition.

4. (e,76) Under the net method, the purchases of inventory on March 1 was journalized with a debit to Purchases (or Merchandise Inventory) for $9,800 and a credit to Accounts Payable for $9,800. Payment on March 10, then, would require a debit to Accounts Payable of $9,800 and a credit to Cash of $9,800.

5. (a,35) The working capital ratio = current assets/current liabilities. Before purchase, WC ratio = $5,000/$2,500 = 2:1. After purchase, WC ratio = ($5,000 + $200)/($2,500 + $200) = 1.93:1.

6. (b,62) This note earns $40 per month [($6,000 x 8%)/12 months]. From September 1 through December 31 is four months. $40 x 4 = $160.

7. (d,55) Although not due for payment until 19C, this bill is an expense of 19B. The complete journal entry at December 31, 19B would be: debit Property Tax Expense, and credit Taxes Payable.

8. (d,67) The period-end journal entry to record Income Tax Expense and Income Tax Payable will include an entry to Deferred Income Tax if the amounts of the expense and payable are not equal. (Remember that Income Tax Expense is debited and Income Tax Payable is credited.) If Income Tax Expense exceeds Income Tax Payable, the debit will exceed the credit and another credit entry (to Deferred Income Tax) is necessary.

9. (a,40) A debit to deferred taxes represents a prepaid expense and arises when the tax liability (amount to be paid to the IRS) exceeds the tax expense (from the income statement).

10. (a,68) Timing differences are recorded as deferred taxes; permanent differences are not.

11. (c,69) Deferred taxes are recorded only when there is a timing difference between the income statement and the tax return.

12. (c,60) The deferred income tax account arises when there are timing differences between recognition of items on the tax return and the income statement. That is, some element of revenue or expense is to be recognized on one of the reports this period but on the other report in some other period.

13. (c,60) Response c is a straightforward description of why the deferred income taxes account arises. The other answers are nonsense.

14. (a,58) Assuming all other taxation factors are held constant, response a is correct. That is, total tax expense recognized on the income statement (cumulatively for the three years) is equal to total taxes payable shown on the tax return.

15. (c,90) Because money has a time value we know that there is no such thing (conceptually) as a non-interest bearing note. Instead, notes either have the interest explicitly stated (e.g. 12%) or the interest is included in the face value of the note. In this second case, since the interest is not explicitly stated it is **implicit** interest.

16. (a,83) Discount on Notes Payable is a contra-account (to Notes Payable) and is used when the note is **supposedly** noninterest-bearing (as in this problem). Since the note itself is a long-term liability for the first seven years, the contra-account will be found in the same section of the balance sheet. Deferred Taxes Payable has no necessary relationship to this question, and responses c and d are nonsense.

17. (d,92) By definition.

18. (c,54) While contingent liabilities **can be** disclosed on the face of the balance sheet, it is usually the case that they are disclosed in the notes to the financial statements.

19. (a,80) It is not yet certain that the company will have to pay more taxes. It is not an "actual" liability, then, it is a **contingent** liability. Responses c, d, and e are nonsense.

20. (c,44) Paying off a liability reduces cash (an asset) and a liability. To do so twice understates both accounts. Income and equity are not involved.

21. (a,77) When a voucher system is in use, an approved voucher is necessary prior to **every** expenditure of cash.

22. (b,74) This is a straightforward statement of the amount at which a liability should be stated.

23. (d,81) One needs to determine the present value of $9,000 discounted at 10% for four periods (the factor is .6830). $9,000 x .6830 = $6,147.

24. (a,43) Present value (of a single sum) = amount x interest factor. PV (single sum) = $10,000 x .6209. Interest = amount ($10,000) - PV of a single sum ($6,209) = $3,791.

25. (c,37) Anne needs $4,000 at some future date. This $4,000 is, therefore, a "future value." The following equation applies: Future Value (of an annuity) = Amount of the Annuity x an Interest Factor. In this problem the Amount of the Annuity is the unknown. It would be determined by dividing the Future Value of an Annuity by the appropriate Interest Factor from the Future Value of an Annuity table.

26. (b,20) Total interest income = amount accumulated in fund - total amount of payments to the fund. Total amount accumulated in the fund at December 31, 19D is calculated as $900 x 3.3744 (3 year annuity factor @ 12%) = $3,036.96. Total amount of payments to the fund is $2,700 (3 payments of $900 each). Therefore, total interest income = $3,036.96 - $2,700 = $337 (rounded).

27. (d,36) The present value of the debt is $28,839 ($30,000 - $1,161). This is also the present value of the payments to be made. PV (of an annuity) = amount of annuity x interest factor, or $28,838 = amount x 3.6048. Amount, then, equals $8,000.

28. (b,79) Compute the future value of $8,900 compounded at 10% for three years (the factor is 1.3310). $8,900 x 1.3310 = $11,846.

29. (d,64) According to the cost principle, assets should be recorded at the present value of all future expenditures necessary to acquire the asset. The present value of $75,000 due in two years = $75,000 x .8264 = $61,980 (discounted two periods at 10%).

30. (b,83) (1) PV of an annuity = amount x interest factor. Therefore, PV = $500 x 5.6502 = $2,825. (2) PV of a single sum = amount x interest factor. Therefore, PV = $10,000 x .3220 = $3,220.

31. (a,83) The future amount of this five year annuity = $2,500 x 16.7220 = $41,805.

32. (c,41) The revenue and receivable must be recorded (valued) at the present value of the expected cash inflows. There will be ten annual receipts of $1,000. The present value of an annuity = the annual cash inflow x interest factor. Therefore, PV = $1,000 x 6.4177 = $6,418.

33. (b,44) First, the size of the payments must be determined. PV (of an annuity) = amount x interest factor. $80,000 = amount x 2.4437; amount = $32,737. Second, the total interest must be determined. Amount of interest = total amount paid - principal. Therefore, ($32,737 x 3) - $80,000 = $18,212.

34. (a,36) To answer this question, you must compute the present value of all the alternatives. P.V. of #1 = $800,000. P.V. of #2 = $760,960 ($200,000 x 3.6048 + $40,000). P.V. of #3 = $796,800 ($2,400,000 x .3320). P.V. of #4 = $784,287 ($105,000 x 7.4694). Therefore, select option #1.

35. (a,47) The six deposits (plus interest) are to add up to the amount due six periods from now (i.e. the maturity value of the bonds). The following formula applies: future value of an annuity = amount x interest factor. Since FV (of an annuity) is the maturity value of the bonds, it must be divided by the interest factor (future value of of an annuity of $1) to yield the amount of the annual deposits.

36. (b,86) Use this formula: future value (of a single sum) = amount x interest factor. Then, FV (single sum) = $5,000 x 1.7138; FV = $8,569. (The 10% interest rate on corporate bonds is irrelevant.)

37. (c,77) The present value of this three-year annuity is $108,081 ($45,000 x 2.4018).

38. (c,74) $25,000 is the present value of the five payments to be made. To determine the size of the payments, divide $25,000 by the interest factor (from the P.V. of an annuity table) for 5 periods and 10% (3.7908). $25,000/3.7908 = $6,594.91 (rounded to $6,595).

39. (c,74) The present value of $20,000 discounted 3 years @ 12% is $14,236 ($20,000 x .7118).

40. (b,67) The $1,000,000 on deposit is the present value of the 20 withdrawals that Mr. Miller wishes to make. Use the following formula: PV (of an annuity) = amount of the annuity x the interest factor. In this problem the annuity is known ($1 million) and the interest factor comes from the table (8.5136). Therefore, $1,000,000/8.5136 = $117,459 which is **approximately** $117,000.

41. (b,57) The remaining balance after the down payment is $37,900 ($40,000 - $2,100). This is the present value of the future payments that must be made. The PV of an annuity = amount of the annuity x the interest factor. From the table, the interest factor is 3.79. Substituting in the numbers (and rearranging algebraically), $37,900/3.79 = $10,000.

42. (a,78) The future value of an annuity = amount of the annuity x the interest factor. In this problem the amount (size) of the annuity is $2,000 and the interest factor (from the table) is 15.9374. Substituting these numbers into the equation, $2,000 x 15.9374 = $31,875 which is **approximately** $31,900

43. (d,81) Determine the present value of $9,000 discounted seven years at 8%. $9,000 x .5835 = $5,252.

44. (e,61) The $60,000 price is the present value of the four payments (an annuity). Since the present value of the annuity is known ($60,000) as is the interest rate (10%) and the number of periods (4), the amount of each annual payment can be determined. Solve the following equation: $60,000 = payment (?) x interest factor (3.1699). $60,000/3.1699 = $18,928.

CHAPTER ELEVEN: MEASURING AND REPORTING BONDS PAYABLE

PART A: Fundamentals of Measuring, Recording, and Reporting Bonds Payable

1. Surf City issued some 12%, 20-year bonds. According to the indenture agreement, the city's street sweeping equipment will be sold and the proceeds distributed to bond-holders if the city does not make interest and principal payments on time. Which of the following terms best describes the type of bonds that have been sold?
   a. registered
   b. redeemable
   c. debenture
   d. callable
   e. secured

2. Top Rank, Inc. has an issue of bonds outstanding for which there is no specific collateral backing. These bonds may be turned in for early retirement at the option of the bondholder. The terms that best describe these bonds are:
   a. redeemable and secured.
   b. callable and registered.
   c. coupon and debentures.
   d. callable and coupon.
   e. unsecured and redeemable.

3. A bond indenture agreement is:
   a. the same as a bond certificate.
   b. written by the bond holders.
   c. written by the trustee.
   d. a specification of the legal provisions of the bonds.

4. The interest rate which determines the amount of interest paid periodically over the life of the bond to the bondholder is called the:
   a. stated rate.
   b. market rate.
   c. effective rate.
   d. yield rate.

5. Which of the following statements regarding the classification of bonds is **incorrect**?
   a. Secured bonds include a mortgage that pledges specific assets as a guarantee of payment.
   b. Redeemable bonds may be turned in for early retirement at the option of the issuer.
   c. Callable bonds may be called for early retirement at the option of the issuer.
   d. Single-payment bonds pay the principal at a single specified maturity date.

6. Each period, bond interest expense is measured, recorded and reported in conformance with the:
   a. cost principle.
   b. objectivity principle.
   c. consistency principle.
   d. matching principle.

7. When the market interest rate for a bond is higher than the stated interest rate, the bond will sell at:
   a. par.
   b. a discount.
   c. a premium.
   d. face value.

8. When the market rate of interest for a bond is lower than the stated interest rate, the:
   a. bond sells at a price above par.
   b. bond sells at par.
   c. bond sells at a price below par.
   d. stated interest rate is decreased to match the market rate.

9. If a company sells bonds at a premium instead of par, the interest expense over the life of the bonds is:
   a. increased.
   b. reduced.
   c. unaffected.
   d. sometimes increased and sometimes decreased.

10. Compared to a bond sold at par, one sold at a discount results in:
    a. more cash being paid out each period.
    b. less cash being paid out each period.
    c. more interest expense being recorded each period.
    d. less interest expense being recorded each period.

11. The market rate of interest is:
    a. usually printed on the face of the bond certificate.
    b. always the same as the stated rate.
    c. always higher or lower than the stated rate.
    d. determined by competitive forces in financial markets.

12. X Company has 10,000 bonds outstanding with a par value of $1,000 each and a stated interest rate of 12%. The bonds mature in 30 years. Currently, the bonds are quoted on the security exchanges at $1,200 each. Which of the following is the nearest approximation to the current market rate of interest?
    a. 10%
    b. 12%
    c. 20%
    d. 24%

13. Which of the following statements is **true** concerning bonds payable?
    a. When the market rate of interest for a bond is less than the stated rate, the bond will sell at a premium.
    b. Bonds can only be sold at their face amount.
    c. When the market rate of interest for a bond is less than the stated rate, the bond will sell at a discount.
    d. Amortization of a bond discount or premium affects both the annual amount of interest expense and the annual cash interest payments.

    REMEMBER: There are interest factor tables available in this book. They are located between the Chapter 10 Questions and the Chapter 10 Solutions.

14. If the market rate of interest were 9% at the date of issue, the selling price of $50,000 par value, 7%, 5 year bonds with interest payable annually would be:
    a. $46,109.
    b. $46,845.
    c. $49,624.
    d. $50,000.

15. Devilish Delights, Inc. sold a $100,000, 10% issue of bonds on January 1,19A at a market rate of 8%. The bonds were dated January 1, 19A and interest is paid each December 31. If these bonds mature in 10 years, their issue price is:
    a. $ 87,707.
    b. $ 95,477.
    c. $ 99,996.
    d. $105,651.
    e. $113,421.

16. Bonds having a face value of $50,000 were sold for $60,000 when they came on the market. Which of the following entries properly reflect this transaction?

    a. | Cash | 50,000 | |
       |---|---|---|
       | Discount on Bonds | | 10,000 |
       | Bonds Payable | | 40,000 |

    b. | Cash | 50,000 | |
       |---|---|---|
       | Discount on Bonds | 10,000 | |
       | Bonds Payable | | 60,000 |

    c. | Cash | 60,000 | |
       |---|---|---|
       | Premium on Bonds | | 10,000 |
       | Bonds Payable | | 50,000 |

    d. | Cash | 40,000 | |
       |---|---|---|
       | Premium on Bonds | 10,000 | |
       | Bonds Payable | | 50,000 |

17. A journal entry is being made to record the annual payment of interest on $100,000 of ten-year, 8% bonds. If the bonds originally sold for $98,000, the credit to Cash would be:
    a. more than the debit to interest expense.
    b. less than the debit to interest expense.
    c. the same as the debit to interest expense.
    d. indeterminable.

18. Which of the following entries would be made at the date of issuance of bonds having a face amount of $100,000 and a selling price of $90,000?

a. Cash   100,000
        Bonds Payable   100,000

b. Bonds Payable   100,000
        Cash   100,000

c. Cash   90,000
    Discount on Bonds Pay. 10,000
        Bonds Payable   100,000

d. Bonds Payable   100,000
        Cash   90,000
        Discount on Bonds Payable   10,000

19. Monsoon, Inc., sold a $100,000, 12% bond issue on July 1, l9D for $112,285. The bonds were dated the same day and pay annual interest. Assuming a 10% market interest rate and a 10 year life, the entry to record issuance of the bonds would include a:
a. debit to Cash of $100,000.
b. debit to Discount on Bonds Payable of $12,185.
c. credit to Bonds Payable of $112,285.
d. credit to Premium on Bonds Payable of $12,285.

20. Hatton Co. issued 100, $1,000 par value, 6% bonds for $112,000. The bonds are dated May 1, were issued May 1, 19C, and have a 10 year life. The semi-annual interest dates are November 1 and May 1. On November 1, 19C, Hatton Company's entry to record the payment of interest (assuming straight-line amortization) would include a:
a. debit to Interest Expense of $2,400.
b. debit to Premium on Bonds Payable of $1,200.
c. credit to Premium on Bonds Payable of $600.
d. credit to Cash of $3,600.

21. The account Premium on Bonds Payable should be shown in the financial statements as a(n):
a. contra asset account.
b. addition to bonds payable.
c. reduction in long-term debt.
d. deferred charge.

22. The account Discount on Bonds Payable appears on the:
a. income statement as an expense.
b. balance sheet as an asset, under deferred charges.
c. income statement as a revenue account.
d. balance sheet as a reduction of a liability.

23. On January 1, Shapiro Company issued $10,000 face amount of bonds payable at $9,500. The stated rate of interest is 10% and is payable semi-annually on July 1 and January 1. The bonds mature in 10 years. The appropriate journal entry for Shapiro Company on each interest payment date is:

a. Interest Expense   525
        Discount on Bonds Payable   25
        Cash   500

b. Interest Expense   1,050
        Discount on Bonds Payable   50
        Cash   1,000

c. Interest Expense   1,000
    Discount on Bonds Payable   50
        Cash   1,050

d. Interest Expense   500
    Discount on Bonds Payable   25
        Cash   525

24. Which of the following statements is **correct** regarding interest rates when bonds sell at a discount?
a. The stated rate is higher than the market rate.
b. The yield rate is less than the market rate.
c. The market rate is less than the yield rate.
d. The market rate is higher than the stated rate.

25. VHR Company issued $150,000 of bonds payable at 96% of par value. The entry to record the sale would include a:
    a. debit to Premium on Bonds Payable of $6,000.
    b. debit to Cash of $144,000.
    c. credit to Discount on Bonds Payable of $6,000.
    d. credit to Bonds Payable of $144,000.

26. $300,000 of 6%, 10-year bonds sold at 101% of face value would require semi-annual cash interest payments and straight-line premium amortization, respectively, of:
    a. $3,000 and $1,800.
    b. $6,000 and $900.
    c. $9,000 and $150.
    d. $1,800 and $300.

27. Mac-Tel-Co. sold ten year bonds having a face value of $100,000 and an 8% stated interest rate for 98% of par value. Assume that straight-line amortization is used. At each annual interest payment date, the sum of any debits to Interest Expense will be:
    a. more than the credit to Cash.
    b. less than the credit to Cash.
    c. the same as the credit to Cash.
    d. indeterminable without knowing the market rate of interest.

28. Using borrowed assets to enhance the return on owner's equity is called:
    a. financial leverage.
    b. the time value of money.
    c. compound discounting.
    d. an indenture.

29. Palm Company reports the following information at year-end.

Total assets	$500,000
Long-term debt	300,000
Stockholders' equity	200,000
Net income	60,000
Return on total assets	18%

    The amount of financial leverage is:
    a. 0%.
    b. 12%.
    c. 18%.
    d. 30%.

USE THE FOLLOWING INFORMATION FOR THE NEXT TWO QUESTIONS.

Toshiba Company issued $100,000 of 10-year, 6% bonds at a price of $112,000. The bonds are dated March 1, and were issued March 1, 19A. Interest payment dates are September 1 and March 1.

30. The entry to record the issuance of the bonds would include a:
    a. credit to Bonds Payable of $112,000.
    b. credit to Cash of $112,000.
    c. credit to Premium on Bonds Payable of $12,000.
    d. debit to Bonds payable of $100,000.

31. On September 1, 19A, Toshiba's entry to record the payment of interest (assuming straight-line amortization) would include a:
    a. debit to interest expense of $2,400.
    b. debit to premium of $1,200.
    c. credit to premium of $600.
    d. credit to cash of $3,600.

32. Leverage:
    a. means that a company is funding operations without incurring debt.
    b. is least desirable for companies with stable earnings records.
    c. is profitable if borrowed funds generate a higher rate of return than the rate paid for use of the funds.
    d. causes a company's income before interest expense and income taxes to be larger than it would be in the absence of leverage.

33. Brett Company has $10,000 of bonds outstanding that pay 8% interest on a semi-annual basis. If Brett Co. is in the 30% income tax bracket, what is the annual net interest cost of these bonds?
    a. $ 240
    b. $ 560
    c. $ 800
    d. $1,240
    e. $1,360

PART B: Additional Problems in Accounting for Bonds Payable

34. A $1,000, 6%, 5-year bond, dated April 1, 19D was sold for $1,055 plus accrued interest on September 1, 19D. The interest is payable each March 31 and September 30. How much cash would the issuer receive on September 1, 19D?
   a. $1,000
   b. $1,030
   c. $1,055
   d. $1,060
   e. $1,080

35. A $1,000 par value bond with a stated rate of 9% was sold for $865 plus accrued interest four months after it first became available for sale. How much cash was collected by the seller on the date of this sale?
   a. $1,030
   b. $1,000
   c. $ 895
   d. $ 865
   e. $ 835

USE THE FOLLOWING INFORMATION FOR THE NEXT THREE QUESTIONS

Bonds dated April 1, 19A were finally sold on June 1, 19A. Additional data is as follows:

Face value	$60,000
Stated interest rate	8%
Annual interest payment date	March 31
Life	10 years

36. Assume the bonds were sold for $57,000 plus accrued interest. The proper journal entry to record the sale on June 1, 19A would include a credit to Bonds Payable of:
   a. $57,800.
   b. $59,200.
   c. $60,000.
   d. $60,800.
   e. $63,800.

37. If the bonds above were sold for $57,000 plus accrued interest, what amount of discount will be amortized every 12 months under the straight-line method?
   a. $305
   b. $300
   c. $240
   d. $224

38. Assume the bonds above were sold instead for $62,000 plus accrued interest. The proper journal entry to record the sale on June 1, 19A would include a credit to Bond Interest Expense of:
   a. $ 400.
   b. $ 800.
   c. $2,000.
   d. $4,800.

39. A $10,000, five-year, 10% bond payable was sold on October 1, 19A (its issue date) for $9,500. The necessary end-of-period adjusting entry at December 31, 19A would include a credit to Discount on Bonds Payable in the amount of:
   a. $ 0.
   b. $ 25.
   c. $100.
   d. $125.

40. Ten-year, 9%, annual bonds having a $50,000 par value were dated and sold (for $53,000) on September 1, 19B. What amount of interest expense will be reported on 19B's income statement regarding these bonds?
   a. $ 0
   b. $1,400
   c. $1,500
   d. $1,600

41. B Co. will make 10 annual deposits to a bond sinking fund to retire $167,220 of bonds coming due in 10 years. The fund will earn 11% interest compounded annually. What total amount of **interest** will the sinking fund earn over the 10 years?
   a. $10,000
   b. $58,892
   c. $67,220
   d. $474,804

42. Peabody Manufacturing sold a $1,000 face value, 5-year, 9% bond for $910. The bond was dated November 1, 19A and sold the same day. Interest expense is paid annually on October 31. On the financial statements for calendar year 19A, Peabody should report what amounts for interest expense and discount on bonds payable? (Assume straight-line amortization.)

	Interest Expense	Discount on Bonds Payable
a.	$15	$90
b.	$15	$87
c.	$18	$90
d.	$18	$87

43. Which combination of the following terms describe a bond sinking fund when reported on the balance sheet?

	Short-Term	Liability
a.	Yes	Yes
b.	Yes	No
c.	No	Yes
d.	No	No

44. Which of the following correctly describes how the amount of interest expense on bonds payable is computed each period under the effective-interest method?
   a. multiply the stated rate times the carrying value of the bond
   b. multiply the market rate times the carrying value of the bond
   c. multiply the stated rate times the par value of the bond
   d. multiply the market rate times the par value of the bond

45. Which combination of the following are used to determine annual bond interest expense under the effective-interest method?

	Stated Rate	Par Value
a.	Yes	Yes
b.	Yes	No
c.	No	Yes
d.	No	No

46. Bidwell Enterprises has the following account balances and other information at December 31 just **before** making the annual adjusting entry for bond interest expense and amortization.

8% Bonds Payable (due in 7 years):

	$100,000
Discount on Bonds Payable:	5,536
Effective interest rate:	9%
Original life of the bonds:	10 years

Using effective-interest amortization, what is the total interest expense for the these bonds during the current year?
   a. $7,557
   b. $8,000
   c. $8,502
   d. $8,554
   e. $9,000

47. Peavy Company uses the effective-interest method to account for bonds payable. On December 31, 19C (just prior to making adjusting entries), Peavy had the following information available.

7% Bonds Payable:	$50,000
Premium on Bonds Payable:	2,647
Effective interest rate:	6%
Original life of the bonds:	5 years

If the bonds were outstanding for the entire year, what amount of premium should be amortized at year-end?
   a. $882
   b. $659
   c. $529
   d. $185

48. Which combination of the following are true when the effective-interest method is used to account for bonds sold at a premium or discount?

	Amortization Amount Differs Each Period	Interest Expense Differs Each Period
a.	Yes	Yes
b.	Yes	No
c.	No	Yes
d.	No	No

49. Zack Company sold 10-year, 6% bonds having a face value of $100,000 at a premium of $12,000. The bonds were dated and sold on April 1, 19A and have semiannual interest payments due each October 1 and April 1. If Zack uses the effective interest method of amortization, which of the following would be true of the journal entry necessary on September 1, 19A?
   a. The debit to Premium would be $600.
   b. The credit to Cash would be different than that for straight-line amortization.
   c. The debit to Interest Expense would be different than that for straight-line amortization.
   d. The effective interest would misstate the true interest cost to Zack.

CHAPTER ELEVEN: ANNOTATED SOLUTIONS

1. e	8. a	15. e	22. d	29. b	36. c	43. d
2. e	9. b	16. c	23. a	30. c	37. a	44. b
3. d	10. c	17. b	24. d	31. a	38. b	45. d
4. a	11. d	18. c	25. b	32. c	39. b	46. c
5. b	12. a	19. d	26. c	33. b	40. b	47. b
6. d	13. a	20. a	27. a	34. e	41. c	48. a
7. b	14. a	21. b	28. a	35. c	42. d	49. c

> *The correct answer and the percentage of students answering the question correctly (when it was used on an introductory accounting examination) are shown in parentheses at the beginning of each annotated solution that follows.*

1. (e,68) By definition, bonds that allow for the liquidation of issuer assets upon default of a bond issue are called **secured** bonds.

2. (e,84) "No specific collateral backing" means that the bonds are unsecured. If they may be "turned in" for retirement at the option of the bondholder, they are redeemable.

3. (d,63) A bond indenture specifies the legal provisions of the bonds to be issued such as the (1) issue date, (2) stated rate of interest, (3) dates that interest payments are due, and (4) any conversion privileges that might exist. Essentially, it's a list of promises made by the company wanting to sell the bonds.

4. (a,51) The stated rate is the rate of interest printed on the bond. That rate times face value determines the amount of cash paid periodically to bondholders.

5. (b,71) Response b is a false statement because redeemable bonds may be turned in for early retirement not at the option of the issuer, but at the option of the **holder**. Responses a, c, and d are correct statements.

6. (d,54) This question requires you to make a very careful judgment. While the objectivity and consistency principles **may** be involved, the **primary** principle involved (the best answer) is the matching principle. The recording of cash interest paid plus (or minus) amortization is an attempt to match bond interest expense to the period(s) benefited. (The cost principle is important when **recording** the bonds at the sale date, but is not directly related to determining periodic interest expense.

7. (b,66) Since investors demand a market rate higher than the stated rate, they will not be willing to pay face value and the bond will sell at a discount.

8. (a,56) Since investors will be receiving more than the market rate of interest, they will be willing to pay more than par value for the bonds. The bonds will sell at a premium.

9. (b,53) Sale of bonds at a premium causes total interest expense over the life of the bonds to be less than if the bonds had been sold at par.

10. (c,45) Selling bonds at a discount raises the "true" cost of borrowing above the face (or stated) rate printed on the bond. Remember, however, that regardless of whether the bonds sell at par, premium, or discount, the cash interest received by the buyer each period is exactly the same.

11. (d,80) Response d is a straightforward description of how the market rate of interest is determined. At any given time, however, it may be higher, lower, or equal to the stated rate of interest that is printed on the face of a bond.

12. (a,40) Response a is the only possible correct answer. If the bonds are selling at $1,200 (a premium), it means that the current market rate is less than the stated rate. Only response a (10%) is less than the 12% stated rate of the bonds.

13. (a,68) If the market rate is less than the stated rate, it means that the bonds are paying **higher** than market rate interest. Buyers will be willing to pay a premium to obtain these bonds that pay more than the market rate of interest.

14. (a,39) The selling price of bonds = present value of the interest payments + present value of the face value of the bonds. Therefore, ($3,500 x 3.8897) + ($50,000 x .6499) = $13,614 + $32,495 = $46,109.

15. (e,36) Bonds contain two promises, each of which has a present value. The first promise is to pay interest. It's present value is $10,000 (the annual interest payments) x 6.7101 = $67,101. The second promise is to return the principal of the bonds at maturity. The present value of that promise is $100,000 (the principal) x .4632 = $46,320. The sum of the present values is the amount someone would be willing to pay to buy the bonds ($67,101 + $46,320 = $113,421). (Note: always discount at the **market** rate of interest.)

16. (c,90) Cash should be debited for the amount received ($60,000); Bonds Payable should be credited for the face value of the bonds sold ($50,000); and Premium on Bonds should be credited for the excess of selling price over face value ($10,000).

17. (b,38) Selling bonds at a discount causes interest expense to increase. Since cash paid out per year is constant (regardless of the price paid for the bonds), the cash paid out per year (when bonds are sold at a discount) is less than the interest expense.

18. (c,88) The problem says that the bonds were sold for $90,000. Response c is the only one that debits (increases) cash by $90,000. It also properly records the Bonds Payable at their face value ($100,000) and sets up the Discount on Bonds Payable account with a debit balance.

19. (d,72) The complete journal entry would be: debit Cash for $112,285, credit Bonds Payable for $100,000 and credit Premium on Bonds Payable for $12,285.

20. (a,27) The interest expense is composed of the $3,000 cash interest to be paid ($100,000 x 6% x 1/2 year) and the $600 amortization of premium [$12,000 x (6 months/120 months)]. The amortization of the premium reduces the interest expense for a net of $2,400 ($3,000 - $600).

21. (b,42) The Premium on Bonds Payable account at a specific point in time represents an additional liability (over and above the face value of the bonds) and is shown on the balance sheet as an addition to Bonds Payable.

22. (d,51) Discount on Bonds Payable is a contra-account to Bonds Payable and is shown on the balance sheet as a reduction of that liability.

23. (a,48) At July 1st, a cash interest payment of $500 ($10,000 x 10% x 1/2 year) must be recorded with a credit entry. Further, the debit to Interest Expense must include the $500 plus amortization of discount for 1/2 year. Total discount is $500 and there are 20 six month periods in the life of the bonds. $500/20 periods = $25 of discount to be amortized each period. Total interest expense, then, is $525.

24. (d,37) When bonds sell at a discount it means that the market rate is greater than the stated rate. Response a is, therefore, incorrect. Responses b and c are nonsense since the yield rate and market rate are merely different terms for the same concept. Only response d can be correct.

25. (b,56) Cash will be debited for the amount received ($150,000 x .96 = $144,000). Discount on Bonds Payable will be debited for the difference between face value and cash received ($6,000); and Bonds Payable will be credited for the face value of the bonds ($150,000).

26. (c,65) Semi-annual interest = 6% x $300,000 x 1/2 year = $9,000. Semi- annual premium amortization = $3,000 premium/10 years x 1/2 year = $150.

27. (a,47) If bonds sell at par, the credit to cash equals the debit to interest expense at each interest payment date. Selling bonds at a discount, however, increases the amount of interest expense to be recognized each period. This means that the debit to Interest Expense will be greater than the credit to Cash.

28. (a,89) By definition, the use of borrowed assets to enhance the return to owners is called financial leverage.

29. (b,17) Financial leverage = return on stockholders' equity ($60,000/$200,000 = 30%) - return on total assets (given = 18%). Therefore, financial leverage in this problem = 30% - 18% = 12%.

30. (c,61) The complete journal entry would be:

Cash	112,000	
Bonds Payable		100,000
Premium on Bonds Payable		12,000

Response c, then, is the correct answer.

31. (a,65) The September 1, 19A entry to record payment of interest would also include amortization of premium for 1/2 year ($12,000 premium/10 years x 1/2 year = $600). The debit to interest expense, then, is reduced by the $600 amortization of premium. Cash interest paid of $3,000 - $600 = $2,400 of interest expense.

32. (c,87) Response a is incorrect since leverage involves using borrowed money. Response b is exactly backwards. Response d is incorrect since leverage can be either positive or negative.

33. (b,37) The **after-tax** cost of interest = interest cost x [1- tax rate]. Here, 1 - tax rate = 70% (1.00 - 30% = 70%). So, $800 x 70% = $560.

34. (e,83) The amount received by the seller would include the $1,055 selling price and the accrued interest since the last interest date of $25 for a total of $1,080. (Interest per year is $60 or $5 per month. Five months have passed since the previous interest payment.)

35. (c,86) On the date of sale, the seller collected the sales price ($865) plus four months accrued interest ($1,000 x .09 x 4/12 = $30) for a total of $895.

36. (c,80) Anytime bonds payable are sold, the credit to Bonds Payable is for par value. Here that amount is $60,000. The complete journal entry would be:

Cash	57,800	
Discount on Bonds Payable	3,000	
Bonds Payable		60,000
Bond Interest Expense		800

37. (a,42) Total discount on bonds payable of $3,000 is to be spread over the remaining 118 months life of the bonds for a monthly amortization of $25.42 ($3,000 / 118 = $25.42). Amortization for 12 months would be $305 ($25.42 x 12).

38. (b,65) The two months of accrued interest since April 1 is credited to Bond Interest Expense. Interest expense per month = $60,000 x .08 x 1/12 = $400. Two months worth, then, is $800. The complete journal entry would be:

Cash	62,800	
Bonds Payable		60,000
Bond Interest Expense		800
Premium on Bonds Payable		2,000

39. (b,68) Total discount of $500 ($10,000 - $9,500) is to be spread over 5 years ($100 per year). Amortization for three months (or 1/4 year), then, is $100 x 1/4 = $25.

40. (b,61) The adjusting entry at December 31 to record 19B interest expense is:

Interest Expense ($1,500 - $100)	1,400	
Premium on Bonds Payable	100	
Interest Payable		1,500

Gross interest expense (before amortization) is $1,500 ($50,000 x .09 x 4/12). Amortization of premium (to be deducted from the debit to interest expense) is $100 (($3,000 / 10 years) x 4/12).

41. (c,46) First, use the FV of $1 Annuity factor to determine the size of the necessary annual deposit to the sinking fund.

FV (of an annuity) = annual deposit x interest factor
$167,220 = annual deposit x 16.7220
annual deposit = $167,220 / 16.7220
annual deposit = $10,000

Since ten deposits of $10,000 will be made, B. Co. will contribute a total of $100,000 to the sinking fund. The other $67,220 ($167,220 - $100,000) will come from **interest earned by the fund.**

42. (d,55) The bond has been outstanding for two months. Interest expense at 9% for two months is $15 ($1,000 x .09 x 2/12) while the amortization of discount adds another $3 to interest expense ($90 x 2 months/60 months). Total interest expense, then, is $18. The discount on bonds payable was originally $90 ($1,000 - $910), but $3 was amortized at December 31, 19A leaving a balance of $87.

43. (d,83) Neither **short-term** nor **liability** are appropriate descriptive terms. A bond sinking fund is classified on the balance sheet as a **long-term asset**.

44. (b,88) Response b is a straightforward description of how annual interest expense is computed under the effective-interest method.

45. (d,73) Neither the stated rate nor par value of the bonds is relevant to determining bond interest expense under the effective-interest method. Instead, the **market rate** is used as is the **carrying value** of the bonds.

46. (c,65) Under the effective-interest method, annual interest expense is computed by multiplying the annual effective rate (9%) times the carrying value of the bonds ($100,000 - $5,536 = $94,464). $94,464 x 9% = $8,502.

47. (b,51) At December 31, 19C, the carrying value of the bonds is $47,353 ($50,000 - $2,647). The amount of premium to be amortized is the difference between effective interest expense ($47,353 x .06 = $2,841) and the cash interest paid ($50,000 x .07 = $3,500). $3,500 - $2,841 = $659.

48. (a,83) When bonds are sold at premium or discount, their carrying value changes each year. Since interest expense and amortization are both derived from the carrying value, they too will differ each period.

49. (c,71) Since the amount of amortization differs between the straight-line and effective interest methods, the accompanying debit to interest expense will also differ. The credit to Cash would remain the same. Conceptually, the effective interest method gives a better measurement of true interest cost than does straight-line.

CHAPTER TWELVE: MEASURING AND REPORTING OWNERS' EQUITY

PART A: Stockholders' Equity

1. Select the one **true** statement regarding corporations.
   a. Corporations are issued a charter by the federal government.
   b. Shareholders generally elect the president and various vice presidents.
   c. A proxy is a temporary manager hired by the Board of Directors.
   d. A corporation is a separate legal entity under the law.

2. Which of the following statements is (are) **false**?

   1. A dividend is a distribution to stockholders by a corporation and, as such, is an expense.
   2. The two fundamental requirements for the payment of a cash dividend are sufficient net income in the current period and sufficient cash.
   3. Dividends are declared by the corporation's Board of Directors.

   a. Only statement #1 is false.
   b. Only statement #2 is false.
   c. Only statement #3 is false.
   d. Statements #1 and #2 are false.
   e. Statements #1 and #3 are false.

3. The maximum number of shares of stock that can be issued (as specified in the charter of the corporation) is known as the:
   a. authorized shares.
   b. issued shares.
   c. outstanding shares.
   d. subscribed shares.

4. Outstanding stock is:
   a. stock that pays a very high dividend.
   b. authorized, sold, and still held by shareholders.
   c. the maximum number of shares that a corporation may sell.
   d. cumulative.

5. The following capital stock data were obtained from the records of Kenny's Electric Shop.
Authorized shares	8,000
Outstanding shares	5,000
Treasury stock shares	2,000

   The number of issued shares is:
   a. 10,000.
   b. 7,000.
   c. 6,000.
   d. 5,000.
   e. 3,000.

6. BAB Corporation has permission via its charter to issue up to 100,000 shares of common stock. To date, 23,000 have been sold and another 2,000 were given to the firm's attorney in exchange for legal services performed. What is the number of issued common shares?
   a. 100,000
   b. 25,000
   c. 23,000
   d. 21,000
   e. 19,000

7. Common stock usually has which combination of the following characteristics?

	Dividend Preference	Liquidation Preference
a.	Yes	Yes
b.	Yes	No
c.	No	Yes
d.	No	No

8. 10,000 shares of $5 par value common stock were sold by Jensen Corp. for $20 per share. Currently, the stock market value of these shares is $26 each. What is the amount of legal capital associated with these shares?
   a. $260,000
   b. $200,000
   c. $150,000
   d. $ 60,000
   e. $ 50,000

9. Which of the following is **not** a true statement about preferred stock?
   a. Preferred shareholders receive a current cash dividend before common shareholders do.
   b. Preferred shareholders will receive a stated dividend each year if there is net income.
   c. Preferred shares generally do not have voting privileges.
   d. Dividends in arrears arise only if preferred stock is cumulative.

10. Which one of the following characteristics would you **least** expect to be associated with preferred stock?
    a. dividends preferences
    b. conversion privileges
    c. asset preferences
    d. voting privileges

11. Elkington Company has just sold 3,000 shares of $10 par value common stock at a price of $15 per share. The firm is authorized to sell 5,000 such shares. In recording this transaction, the Common Stock account should be credited for:
    a. $75,000.
    b. $50,000.
    c. $45,000.
    d. $30,000.

12. On July 1, 19X7, Tom, Dick, and Harry each invested $1,000 to start TDH, Inc. Each of these investors was issued one share of common stock with a par value of $10. TDH, Inc. should record this transaction by which of the following?
    a. Dr. Cash; Dr. Contributed Capital in Excess of Par; Cr. Common Stock, par $10.
    b. Dr. Contributed Capital in Excess of Par; Dr. Common Stock, par $10; Cr. Cash.
    c. Dr. Cash; Dr. Common Stock, par $10; Cr. Contributed Capital in Excess of Par.
    d. Dr. Cash; Cr. Common Stock, par $10; Cr. Contributed Capital in Excess of Par.

13. The journal entry to record the original issuance of 1,000 shares of common stock at a sales price of $13 per share when the par value is $10, would be:
    a. debit Cash $13,000; credit Common Stock, $3,000 and Contributed Capital in Excess of Par Value $10,000.
    b. debit Cash $13,000; credit Common Stock $13,000.
    c. debit Cash $13,000; credit Common Stock $10,000 and Contributed Capital in Excess of Par Value $3,000.
    d. debit Common Stock $13,000; credit Cash $13,000.

14. 100 shares of common stock with a par value of $1 per share are sold for a total of $500. The entry to record the transaction is:

    a. Cash   100
        Common Stock   100

    b. Cash   500
        Common Stock   100
        C.C.--Excess over Par   400

    c. Common Stock   100
        Cash   100

    d. Cash   500
        Common Stock   500

15. Active, Inc. acquired machinery having a fair market value of $28,000 by giving the seller 1,000 shares of Active's $25 par value common stock. The correct journal entry to record this transaction would include a:
    a. credit to Common Stock of $28,000.
    b. debit to Machinery of $25,000.
    c. credit to Contributed Capital in Excess of Par of $3,000.
    d. debit to Allowance on Purchase Price of $3,000.

16. Which of the following is **not** a reason why companies acquire treasury stock?
    a. to reduce the size of operations
    b. to increase earnings per share
    c. to have shares available for stock bonus or stock option plans
    d. to increase market price per share
    e. to increase net income

17. The Hansen Company issued 500 shares of common stock to Levi Carlile in exchange for land that Carlile had recorded at $30,000. Hansen's common stock has a $5 par value and closed yesterday at $40 on the New York Stock Exchange. Hansen Company should record the land on its books at:
    a. $ 2,500.
    b. $17,500.
    c. $20,000.
    d. $30,000.
    e. $40,000.

18. Walter Corp. exchanged 500 shares of its $10 par value common stock for a new word processor with a fair value of $15,000. No open market sales of Walter Corporation stock have occurred in the last three years. Prior to that time, however, the stock was selling at $28 per share. In recording this transaction, the credit to Contributed Capital in Excess of Par should be for:
    a. $15,000.
    b. $10,000.
    c. $ 9,000.
    d. $ 8,000.
    e. $ 5,000.

19. Barb and Phyllis each own $1,000 in stock of Medium Corporation. If Barb sells her stock directly to Phyllis, which of the following statements is true?
    a. An equity account of Medium Corporation increases.
    b. An equity account of Medium Corporation decreases.
    c. An asset account of Medium Corporation increases.
    d. An asset account of Medium Corporation decreases.
    e. No account of Medium Corporation is affected.

20. Treasury stock is considered to be:
    a. an asset of the corporate treasury.
    b. a liability of the federal government.
    c. a contra stockholders' equity account with a debit balance.
    d. an equity account with a normal credit balance.

21. Treasury stock is an:
    a. owners' equity account with a debit balance.
    b. asset account with a debit balance.
    c. owners' equity account with a credit balance.
    d. asset account with a credit balance.

22. Westerburg Company temporarily reacquired 700 shares of its own common stock. Assuming the firm properly accounted for this event, which of the following were **decreased** by this reacquisition?

	Total Assets	Common Stock Account
a.	Yes	Yes
b.	Yes	No
c.	No	Yes
d.	No	No

23. The following excerpts from Bayou Company's stockholders' equity section are available.

Contributed Capital From Treasury Stock Transactions:	$ 500
Treasury Stock (100 shares):	$1,000

   If the company originally had 600 shares of treasury stock, then the treasury stock must have been sold for:
    a. $1 above its cost.
    b. $2 above its cost.
    c. $1 above its market value.
    d. $2 above its market value.

24. 100 shares of treasury stock ($10 par, common) were reacquired at $8 per share and later reissued at $13 per share. After reissuance, contributed capital from treasury stock transactions would equal:
    a. $1300.
    b. $ 800.
    c. $ 500.
    d. $ 200.
    e. $ 0.

PART B: Accounting for Dividends, Retained Earnings, and Unincorporated Businesses

25. In order to be able to pay a cash dividend, a corporation:
    a. must have operated at a profit for the year.
    b. must be able to cover the amount of dividends with cash **and** retained earnings.
    c. need only have a sufficient amount of retained earnings since cash will always exceed retained earnings.
    d. need not consider the amounts in balance sheet accounts.

26. Retained earnings:
    a. is equal to all the profits a corporation has ever made.
    b. must (in most states) have a credit balance in order for a dividend to be declared.
    c. represents a pool of cash that can be distributed to stockholders.
    d. must always exceed the amount of legal capital.

27. Evans Company has just declared a cash dividend. The necessary journal entry will include a:
    a. credit to Retained Earnings.
    b. debit to Contributed Capital in Excess of Par.
    c. credit to Dividends Payable.
    d. debit to Cash.

28. If a company failed to record the declaration of a cash dividend:
    a. assets and stockholders' equity would both be overstated.
    b. cash and liabilities would be overstated.
    c. there would be no effect since the double-entry system is designed to identify such errors.
    d. liabilities would be understated and retained earnings would be overstated.

29. You are given the following information.

Year	Net Income	Cash Dividends
B	$6	$4
C	$5	$2

If retained earnings after closing the books on December 31, 19C is $10, then retained earnings after closing the books on **December 31, 19A** must have been:
a. $ 3.
b. $ 5.
c. $12.
d. $15.

30. Melrose Company reported the following asset and liability balances at the end of 19B and 19C.

	19B	19C
Assets	$250,000	$500,000
Liabilities	$120,000	$180,000

During 19C, dividends of $10,000 were declared and paid. Additional common stock was issued for $50,000 and additional preferred stock for $80,000. Net income for 19C, therefore, must have been:
a. $200,000.
b. $150,000.
c. $ 70,000.
d. $ 60,000.

31. Dividends in arrears on preferred stock:
    a. are classified in the balance sheet as a current liability.
    b. are paid only after all current dividends on common stock stock have been paid.
    c. will exist only on noncumulative preferred stock.
    d. means cash dividends have been omitted in past years on cumulative preferred stock.

32. Which **one** of the following statements about the declaration and distribution of a stock dividend is **false**?
    a. contributed capital is increased
    b. par value remains the same
    c. retained earnings is increased
    d. common stock is increased

33. The records of Aspen Company contain the following data at Dec. 31, 19C.

   1. Common stock, par $25, 10,000 shares outstanding;
   2. 10% preferred stock, par $10, 2,000 shares outstanding;
   3. retained earnings, $100,000

On Dec. 31, 19C, the Board of Directors declared a cash distribution of $16,000. (While dividends had been paid to both classes of stock in 19A, no dividends had been paid during 19B.) Determine the total amounts that would be paid to the common and preferred stockholders, respectively, assuming the preferred stock is cumulative and non-participating.
   a. $14,000; $ 2,000
   b. $12,000; $ 4,000
   c. $10,000; $ 6,000
   d. $ 8,000; $ 8,000
   e. $ 6,000; $10,000

34. Assume the following stockholders' equity section at December 31, 19C.

   Pref. Stock (8%, cumulative, $50 par):
   $500,000
   Common Stock, $1 par: 50,000
   C. C. In Excess of Par, Common: 300,000
   Retained Earning: 165,000

If dividends on preferred stock are two years in arrears, what amount will go to common stockholders if dividends totaling $120,000 are declared?
   a. $ 0
   b. $ 40,000
   c. $ 50,000
   d. $ 80,000
   e. $120,000

35. Stock dividends **decrease** which (if any) of the following?

	Assets	Stockholders' Equity
a.	Yes	Yes
b.	Yes	No
c.	No	Yes
d.	No	No

36. The declaration and issuance of a stock dividend will:
   a. reduce owner's equity.
   b. increase owner's equity.
   c. reduce retained earnings.
   d. increase retained earnings.

USE THE FOLLOWING INFORMATION FOR THE NEXT TWO QUESTIONS.

On December 1, EZ Company declared and issued a 10% stock dividend to all common shareholders as of that date. The market value of the stock on that date was $75 per share. The stockholders' equity section of the balance sheet as of November 30 reflected the following:

Common Stock, (100 shares issued & outstanding):	$2,000
C. C.--Excess over Par, Common:	$3,000
Retained Earnings:	$4,000
Total Stockholders' Equity:	$9,000

37. Following issuance of the stock dividend, the Common Stock, Contributed Capital-- Excess over Par, and Retained Earnings accounts will have which of the following balances, respectively?
   a. $2,000; $3,000; $4,000
   b. $2,200; $3,300; $3,500
   c. $2,200; $3,550; $3,250
   d. The balances cannot be determined from the information given.

38. If, rather than a stock dividend, EZ Company had declared a 3 for 1 stock split, the Common Stock, Contributed Capital-- Excess over Par, and Retained Earnings accounts would have which of the following respective balances just after the split?
   a. $2,000; $3,000; $4,000
   b. $2,200; $3,000; $3,800
   c. $2,200; $3,300; $3,500
   d. The balances cannot be determined from the information given.

39. Common, Inc. has just issued a 10% stock dividend. The following information was available just prior to issuance of the dividend.

    Market value of common shares: $25 each
    Number of common shares outstanding: 100,000
    Par value of common shares: $10 per share
    Retained earnings: $2,500,000

    What is the proper balance in Retained Earnings immediately **after** issuing the stock dividend?
    a. $2,750,000
    b. $2,600,000
    c. $2,500,000
    d. $2,400,000
    e. $2,250,000

40. When a corporation has a 2 for 1 stock split, this action doubles:
    a. total stockholders' equity.
    b. the number of shares outstanding.
    c. the amount of retained earnings.
    d. the per share market price of outstanding stock.

41. Which of the following is true about stock splits?
    a. the number of shares outstanding increases
    b. the par value increases
    c. total contributed capital increases
    d. working capital increases

42. Bart Howard Company has 6,000 shares of $10 par value common stock outstanding. Assume that a 3 for 1 stock split is declared. Which of the following is **true** concerning a journal entry to record the stock split?
    a. Retained Earnings will be debited
    b. Retained Earnings will be credited
    c. Stock Split Payable will be debited
    d. Stock Split Payable will be credited
    e. no journal entry is needed

43. Journal entries related to dividends are made on the date of:
    a. record and date of payment.
    b. declaration and date of record.
    c. declaration and date of payment.
    d. declaration, record, and payment.

44. Prior period adjustments are reported as an:
    a. adjustment to the ending balance of retained earnings.
    b. extraordinary item.
    c. adjustment to the current year's revenues (or expenses).
    d. adjustment to the beginning balance of retained earnings.

45. Which of the following is true regarding owners' equity transactions?
    a. The dividend payment date usually preceeds the date of record.
    b. Stock splits are often used by management to permanently capitalize a portion of retained earnings.
    c. A stock dividend maintains each owner's proportionate ownership percentage.
    d. Authorized shares minus issued shares equal outstanding shares.

46. The Ted. E. Bear Co. has 5000 shares of $10 par, 6%, cumulative, nonparticipating preferred stock outstanding. They also have issued 6000 shares of $15 par value common stock and hold 1000 as treasury shares. The company has not paid dividends for 2 previous years. Calculate the total dividend amount the Board of Directors must declare in order for each common share to receive a divided of $0.80.
    a. $4,900
    b. $10,000
    c. $10,800
    d. $13,000
    e. $13,800

47. A 3 for 1 stock split:
    a. reduces total stockholders' equity.
    b. increases earnings per share.
    c. increases the number of shares outstanding.
    d. capitalizes retained earnings.

CHAPTER TWELVE: ANNOTATED SOLUTIONS

1. d	8. e	15. c	22. b	29. b	36. c	43. c
2. d	9. b	16. e	23. a	30. c	37. c	44. d
3. a	10. d	17. c	24. c	31. d	38. a	45. c
4. b	11. d	18. b	25. b	32. c	39. e	46. d
5. b	12. d	19. e	26. b	33. b	40. b	47. c
6. b	13. c	20. c	27. c	34. a	41. a	
7. d	14. b	21. a	28. d	35. d	42. e	

> *The correct answer and the percentage of students answering the question correctly (when it was used on an introductory accounting examination) are shown in parentheses at the beginning of each annotated solution that follows.*

1. (d,87) Corporations are chartered by the **state** governments. Shareholders elect the Board of Directors that, in turn, appoints a president. Response c is complete nonsense.

2. (d,41) A dividend is **not** an expense. A firm does not have to have earned net income in the **current** period; it is sufficient that profits merely have been earned in some prior period and not yet distributed.

3. (a,82) This question gives the definition of authorized shares. Issued shares are those that have been sold (or given away), while outstanding shares are those that have been sold (or given away) and still remain in shareholders' hands. Subscribed shares are those that potential shareholders have **promised** to buy.

4. (b,65) By definition, the answer to this question is response b. Outstanding shares have been sold and are still held by stockholders. The difference between the number of issued shares and the number of outstanding shares is the number of treasury shares that have been reacquired by the firm.

5. (b,53) Issued shares = outstanding shares + treasury shares; 5,000 + 2,000 = 7,000.

6. (b,53) Issued shares are those that have been (1) sold, or (2) otherwise given out in exchange for goods or services. Here, 23,000 have been sold and another 2,000 given in exchange for services for a total of 25,000 shares issued.

7. (d,70) Common stock generally does not have either of the two preferences listed. These preferences usually are associated with preferred stock.

8. (e,38) Generally, legal capital is merely the par value of shares issued. Here, 10,000 shares having a par value of $5 each have been issued resulting in legal capital of $50,000.

9. (b,43) Response b is false because there is no requirement for a company to declare dividends (on either common or preferred stock) just because there has been net income.

10. (d,85) It is very unusual for preferred stock to have voting privileges.

11. (d,59) The Common Stock account should be credited for the number of shares issued times par value of the stock; 3,000 x $10 = $30,000.

12. (d,62) Cash should be debited for the full amount received. Common Stock is credited for the par value of each share issued. Contributed Capital in excess of par is credited for the difference.

13. (c,79) Cash would be debited (increased) for the amount received ($13,000); the Common Stock account would be credited (increased) for the par value of the shares sold ($10 x 1,000 = $10,000); and Contributed Capital in Excess of Par would be credited (increased) for the difference between selling price and par value of the shares ($13 - $10 x 1,000 shares = $3,000).

14. (b,90) The key here is that only the par value of the stock (100 shares x $1 = $100) can be credited to the common stock account. The excess must be credited to a contributed capital account.

15. (c,82) The complete journal entry would be: debit Machinery, $28,000; credit Common Stock, $25,000; and credit Contributed Capital in Excess of Par, $3,000.

16. (e,49) Responses a through d are all common reasons why a company might acquire treasury stock. Response e, however, is basically nonsense. There is no way to increase net income by acquiring treasury stock.

17. (c,53) The land should be recorded at the fair market value of the stock issued at the date of the transaction. Therefore, 500 shares x $40 = $20,000.

18. (b,71) The key to this problem is that the word processor should be recorded on the books at its fair market value of $15,000 with a debit entry. The Common Stock account would be credited for par value of the shares (500 shares x $10 = $5,000) while the Contributed Capital in Excess of Par would be credited for the difference ($15,000 - $5,000 = $10,000).

19. (e,73) When one shareholder sells his or her shares to another shareholder, the books of the corporation involved are not affected. No entry is made thereon.

20. (c,66) By definition, treasury stock is considered to be a reduction of stockholders' equity. **It is not an asset.** It is shown on the balance sheet as a contra-account to the stockholders' equity section; it has a debit balance.

21. (a,63) Repeat after me..."**Treasury stock is not an asset.**" It is an equity account that has a debit balance. As such, it is sort of like a contra-account to owner's equity.

22. (b,34) The journal entry to record acquisition of treasury stock would include a debit to Treasury Stock (a negative equity account) and a credit to Cash (an asset account). The credit to Cash reduces total assets. Notice that the Common Stock account is not even involved.

23. (a,49) If the company originally had 600 shares of treasury stock and has an ending balance of 100 shares, 500 shares were sold during the year. A credit balance in Contributed Capital from Treasury Stock Transactions represents an amount realized upon sale that exceeded the cost of the treasury stock. Therefore, treasury stock was sold for $1 above cost ($500/500 shares).

24. (c,80) The selling price of treasury stock exceeded its cost by $5 per share. $5 per share x 100 shares = $500.

25. (b,81) In addition to being able to cover the amount with retained earnings, sufficient cash is necessary to pay a cash dividend.

26. (b,68) Generally, retained earnings represent prior profits of the firm that have not yet been paid out as dividends. If there is not a credit balance in that account, it means that there are no undistributed profits to distribute. Hence, no dividends can be paid.

27. (c,80) When a dividend is declared, the Retained Earnings account is debited (decreased) and the Dividends Payable account is credited (increased).

28. (d,63) The proper entry would include a debit to retained earnings (a decrease) and a credit to dividends payable (an increase). Failure to make this entry, then, would mean liabilities were understated and retained earnings was overstated.

29. (b,44) Let X = retained earnings on December 31, 19A. X + net income ($6 + $5) - dividends ($4 + $2) = $10 (retained earnings on December 31, 19C). So, X + $11 - $6 = $10. X = $5.

30. (c,30) Since assets increased by $250,000, the question is "where did those assets come from?" $60,000 came from an increase in liabilities and $130,000 from sale of stock. The other $60,000 had to come from net income, but remember that $10,000 of net income was paid out in dividends. This means that net income had to have been $70,000 in order to have $60,000 left after dividends to increase assets.

31. (d,67) Dividends in arrears means that there is cumulative preferred stock involved and that dividends on those cumulative shares have not been paid in some prior period. Those "missed" dividends must be made up before any dividends can be paid to common shareholders. Dividends are **not** a liability until declared.

32. (c,55) With a stock dividend, retained earnings are transferred to a contributed capital account. Therefore, retained earnings are decreased.

33. (b,66) The preferred dividend is $4,000 (2,000 shares x $10 par value x 10% x 2 years) with the difference of $12,000 ($16,000 - $4,000) being distributed to common shares.

34. (a,67) The annual dividend on preferred stock is $40,000 (8% x $500,000). If (at December 31, 19C) dividends are two years in arrears it means that no preferred dividends were paid in 19A or 19B. Before any dividends can go to common shareholders in 19C, the two year arrearage must be made up (2 x $40,000 = $80,000) and the current preferred dividend for 19C must be paid ($40,000). Since only $120,000 is to be paid in dividends, this leaves nothing for the common shareholders.

35. (d,32) A stock dividend results in a portion of the retained earnings balance being transferred to the paid-in capital section of stockholders' equity. Overall, then, stockholders' equity is not changed. No assets are involved when a stock dividend is declared and distributed.

36. (c,64) Declaration and issuance of a stock dividend has no effect on owner's equity. It does, however, reduce retained earnings since the entry to record a stock dividend includes a debit to retained earnings.

37. (c,36) Ten new shares were issued. The Common Stock account, then, increased by $200 to $2,200 (10 shares x $20 par value). Contributed Capital--Excess Over Par increased by $550 to $3,550 (10 shares x $55). Retained Earnings decreased by $750 to $2,250 (10 shares x $75).

38. (a,75) When a stock split occurs, no account balances change.

39. (e,49) Small stock dividends (up to 20%) are capitalized at fair market value of the shares distributed. 10,000 shares distributed x $25 per share = $250,000. The new retained earnings balance is $2,250,000 ($2,500,000 - $250,000).

40. (b,86) By definition, the number of shares doubles. Neither total equity nor retained earnings are affected. The per share market price will be cut in half.

41. (a,89) In a stock split, the number of shares outstanding increases, the par value **decreases,** while the contributed capital and working capital remain unchanged.

42. (e,86) No journal entry need be made when a stock split occurs.

43. (c,60) No journal entry is necessary on the date of record. That is merely the day that establishes who will get the dividend.

44. (d,57) By definition, prior period adjustments are reported as an adjustment to beginning retained earnings.

45. (c,67) The dividend payment date must come **after** the date of record becasue the date of record establishes to whom the dividends will be paid.

46. (d,22) The Board of Directors must declare enough in dividends to pay three years of dividends to the preferred stockholders (two years in arrears plus the current year) as well as $0.80 per share to common. The amount to preferred is: (5000 shares x $10 par) x 6% x 3 = $9,000. The amount necessary for common stock is 5000 shares x $0.80 = $4,000 (the 1,000 treasury shares do not receive a dividend). Total dividend necessary, then, is $9,000 + $4,000 = $13,000.

47. (c,80) A 3 for 1 stock split results in three times as many shares being outstanding. A stock split has no effect on total stockholders' equity and has the effect of decreasing earnings per share. It is a **stock dividend** that capitalizes retained earnings.

CHAPTER THIRTEEN: MEASURING AND REPORTING LONG-TERM INVESTMENTS

PART A: Long-Term Investments in Equity Securities (Stocks)

1. Which of the following describes the level of ownership which requires the equity method of accounting for long-term investments?

	Significant Influence	Control
a.	Yes	Yes
b.	Yes	No
c.	No	Yes
d.	No	No

2. Which of the following is a proper match of a measuring and reporting method with a level of ownership in voting capital stock?
   a. significant influence exists but not control; use cost method
   b. control exists; use cost method
   c. significant influence exists but not control; use equity method
   d. neither significant influence nor control; use equity method

3. APB Opinion #18 calls for use of the **equity** method of accounting for a stock investment in an unconsolidated company when the proportion of its stock held is as low as:
   a. 10%.
   b. 20%.
   c. 25%.
   d. 50%.

4. Company R owned 13% of the voting capital stock issued and outstanding by Company S at year-end 19D. At that date, the measurement and reporting approach which should be used by Company R for the long-term investment is known as the:
   a. cost method.
   b. equity method.
   c. consolidated method.
   d. significant influence method.

5. Concerning long-term investments in marketable equity securities, the equity method is used when the level of ownership indicates:
   a. significant influence but not control.
   b. significant influence and control.
   c. no significant influence or control.
   d. no significant influence but indicates control.

6. During a recent year the following events took place:

   ---Jones, Inc. purchased 1,000 shares of Mason Corp.'s 20,000 outstanding common shares for $56 per share.
   ---Dividends of $2.50 per share were received from Mason Corp.
   ---The December 31 market price for Mason shares was $52 each.
   ---Mason Corporation reported net income for the year of $25,000.

   Based on the information given, Jones Inc. stockholders' equity increased (decreased) by what amount during the year?
   a. $ -0-
   b. $2,500
   c. ($1,500)
   d. $4,000

7. During July of 19A, XYZ Company purchased 10,000 of the 100,000 outstanding common shares of ABC Corp. at $5 per share as a long-term investment. On December 31, 19A, ABC Corp. reported net income of $40,000 and declared a $30,000 dividend. On December 31, 19A the market value of each share was $4. The amount to be reported as net long-term investment on December 31, 19A is:
   a. $10,000.
   b. $30,000.
   c. $40,000.
   d. $50,000.

CHAPTER THIRTEEN QUESTIONS

8. Company A owns 15% of the outstanding common stock of Tall Corp. On December 15, 19A, Tall declared dividends of $50,000. For 19A, Tall had net income of $200,000. Which of the following is true concerning Company A for 19A?
   a. Investment Revenue is $7,500.
   b. Investment Revenue is $37,500.
   c. The Investment in Tall Corp. account increased by $22,500 during the year.
   d. Investment Revenue is $22,500.

9. Unrealized losses on the write-down of long-term investments in common stock:
   a. will be shown on the income statement and are included in the calculation of net income for the period.
   b. are not recorded.
   c. reduce stockholders' equity.
   d. allow the firm to show a conservative net income figure.

10. Epstein Co. acquired a long-term investment in common stock during the year and properly accounted for it using the cost method. At year end, the cost of this investment (Epstein's only such long-term investment) exceeds market value. The resulting account balance in Unrealized Loss on Long-Term Investment will be reported on the:
    a. balance sheet under stockholders' equity.
    b. balance sheet under assets.
    c. income statement as an ordinary loss.
    d. income statement as an extraordinary loss.

11. On January 1, 19A, Hilton Company acquired 25% of Biltmore's common stock for $150,000. During 19A, Biltmore paid a total of $20,000 dividends to its shareholders and reported total net income of $36,000. Hilton Company appropriately uses the equity method to account for this investment. What is the proper balance of the Investment in Biltmore account at the end of 19A?
    a. $145,000
    b. $150,000
    c. $154,000
    d. $159,000
    e. $166,000

12. At December 31, 19C, Kowalski Corp. reported the following account balances related to its only long-term investment in equity securities:

Long-term Investment (500 shares): $8,000
Allowance to Reduce L-T Investment to Market: $2,000

On March 15, 19D, Kowalski sold 100 of these shares for $15 per share. The proper journal entry on March 15, 19D to record the sale will include a:
    a. Loss on Sale of $100.
    b. Gain on Sale of $300.
    c. Gain on Sale of $100.
    d. Loss on Sale of $300.

13. Big Company owns 30% of the outstanding common shares of Little Corp. On December 31, 19A, Little Corp. declared dividends of $50,000 and reported net income of $200,000. Concerning Big Company, which of the following statements would be true?
    a. Investment Revenue for 19A is $15,000.
    b. Investment Revenue for 19A is $75,000.
    c. The Investment in Common Stock account increased by $45,000 during the year.
    d. Investment Revenue for 19A is $45,000.

14. On January 1, 19B, Lisa Company acquired 14,000 of the 40,000 outstanding voting shares of O'Rourke, Inc. for $100,000. During 19B, O'Rourke had net income of $50,000 and paid $10,000 in dividends. At December 31, 19B, what amount should be in Lisa Company's "Investment in O'Rourke" account?
    a. $ 96,500
    b. $103,500
    c. $114,000
    d. $117,500
    e. $140,000

15. W Corp. uses the equity method for it's investment in J Corp. This year, J earned $5,000 and paid $400 in dividends. Upon receipt of the dividend, W's accountant credited Investment Revenue. This procedure:
   a. is correct.
   b. will cause an overstatement of net income.
   c. will cause an understatement of net income.
   d. is incorrect according to GAAP, but will not cause any errors on the financial statements.

USE THE FOLLOWING INFORMATION FOR THE NEXT TWO QUESTIONS.

Agresto Inc. purchased 500 common shares of Sun, Inc. as a long-term investment on January 1, 19A for $5,000. Data for Sun Inc. follows.

Year	Net Income	Dividends Paid
19A	$20,000	$4,000
19B	$24,000	$6,000
19C	$26,000	$4,000

Sun had 2,000 common and 1,000 preferred shares outstanding during these three years.

16. How much revenue should Agresto report on the 19B income statement from the investment in Sun Inc.?
   a. $0
   b. $4,500
   c. $6,000
   d. $7,500

17. What should be the balance in Agresto's "Investment in Sun Inc." account at December 31, 19C?
   a. $ 5,000
   b. $18,500
   c. $19,000
   d. $25,500

USE THE FOLLOWING INFORMATION FOR THE NEXT TWO QUESTIONS.

Togo Company has made investments in long-term marketable equity securities as follows. (Assume voting stock is involved.)

Company	# of Shares	Percent of voting Stock	Unit Cost	Year-end Market
Xerox	500	10%	$10	$12
Chrysler	2000	40%	$30	$25
Texaco	1000	30%	$20	$10

18. Assume Chrysler declared a $1 per share cash dividend on 12-15-19C, payable on 1-20-19D. How should Togo record this event on 12-15-19C?

   a. Dividends Receivable   2,000
       Investment Revenue   2,000

   b. Cash   2,000
       Investment Revenue   2,000

   c. Dividends Receivable   2,000
       Investment in Chrysler   2,000

   d. Investment in Chrysler   2,000
       Investment Revenue   2,000

19. Togo's Allowance to Reduce Long-Term Investments to Market account at year-end should have which of the following balances after all adjusting journal entries have been made?
   a. $0
   b. $10,000
   c. $19,000
   d. $20,000

20. Which of the following statements is **not** correct regarding the measurement and reporting of long-term investments in marketable securities?
    a. At acquisition date, the cost recorded for a bond investment is the purchase cost plus any incidental costs such as brokerage fees.
    b. If an investor corporation purchases 25% of the outstanding shares of common stock of another company, it should treat any cash dividends received from that company as a reduction of the investment account.
    c. An investor corporation purchases 15% of the outstanding common shares of another firm. Subsequent to that acquisition, it will report the value of the investment at the lower-of-cost-or-market.
    d. An investor corporation purchases 25% of the outstanding shares of preferred stock of another company. Each year, it will recognize 25% of the net income of the investee company as a part of its own net income.

PART B: Long-Term Investments in Debt Securities (Bonds)

21. The _____ value of a bond fluctuates _____ with changes in the market rate of interest.
    a. maturity; directly
    b. market; directly
    c. maturity; inversely
    d. market; inversely

22. On October 1, 19C, Fralic Co. purchased $50,000 face value of 9%, 20-year bonds at par. The bonds pay interest annually on September 30. Assuming Fralic's accounting year ends on December 31 each year, what amount of interest revenue will Fralic report on **19D's** income statement from these bonds?
    a. $ 0
    b. $1,125
    c. $3,375
    d. $4,500

23. Which of the following statements is (are) true?

    1. When investors demand a higher rate of interest on bonds than the stated rate, bonds will sell in the market at a premium.
    2. When investors demand a lower rate of interest on bonds than the stated rate, bonds will sell in the market at a discount.

    a. Only statement #1 is true.
    b. Only statement #2 is true.
    c. Both statements are true.
    d. Neither statement is true.

24. A bond is purchased at a discount. What will happen to the net carrying value of the bond on the balance sheet as its maturity date approaches?
    a. increases
    b. stays the same
    c. decreases
    d. cannot be determined from the information given

25. If a bond is purchased at a discount, the carrying value of the investment reported on successive balance sheets:
    a. remains constant.
    b. increases each year.
    c. decreases each year.
    d. increases or decreases from year to year depending on the market rate of interest at the time.

26. An investor purchased an 8%, $1,000 face value bond for $856 on July 1, 19A. The bond pays interest every June 30. The investor intends to keep the bond until it matures June 30, 19G. On December 31, 19A, the investor will recognize what amount of interest revenue? (Assume straight-line amortization.)
    a. $ 40
    b. $ 52
    c. $ 80
    d. $104
    e. $144

27. Seedman Company purchased $500,000 of 5%, 10-year bonds on Jan. 1, 19G for $490,000. Assuming straight-line amortization, what is the approximate total **interest revenue** on this investment for 19G?
    a. $24,000
    b. $25,000
    c. $26,000
    d. $29,000
    e. $30,000

28. Subsequent to acquisition, a long-term bond investment:
    a. is valued at lower of cost or market.
    b. is reported at par value plus or minus any unamortized discount or premium.
    c. that is acquired at a premium will be valued at the maturity amount.
    d. that is acquired at par will have an increasing carrying value over its life.

29. Which of the following statements are true?
    1. Through amortization of discount, the carrying value of the investment account is increased each period.
    2. Amortization of the discount each period over the remaining life of the bond also decreases the amount of interest revenue earned.
    3. Through amortization of the premium, the balance in the investment account must be increased each period.
    4. Amortization of the premium each period over the remaining life of the bond also decreases the amount of interest revenue earned.
    a. Statements #1 and #4 are true.
    b. Statements #1 and #2 are true.
    c. Statements #3 and #4 are true.
    d. Statements #2 and #3 are true.

30. Phyllis purchased a $1,000 bond at a premium. This means that:
    a. she made a poor investment.
    b. she made a good investment.
    c. the bond returns more cash interest to her each year than if she had purchased it at a discount.
    d. the bond returns less cash interest to her each year than if she had purchased it at a discount.
    e. the stated rate on the bond exceeds the market rate.

31. Which of the following statements is **true** when bonds are purchased at a premium?
    a. The investor earns more than the stated rate on the bonds.
    b. Each period a credit adjustment must be made to the Investment in Bonds account.
    c. Cash interest is paid out each period equal to the market rate of interest.
    d. The net carrying value of the bonds increases each period over the life of the bonds.

32. On January 1, 19A, Hong Company purchased ten $1,000 face value, 10% bonds of Smith Company at 110 as a long-term investment. The bonds mature ten years from date of acquisition and were held during all of 19A and 19B. The carrying value of these bonds on **January 1, 19C** is:
    a. $ 9,200.
    b. $10,000.
    c. $10,800.
    d. $11,000.

33. Ms. Jones purchased a 5%, $1,000, 10-year bond for $1,040 at its issue date. The cumulative amount of interest revenue that will appear on Ms. Jones' income statement over the life of the bond is:
    a. $460.
    b. $500.
    c. $520.
    d. $540.

34. On July 1, 19C, Jackson Company purchased a five-year, 10%, $1,000 bond at 110. Assuming straight-line amortization, what amount of interest revenue will Jackson Company report on the income statement each year concerning this investment?
    a. $278
    b. $120
    c. $110
    d. $100
    e. $ 80

USE THE FOLLOWING INFORMATION FOR THE NEXT TWO QUESTIONS.

On July 1, 19A, Burkett Corp. purchased (as a long-term investment) bonds of Miller Co. having a face value of $10,000. Burkett Corp. paid $10,440 plus a $160 brokerage fee. The bonds have a 12% stated rate of interest and an annual interest payment date of December 31. The bonds mature on July 31, 19C.

35. What amount should Burkett Corp. report as interest revenue from these bonds in 19A?
   a. $636
   b. $626
   c. $600
   d. $490
   e. $450

36. What is the proper balance in the long-term investment account after all entries have been made on December 31, 19A?
   a. $10,000
   b. $10,360
   c. $10,440
   d. $10,450
   e. $10,600

37. On January 1, 19A, Wong Enterprises purchased (as a long-term investment) 100, $1,000 par value, 9% bonds due in ten years with interest payable each December 31. The bonds were purchased at 105. How much investment revenue will Wong report each year assuming straight-line amortization is used?
   a. $8,500
   b. $9,000
   c. $9,450
   d. $9,500

38. As compared to the straight-line method of amortizing a discount, the effective-interest method has which effect in the first year?
   a. more discount is amortized
   b. less discount is amortized
   c. the same amount of discount is amortized
   d. cannot be determined without more information

39. On August 1, 19A, Benke Company purchased bonds having a face value of $10,000. The price was 97 plus accrued interest with interest due each April 30. The amount that should be recorded in the Long-Term Investment in Bonds account at August 1, 19A is:
   a. $10,150.
   b. $10,000.
   c. $ 9,850.
   d. $ 9,700.

40. Gomez Co. made a long-term investment in bonds. Relevant facts are as follows:

Face Value	$10,000
Date of bonds	July 1, 19A
Purchase date	September 1, 19A
Purchase price	Par
Stated interest rate	9%
Life of bonds	10 years

The journal entry to record this purchase of bonds will include a:

	dr. to Invest. in Bonds for $10,150	*cr. to Cash for $10,150*
a.	Yes	Yes
b.	Yes	No
c.	No	Yes
d.	No	No

41. Stonebridge Financial Corp. made a long-term investment in bonds as follows:

Face value	$750,000
Stated rate	8%
Interest payment date	July 1 (annually)
Purchase date	November 1

The bonds were purchased at 100 plus accrued interest. The proper journal entry on November 1 will include a:
   a. debit to Cash for $750,000.
   b. credit to Investment in Bonds for $770,000.
   c. debit to Revenue from Investments of $20,000.
   d. credit to Bond Interest Receivable for $10,000.

42. Carlucci Co. purchased (on the issue date) 20-year, 9% bonds having a par value of $100,000 for $109,813. The bonds yield 8% effective-interest paid annually. During the first twelve months these bonds are held, what amount of premium should be amortized under the effective-interest method?
    a. $ 215
    b. $ 491
    c. $1,000
    d. $1,883

43. On January 1, 19A, Poindexter Co. paid $40,870 for 50 ten-year bonds each having a face value of $1,000. The stated rate is 7% and the effective rate is 9%. Interest is paid annually and the effective-interest method of amortization is used. Assuming this long-term investment was held throughout the year, at what amount should it be reported on the December 31, 19A balance sheet?
    a. $40,692
    b. $40,870
    c. $41,048
    d. $41,783
    e. $49,822

CHAPTER THIRTEEN: ANNOTATED SOLUTIONS

1. b	8. a	15. b	22. d	29. a	36. d	43. c
2. c	9. c	16. c	23. d	30. e	37. a	
3. b	10. a	17. c	24. a	31. b	38. b	
4. a	11. c	18. c	25. b	32. c	39. d	
5. a	12. a	19. a	26. b	33. a	40. c	
6. c	13. c	20. d	27. c	34. e	41. c	
7. c	14. c	21. d	28. b	35. e	42. a	

> *The correct answer and the percentage of students answering the question correctly (when it was used on an introductory accounting examination) are shown in parentheses at the beginning of each annotated solution that follows.*

1. (b,78) The equity method requires that significant influence exist (at least 20% ownership), not control (which would be more than 50% ownership).

2. (c,91) For holdings of less than 20% of outstanding shares, an investor is presumed to lack "significant influence" over an investee; and the cost method should be used. For a holding of between 20% and 50% an investor is presumed to **have** significant influence and the equity method should be used. For a holding of over 50%, an investor is presumed to have control and consolidated statements should usually be prepared.

3. (b,92) The equity method should be used when the investor company has significant influence over the investee. Such influence is presumed to exist when the percentage ownership of voting shares reaches 20%.

4. (a,84) The cost method is to be used when the investor company does **not** have significant influence over the investee. If the percentage of ownership of voting shares is less than 20%, significant influence is presumed not to exist. In this question, the ownership was 13%.

5. (a,77) According to GAAP, the equity method should be used when the investor company has "significant influence" over the investee. If the investor company has control (i.e. more than 50% of the voting stock), the consolidation method should be used.

6. (c,31) Jones should use the cost method because it purchased only 5% of Mason's shares. The dividends received of $2,500 (1,000 shares x $2.50) are revenue and increase stockholders' equity. At year-end, LCM should be used to recognize a $4,000 loss ($56 - $52 = $4 loss per share; $4 x 1,000 shares = $4,000 loss). The loss decreases stockholder's equity. Net, the change is a decrease of $1,500.

7. (c,66) Since the investment represents only 10% of the outstanding shares of ABC Corp., the lower-of-cost-or-market method should be used. The market value ($40,000) is lower than the cost ($50,000).

8. (a,85) Since neither significant influence nor control exists (less than 20% ownership), the cost method is used for measuring and reporting. Therefore, revenue from this investment = 15% of the dividends paid out by the investee. 15% x $50,000 = $7,500.

9. (c,34) Write-downs on the long-term portfolio are not recorded on the income statement, hence, responses a and d are incorrect. They must be reported, per GAAP, as a contra-account to stockholder's equity.

10. (a,55) For long-term investments, the Unrealized Loss account is reported on the balance sheet as a contra-equity account. The **other** half of the adjusting entry (the Allowance account) is reported under assets as a contra account to the Long-Term Investments account.

11. (c,35) Since Hilton's ownership is greater than 20%, the equity method should be used. The investment account ($150,000) must be increased for Hilton's pro-rata share (25%) of Biltmore's net income and decreased by the pro-rata share of dividends paid. $150,000 + (25% x $36,000) - (25% x $20,000) = $154,000.

12. (a,48) The key to this question is that the shares are (before sale) recorded in the investment account at $16 each ($8,000 / 500 shares = $16). When they are sold for $15 each, a loss of $1 per share is realized. (Remember that the Allowance account is updated **only** at the end of the accounting period.)

13. (c,35) With 30% ownership, the equity method should be used by Big Company. The investment account increased by $60,000 (30% of $200,000) when Little reported net income and decreased by $15,000 (30% of $50,000) when Little paid dividends. The net change, then, is a $45,000 increase.

14. (c,44) The equity method should be used because Lisa acquired 35% of O'Rourke voting stock (14,000 shares out of 40,000). At purchase, the Investment account is debited for the $100,000 cost. When O'Rourke reports net income, Lisa debits the Investment account $17,500 (35% x $50,000) for its 35% share. When O'Rourke pays dividends, Lisa receives $3,500 (35% x $10,000) and credits this to the Investment account. The ending balance, then, is $114,000.

15. (b,59) Under the equity method, the investor company recognizes its share of investee earnings at the time they are reported. If W's accountant credits the dividend received to Investment Revenue there will be a double counting and net income will be overstated. Dividends, under the equity method, should be credited to the Investment account.

16. (c,40) Agresto would report as revenue its 25% share of Sun's $24,000 net income (25% x $24,000 = $6,000).

17. (c,45) Use the equity method because 25% of the common shares (voting shares) were owned (500/2000 shares = 25%). The Investment in Sun, Inc. account is first debited for the $5,000 original cost. Further, it is debited at each year end for 25% of Sun's reported net income (19A = $5,000; 19B = $6,000; 19C = $6,500). Also, it is credited each year for Agresto's share of dividends received (19A = $1,000; 19B = $1,500; 19C = $1,000). The December 31, 19C balance, then, is $19,000 ($5,000 + $5,000 + $6,000 + $6,500 - $1,000 - $1,500 - $1,000).

18. (c,33) Since 40% of Chrysler shares are owned, the equity method should be used. At the dividend declaration date, Togo would debit Dividends Receivable and credit the Investment in Chrysler account.

19. (a,37) Only the Xerox stock should be accounted for by the lower-of-cost-or-market method. At 12-31-19C, however, the market value is **above** cost so there is no need for an allowance account.

20. (d,41) Response d describes use of the equity method. That method, however, is to be used when the investor company can exercise "significant influence" over the investee. Since preferred stock usually does not have voting rights, such influence cannot be obtained. Therefore, the equity method is not used with preferred stock.

21. (d,49) When interest rates increase, bond prices decrease and vice-versa. Hence, the **market** value of a bond fluctuates **inversely** with changes in the market rate of interest.

22. (d,60) During 19D, Fralic Co. will have held these bonds for all 12 months, hence, one full year's interest revenue will be reported $50,000 x .09 = $4,500). (Since the bonds were purchased at par, there is no amortization of premium or discount.)

23. (d,75) An inverse relationship exists between the rate of interest demanded and the selling price of the bonds. Therefore, if a higher interest rate is demanded, the bonds will sell below par (at a discount). If a lower rate is demanded, the bonds will sell at a premium.

24. (a,71) Since the bond was purchased at a discount, its initial carrying value (book value) is less than the face value. Each year during its life, however, a portion of the discount will be amortized and the carrying value will gradually be increased. On the maturity date, the carrying value will equal its face value.

25. (b,52) When a bond is purchased at a discount, it is recorded at **less than** face value. Over the period held, the discount is amortized by debiting the Investment account and crediting the Interest Revenue account. This causes the Investment account to increase each period.

26. (b,37) Interest revenue will consist of cash interest earned plus the pro-rata amortization of discount. The total discount is $144 ($1,000 - $856). The cash interest earned since July 1 is $40 ($1,000 x 8% x 1/2 year), and the pro-rata amortized discount for six months is $12 ($144 x 6/72) for a total of $52.

27. (c,63) Interest revenue would include the cash interest received plus a portion of the amortized discount. Cash interest received is $25,000 ($500,000 x 5%) while the amortization is $1,000 ($10,000 discount/ 10 years). Total interest revenue, then, is $26,000.

28. (b,71) The lower-of-cost-or-market (LCM) procedure is not applied to long-term bond investments. Bonds acquired at a premium are valued **above** maturity value. Bonds acquired at par have a **constant** carrying value over their life.

29. (a,65) Through amortization of the discount, the carrying value of the investment account is increased; this also increases the amount of interest revenue earned. Amortization of premium decreases the carrying value and decreases interest revenue earned. Therefore, #1 and #4 are true.

30. (e,58) Responses a and b are nonsense because the mere existence of a premium or discount says nothing about the quality of the investment. Responses c and d are nonsense because the cash interest payments to be received remain constant regardless of whether a premium or discount (or neither) exist. Response e is a true statement explaining why someone would be willing to pay a premium.

31. (b,65) When bonds are purchased at a premium, the initial carrying value is greater than face value. Over the life of the bonds, that excess (or premium) must be gradually amortized away so that the carrying value of the bonds is equal to face value on the maturity date. This is done by crediting the Investment in Bonds account at each amortization date.

32. (c,47) The carrying value will be cost minus amortized premium. Total premium was $1,000 to be spread over 10 years (or $100 per year). Two years have passed, so $200 of premium has been amortized. Cost ($11,000) - amortized premium ($200) = $10,800.

33. (a,77) The bond was purchased at a $40 premium. The premium will reduce interest revenue (via amortization) during the life of the bond. Without considering the premium, the bond would earn $500 interest over its life ($1,000 x 5% x 10 years = $500). Subtracting the $40 premium leaves total interest revenue over the life of the bond at $460 ($500 - $40).

34. (e,42) There is $100 of bond premium since the bond was purchased at 110% of face value (110% x $1,000 = $1,100). This will be amortized over 5 years ($100/5 years = $20 per year). Cash interest received per year of $100 minus the $20 premium amortization yields $80 net interest revenue per year.

35. (e,25) Interest revenue will include 1/2 year's worth of cash interest ($10,000 x .12 x 1/2 year = $600) less 1/2 year's amortization of premium ($600/24 months = $25 per month; $25 x 6 months = $150). $600 interest - $150 amortization of premium = $450.

36. (d,31) The beginning balance at 7-1-19A is $10,600 ($10,440 + $160). When 19A's premium amortization of $150 is recorded, the investment account will be reduced to an ending balance of $10,450.

37. (a,41) Each year the bonds pay $9,000 interest ($100,000 x 9%). From this, however, must be deducted the amortization of premium of $500 per year (price paid = $105,000; deduct face value of $100,000 leaving $5,000 of premium to be amortized over 10 years). Cash interest received, then, of $9,000 less $500 amortization of premium leaves Revenue From Investments each year of $8,500.

38. (b,43) Under the effective-interest method, the amount of discount to be amortized in any year is the difference between (1) the cash interest received (a constant amount each year), and (2) the product of the effective rate times the carrying value of the bonds. Since the carrying value increases each year (and eventually grows to equal face value), this second amount gets larger and larger each year. Hence, less discount is amortized in early years and more in later years. Straight-line method, however, results in the **same** amount being amortized each year.

39. (d,66) The problem clearly says that the price paid was 97 (meaning 97% of face value). This is the amount that should be recorded in the Long-Term Investment account (97% x $10,000 = $9,700). The buyer will also have to compensate the seller for interest that has accrued since the last interest date, but this amount should not be included in the Investment account.

40. (c,70) The necessary journal entry is as follows:

Investment in Bonds	10,000	
Revenue from Investments	150*	
Cash		10,150

*The amount of the debit to Revenue from Investments is computed as: $10,000 x 9% x 2/12.

41. (c,60) The complete journal entry would include a debit to Investment in Bonds for $750,000 (par value), a debit to Revenue from Investments for $20,000 (accrued interest = $750,000 x 8% x 4/12), and a credit to Cash for $770,000 (the sum of par value and accrued interest).

42. (a,50) The premium to be amortized is the difference between (1) the cash interest received (9% x $100,000 = $9,000) and, (2) the effective interest earned the first year (8% x $109,813 = $8,785). $9,000 - $8,785 = $215.

43. (c,55) This long-term investment will be reported at purchase price plus amortized discount to date ($40,870 + $178 = $41,048). The amount of amortized discount in year 19A is computed as "effective interest revenue (9% x $40,870 = $3,678) minus cash interest received (7% x $50,000 = $3,500)."

CHAPTER FOURTEEN: CONSOLIDATED STATEMENTS – MEASURING AND REPORTING

PART A: Acquiring a Controlling Interest

1. Control of a corporation is presumed to exist when the percent ownership of voting shares passes what level?
   a. 20%
   b. 35%
   c. 50%
   d. 75%

2. Consolidated financial statements are generally required when one firm's ownership of another's common stock passes what percent?
   a. 20%
   b. 35%
   c. 50%
   d. 75%

3. What two factors must be present in order for consolidated statements to be prepared?
   a. control and economic compatibility
   b. significant influence and economic compatibility
   c. control and financial compatibility
   d. significant influence and financial compatibility

4. Which one of the following statements about consolidated reporting is true?
   a. Consolidated statements relate only to the reporting phase of accounting.
   b. Consolidated financial statements are prepared from information recorded in the consolidated ledger.
   c. As long as economic compatibility is present, consolidated statements may be prepared with as small an ownership as 40%.
   d. If consolidated statements are prepared, the individual companies no longer prepare individual or separate statements.

5. When one company owns more than 50% of the voting shares of another company but does not have control because of foreign government restrictions, how should the first company report its investment in the second company?
   a. by the cost method
   b. by the lower-of-cost-or-market method
   c. by the consolidation method
   d. by the equity method
   e. by the effective-interest method

6. Which of the following requirements must be met before consolidated financial statements can be prepared for a parent and subsidiary?

	Economic Compatibility	Similar Size
a.	Yes	Yes
b.	Yes	No
c.	No	Yes
d.	No	No

7. When one company acquires a controlling interest in another company by exchanging unissued capital stock for shares in the acquired firm, what kind of business combination has taken place?
   a. purchase
   b. direct exchange
   c. book value swap
   d. leveraged buyout
   e. pooling of interests

8. The cost principle is applied to business combinations under which of the following methods?

	Pooling	Purchase
a.	Yes	Yes
b.	Yes	No
c.	No	Yes
d.	No	No

9. Nancy Corporation acquired all the outstanding shares of Tang Company in exchange for 5,000 $10 par value shares of Nancy Corp. Prior to the buyout, Tang's stockholders' equity section was composed of common stock of $75,000 and retained earnings of $30,000. The common stock had a market value of $140,000. On Nancy's books, the Investment in Tang should be recorded at what amount?
   a. $ 75,000
   b. $105,000
   c. $110,000
   d. $140,000
   e. $170,000

10. Bildad Corporation has just acquired the Shuhite Company via a pooling of interests. When the consolidated balance sheet is prepared on the date of the pooling, which of the following combinations of account values will be used?

	Bildad Corp.	Shuhite Co.
a.	book	book
b.	market	book
c.	book	market
d.	market	market

11. Big Company has just acquired the Ben Corporation via the purchase method. If a consolidated balance sheet is prepared on the date of purchase, which of the following combinations of account values will be used?

	Big Company	Ben Corporation
a.	book	book
b.	market	book
c.	book	market
d.	market	market

12. Not recognizing goodwill generally reflects which of the following?
   a. pooling of interests
   b. purchase
   c. subsidiary
   d. amortization

USE THE FOLLOWING INFORMATION FOR THE NEXT FOUR QUESTIONS.

Beier Company is considering acquisition of the Buyee Company. The following data is accurate **just prior** to any acquisition.

	Beier	Buyee
Cash	$400	$100
Accounts Receivable ($30 due from Buyee)	110	30
Plant and Equipment	290	200
Total Assets	$800	$330
Accounts Payable ($30 due to Beier)	$110	$ 50
Bonds Payable	300	90
Common Stock, Beier Co. ($5 par)	300	--
Common Stock, Buyee Co. ($10 par)	--	150
Retained Earnings	90	40
Total Liabilities and Equity	$800	$330

Market values at the date of proposed acquisition are as follows:

Beier common stock	$15 per share
Buyee common stock	$25 per share
Beier plant and equipment	$320
Buyee plant and equipment	$250

13. Assume that (1) Beier exchanges two of its shares for each share of Buyee's stock, (2) no cash changes hands, and (3) this event should be accounted for as a pooling of interests. Beier should debit its Investment in Buyee account for what amount?
   a. $150
   b. $190
   c. $210
   d. $450
   e. $750

14. Assume, instead, that Beier acquires all of Buyee's stock at a total price of $375 cash. If Buyee then prepares a separate balance sheet for itself, how much should be recorded for goodwill on that statement?
   a. $-0-
   b. $135
   c. $185
   d. $215

15. If the proposed acquisition is accounted for as a pooling of interests and Beier gives up two shares for every one share of Buyee, what will be the amount of consolidated retained earnings immediately thereafter?
    a. $ 40
    b. $ 90
    c. $130
    d. $280

16. Assume the acquisition is made, but that we don't know if it was a purchase or a pooling of interests. What will be the amount of consolidated Accounts Receivable and consolidated Accounts Payable?

	Accounts Receivable	Accounts Payable
a.	$140	$160
b.	$110	$130
c.	$140	$130
d.	$110	$160

    e. The balances cannot be determined without further information.

17. Purchase as a method for combining firms means that:
    a. the fair market value of assets and liabilities are added.
    b. the book value of assets and liabilities are added.
    c. goodwill will be reported on the subsidiary's balance sheet.
    d. the fair market value of the acquired firm is added to the book value of the dominating firm.

18. On January 2, 19A, Ortega purchased 100% of Kelliher Company for $60,000 cash. Book value of Kelliher's net assets was $40,000 and fair value was $55,000. At December 31, 19A, Ortega wishes to report the highest possible consolidated net income allowable by generally accepted accounting principles. Under this objective, what is the minimum amount of goodwill that can be amortized to expense during 19A?
    a. $-0-
    b. $100
    c. $125
    d. $375
    e. $500

19. Purchase accounting and pooling of interest accounting differ most in the application of which of the following accounting principles?
    a. matching principle
    b. time-period principle
    c. continuity principle
    d. cost principle

PART B: Reporting Consolidated Operations after Acquisition

20. When the pooling of interests method is used, certain accounts on the resulting consolidated balance sheet usually have higher amounts than if the purchase method had been used. For which set of accounts below is this true?
    a. cash, accounts receivable, plant and equipment
    b. accounts payable, common stock, retained earnings
    c. accounts payable, plant and equipment, retained earnings
    d. cash, common stock, retained earnings

21. Parent Company acquired all the voting shares of Subsidiary, Inc. One year later, which one of the following accounts is most likely to have a larger balance just because a purchase occurred rather than a pooling?
    a. sales revenue
    b. cash
    c. accounts receivable
    d. common stock
    e. depreciation expense

22. Abercrombie acquired 100% of Fitch via a pooling of interests. One year later, the consolidated balance sheet is being prepared. The amount reported for retained earnings has what relationship to the amount that **would have been reported** if a purchase had taken place.
    a. higher
    b. lower
    c. the same
    d. cannot be determined without more information

23. Wallace Incorporated will acquire 100% of the outstanding common stock of Ladmo Company during the current accounting period. Assume that the pooling of interests method is used and that immediately after acquisition a consolidated balance sheet will be prepared. Which of the following statements is **true** concerning that balance sheet?
    a. Goodwill is likely to be included.
    b. Retained earnings will probably be larger than if the purchase method had been used.
    c. Ladmo Company assets will be included at their market values as of the date of acquisition.
    d. The Common Stock account will be smaller than if the purchase method had been used.

24. Goodwill might be found on a consolidated balance sheet if the business combination was accounted for as a:

	Pooling	Purchase
a.	Yes	Yes
b.	Yes	No
c.	No	Yes
d.	No	No

25. Concerning a consolidated balance sheet, which one of the following categories is usually larger simply because a purchase took place rather than a pooling?
    a. current assets
    b. operational assets
    c. intangible assets
    d. current liabilities
    e. long-term liabilities

26. How many of the following statements are true of the pooling method?

    -- requires little or no cash disbursement
    -- results in higher reported net income
    -- reports higher retained earnings
    -- is susceptible to manipulation

    a. one
    b. two
    c. three
    d. four

27. "Instant earnings," "escalating EPS," and "tricky mixes" are terms historically associated with which of the following methods?

	Pooling	Purchase
a.	Yes	Yes
b.	Yes	No
c.	No	Yes
d.	No	No

28. Which of the following statements are true of the pooling method?

    (1) It avoids the necessity of recognizing goodwill and amortizing of it.
    (2) It is conceptually preferable to the purchase method.
    (3) It yields higher asset valuations than does the purchase method.

    a. Statement #1 only.
    b. Statement #2 only.
    c. Statement #3 only.
    d. Both statements #1 and #2.
    e. Both statements #2 and #3.

29. Which one of the following consolidated financial statement accounts is usually **not** effected in the years following a business combination by whether the combination was a pooling or a purchase?
    a. plant and equipment
    b. accounts receivable
    c. amortization expense
    d. depreciation expense
    e. goodwill

30. Two years ago, Company A acquired all the voting stock of Company B via a pooling of interests. Which of the following accounts from the current consolidated balance sheet is most likely to have a higher balance today than it would have had if the business combination had been a purchase?
    a. accounts receivable
    b. plant, property, and equipment
    c. goodwill
    d. contributed capital from treasury stock transactions
    e. retained earnings

CHAPTER FOURTEEN: ANNOTATED SOLUTIONS

1. c	8. c	15. c	22. a	29. b
2. c	9. b	16. b	23. b	30. e
3. a	10. a	17. d	24. c	
4. a	11. c	18. c	25. b	
5. d	12. a	19. d	26. d	
6. b	13. b	20. d	27. b	
7. e	14. a	21. e	28. a	

The correct answer and the percentage of students answering the question correctly (when it was used on an introductory accounting examination) are shown in parentheses at the beginning of each annotated solution that follows.

---

1. (c,81) By definition, control of a corporation is presumed to occur once the percentage of ownership of outstanding **voting** stock reaches 50%.

2. (c,85) A controlling interest is usually deemed to exist if one firm owns 50% or more of another. If the economic compatibility test is satisfied, the consolidated method should then be used to report this investment.

3. (a,75) The two factors that must be present are (1) control, and (2) economic compatibility. Economic compatibility means that the activities of the two organizations are related and complementary. For example, a manufacturer of sporting goods might also own a chain of retail sporting goods shops. A retail food store and a bank would probably **not** meet the test of economic compatibility.

4. (a,69) Response a is the only true statement. There is no such thing as a consolidated ledger; control starts at 50% ownership; and even after a business combination the individual companies continue to prepare separate statements.

5. (d,78) Under the terms of APB #18, the equity method should be used when more than 50% of the voting shares are owned but control cannot be exercised.

6. (b,78) There are two requirements: (1) control and (2) economic compatibility. Similar size is **not** a requirement.

7. (e,79) In general, if the business combination is achieved by exchanging shares of stock, it qualifies as a pooling of interests. If cash is involved, the business combination must usually be accounted for as a purchase.

8. (c,71) The cost principle is applied under a purchase since the assets of the acquired company are brought on to the consolidated balance sheet at their market values. For a pooling, those assets are brought on at book values.

9. (b,49) This event most likely qualifies as a pooling of interests since it involves an exchange of stock. Under a pooling, the investment is recorded at the book value of the subsidiary's equity ($75,000 + $30,000 = $105,000). This amount is also the book value of net assets.

10. (a,69) When a pooling of interests has taken place, the subsequent consolidated balance sheet will be based on the **book** values of each company. If the purchase method had been used, the assets etc. of the acquired company would be recorded on the consolidated balance sheet at their market values as of the date the purchase took place.

11. (c,65) Since the purchase method was used, the resulting consolidated balance sheet will include Big Company accounts at their historical book values while the Ben Company accounts will be stated at their market values as of the date of purchase.

12. (a,89) Under the pooling of interests method of business combination, goodwill is never recorded since, conceptually, no purchase (or sale) of assets has taken place. The terms subsidiary and amortization are not methods of business combination.

13. (b,57) Since the pooling method has been used, Beier's debit to the Investment in Buyee account should be based on the book value of Buyee's equity (common stock of $150 + retained earnings of $40 = $190).

14. (a,43) Since cash was involved, the purchase method was used. Even so, the question asks about goodwill on Buyee's balance sheet. No goodwill from Beier's purchase would appear there; goodwill would appear only on the **consolidated** balance sheet.

15. (c,67) Since a pooling took place, consolidated retained earnings would be the sum of the individual retained earnings amounts just prior to the business combination ($90 + $40 = $130).

16. (b,71) Intercompany debt is always eliminated regardless of whether a pooling or purchase took place. Total accounts receivable is $140 ($110 + $30) less the $30 intercompany debt for a consolidated accounts receivable of $110. By the same process, consolidated accounts payable is $130.

17. (d,78) When the purchase method has been used in a business combination, the resulting consolidated balance sheet will combine the fair values of the firm acquired with the book values of the dominating firm.

18. (c,57) Goodwill in this problem is $5,000 ($60,000 cash paid for net assets minus their $55,000 fair value.) Such goodwill must be amortized to expense over a period not to exceed 40 years. Maximum income is reported when the longest allowable amortization period (40 years) is used. $5,000/40 years = $125 amortization per year.

19. (d,73) A fundamental difference between the purchase and pooling of interests methods is that the cost principle is used to value assets acquired under the purchase method while the cost principle is **not** used to value assets acquired via a pooling of interests.

20. (d,51) Cash will have a higher balance sheet amount since, under a pooling, no cash was used to acquire ownership of the other firm. The common stock account will be higher because additional shares were issued in the pooling. The retained earnings account will be higher because consolidated retained earnings is the sum of both companies individual retained earnings under a pooling. (Under a purchase, the retained earnings of the acquired firm are "eliminated.")

21. (e,58) Sales revenue and accounts receivable do not differ because of purchase versus poolng. The cash balance under the purchase method would be **lower** because of the cash expended in the purchase. The common stock balance would also be **lower** under purchase because additional stock would **not** have been issued as in a pooling.

22. (a,63) After a pooling of interests, the consolidated balance sheet reports retained earnings as the sum of the parent and subsidiary individual retained earnings. After a purchase, subsidiary retained earnings are "eliminated" in the consolidation process.

23. (b,46) Consolidated retained earnings include the retained earnings of **both** firms when a pooling has taken place. It includes only those of the acquiring firm under a purchase. Goodwill is **not** recognized under a pooling and Ladmo assets will be included at **book** values. The common stock account will be **larger** than if the purchase method had been used.

24. (c,80) By definition of the concept and measurement of goodwill, it can **only** arise when a purchase has been made. It is **never** recognized in a pooling.

25. (b,74) Of the options given, only operational assets necessarily differ between pooling and purchase. They are usually larger under a purchase because they are brought onto the consolidated balance sheet at market values whereas under a pooling they are brought on at book values (which are usually lower).

26. (d,50) All four statements are true concerning the pooling method.

27. (b,85) These terms (and underlying concepts) are often cited as problems that have been caused at one time or another by use of the pooling method.

28. (a,67) Only statement #1 is true. Concerning statement #2, it is the **purchase method** that is conceptually preferable. Statement #3 is false because just the opposite is true.

29. (b,61) Of the options given, only accounts receivable is unaffected by whether a pooling or purchase was involved. Plant and equipment would probably be higher under a purchase since the subsidiary's assets would be brought onto the consolidated balance sheet at market values rather than book values. This also causes depreciation expense to be higher under the purchase method. Since goodwill is not recorded under a pooling, that account (and the related amortization expense) are likely to be higher under a purchase.

30. (e,48) Accounts receivable and contributed capital from treasury stock transactions are **not** affected by whether a pooling or purchase occurred. Plant, property, and equipment are likely to have **lower** values today because of the pooling. Retained earnings is likely to have a higher balance under pooling since no portion of either parent or subsidiary retained earnings is "eliminated" during the consolidation process. (Remember that under a purchase, subsidiary retained earnings are "eliminated" during preparation of the consolidated balance sheet.)

CHAPTER FIFTEEN: THE STATEMENT OF CHANGES IN FINANCIAL POSITION

PART A: Statement of Changes in Financial Position, Cash Basis

1. The primary purpose of the Statement of Changes in Financial Position is to:
    a. explain the results of operations for the period.
    b. explain the sources and uses of cash or working capital for the period.
    c. show the financial position of the firm at the end of the period.
    d. explain changes in the retained earnings account during the period.

2. The statement of changes in financial position is designed to provide an answer to which one of the following questions?
    a. Was the firm's gross margin acceptable?
    b. What amount of short-term obligations of the firm are coming due within the next acounting period?
    c. What is the amount of the company's total indebtedness at the end of the current accounting period?
    d. How has the company been financing its activities during the past accounting period?

3. Which of the following statements is **false**?
    a. The income statement and balance sheet are developed on the accrual basis.
    b. The statement of changes in financial position reports on the liquidity of the entity.
    c. The statement of changes in financial position reports on the financing and investing activities of the entity.
    d. The statement of changes in financial position is a good substitute for either the balance sheet or income statement.

4. The statement of changes in financial position is designed to report:
    a. the liquidity dimension of entity performance but **not** the financing and investing activities of the entity.
    b. additional accrual basis information similar to the balance sheet and income statement.
    c. the liquidity of an entity as of a specific point in time.
    d. the liquidity dimension of an entity and the relation between sources and uses of funds during the period.

5. When analyzing the statement of changes in financial position, which of the following would most likely result in a source of cash?
    a. an increase in the land account
    b. an increase in the long-term notes payable account
    c. a direct exchange
    d. the reporting of a net loss from operations

6. Greenberg Company acquired a machine by giving up 100 shares of the common stock of another corporation that Greenberg owned as a long-term investment. This transaction should be reported on the statement of changes in financial position as:
    a. part of cash provided by operations.
    b. a use of cash.
    c. a source of cash (from "other sources").
    d. both a source of cash (from "other sources") and a use of cash.

7. Robert's Company is preparing the statement of changes in financial position on a cash basis. An issuance of common stock in exchange for the acquisition of land would:
    a. be reported as a use of cash.
    b. not be reported since neither cash nor working capital is affected.
    c. be reported as a source of cash.
    d. be considered as both a financing and an investing activity.

8. A firm's predominant recurring source of cash over the long-run should be:
   a. operations.
   b. sale of noncurrent assets.
   c. sale of capital stock.
   d. borrowing.

9. You are preparing the Statement of Changes in Financial Position for Garcia Company and while reviewing the general journal you notice the following entry:

Bonds Payable, L-T	1,000	
Common Stock		100
Contrib. Cap. in Excess of Par		900

   How will this transaction affect the Statement of Changes in Financial Position?
   a. Will be no effect because no working capital or cash accounts were involved.
   b. Will be reported as a source of funds because owners' equity increases and assets remain unchanged.
   c. Will be reported as both a source of funds and as a use of funds.
   d. Will be reported as a use of funds because the amount owed to creditors has decreased while owners' equity has increased.

10. As the accountant for the Small Corp. you are attempting to prepare the Statement of Changes in Financial Position at year end. While reviewing the general journal you notice the following journal entry:

Bonds Payable, L.-Term	30,500	
Land		30,500

   How should this transaction be reported on the Statement of Changes in Financial Position?
   a. It should not be reported because no working capital accounts were affected.
   b. As a source of funds because an asset was used to decrease liabilities.
   c. Both as a source and as a use of funds even though no cash or working capital accounts were involved.
   d. As a use of funds since liabilities decreased and the amount of assets also decreased.

11. McHale Company bought a $10,000 machine and paid for it with 200 shares of its own $10 par value common stock (market value $50 per share). The Statement of Changes in Financial Postion (cash basis) should show which of the following?
   a. a $10,000 source and a $10,000 use
   b. a $2,000 source and a $2,000 use
   c. a $10,000 use
   d. nothing, because no cash was involved

12. Which of the following statements concerning direct exchanges is **not** true?
   a. Some transactions that cause neither an inflow or outflow of funds are called direct exchanges because they involve the exchange of nonfund assets, liabilities or equity.
   b. A direct exchange should be reported when a firm acquires a machine and pays in full by issuing shares of its own common stock.
   c. A direct exchange should be reported on the statement of changes in financial position "as if" two separate transactions occurred concurrently.
   d. The statement of changes in financial position must report either a source of funds or a use of funds, but not both for a direct exchange.

13. The balance in the accumulated depreciation account of a company increased by $8,000 during the year. During this period the company sold machinery originally costing $20,000 for $12,000 (its book value). In determining cash provided by operations:
   a. $16,000 depreciation expense would be added to net income.
   b. $20,000 depreciation expense would be subtracted from net income.
   c. $8,000 depreciation expense would be added to net income.
   d. $8,000 depreciation expense would be subtracted from net income.
   e. $20,000 depreciation expense would be added to net income.

14. Calculate "net cash flow from normal operations."

Net income	$10,000
Depreciation expense	1,000
Patent amortization	500
Payoff of long-term note payable	5,000
Decrease in accounts receivable	3,000

   a. $ 8,500
   b. $ 9,500
   c. $11,500
   d. $14,500
   e. $19,500

15. Deep Purple Crawling Company had total sales in 19B of $750,000 of which 60% were on credit. The balance in accounts receivable was $100,000 at the end of 19A and $125,000 at the end of 19B. During 19B, what was the total cash inflow from sales?
   a. $300,000
   b. $450,000
   c. $725,000
   d. $775,000

16. The Tylenol Co. reported a net loss for 19B of $600 using the accrual basis of accounting. The following information is available.

Depreciation expense	$400
Accounts payable increase	300
Inventory increase	100

   The net cash inflow (or outflow) from normal operations during 19B was:
   a. $ -0-.
   b. $ 600 outflow.
   c. $1,400 outflow.
   d. $ 200 inflow.

17. Which of the following transactions will **not** be shown on a Statement of Changes in Financial Position prepared on the cash basis?
   a. cash dividends paid
   b. sale of an operational asset
   c. the amount of depreciation expense
   d. a stock dividend

18. Cactus Company reported revenue of $200 and expenses of $212 for the year ended December 31, 19C. During 19C, accounts receivable decreased by $1, trade payables increased by $5, accrued wages decreased by $3, and $8 in depreciation expense was recorded. Assuming there is no other relevant information, what is the net cash flow from operations?
   a. $1
   b. ($1)
   c. $5
   d. $7
   e. ($2)

19. The Janice Stemmler Carr Company is preparing the statement of changes in financial position on a cash basis. Which of the following is a **true** statement?
   a. A decrease in net accounts receivable should be reported as a use of funds.
   b. An increase in accounts payable should be reported as a source of funds.
   c. Depreciation expense for the year is deducted from net income in computing cash provided by operations.
   d. Over the long-run, the largest source of cash should be operations.

20. The accountant at ABC Company is preparing the statement of changes in financial position and has gathered the following information:

Gain on sale of equipment	$ 5,000
Net Income	52,000
Common stock issued for cash	100,000
Depreciation expense	20,000
Sale of equipment	40,000
Increase in inventory	2,000

   Based only on the above information, the amount of cash generated from normal operations during the year was:
   a. $ 32,000.
   b. $ 65,000.
   c. $ 72,000.
   d. $165,000.

21. Harriet Company reported net income of $300,000 for the year on the accrual basis. Depreciation expense amounted to $31,500. The beginning and ending balances of current asset and current liability accounts were as follows:

	Beginning	Ending
Accounts Receivable	$50,000	$56,500
Inventories	75,200	76,600
Accounts Payable	45,800	40,400

In a Statement of Changes in Financial Position (cash basis) the cash provided by operations would be:
a. $318,200.
b. $329,000.
c. $334,000.
d. $344,800.

(handwritten: 300000, 31500, -6500, -1400, -5400)

22. Katie Corp. is preparing the statement of changes in financial position (cash basis). When doing so, depreciation expense for the year was added to net income. This was done because depreciation expense:
a. is a source of cash.
b. reduces reported net income but is **not** a use of cash.
c. reduces net income for a period and represents an inflow of cash.
d. represents an inflow of cash to a reserve account that is maintained for the replacement of assets.

23. Barry's Brake Shop just completed its first year in business and uses the accrual basis of accounting. Net income for the year (accrual basis) was $30,000. The year-end balance sheet shows the following relevant account balances:

Prepaid Advertising	$1,200
Prepaid Insurance	1,300
Rent Collected in Advance	1,800

If Barry's Brake Shop had used the cash basis of accounting, net income of the year just ended would have been:
a. $ 700 lower.
b. $1,800 higher.
c. $2,500 lower.
d. $4,300 higher.

USE THE FOLLOWING INFORMATION FOR THE NEXT THREE QUESTIONS.

Bojangles Company reports the following comparative information:

Balance Sheets	12-31-19B	12-31-19A
Cash	$ 15,000	$ 10,000
Inventory	40,000	36,000
Equipment	50,000	45,000
Accumulated Dep.	(10,000)	(6,000)
	$ 95,000	$ 85,000
Accounts Payable	$ 21,000	$ 23,000
Bonds Pay. (L-T)	24,000	20,000
Common Stock	30,000	30,000
Retained Earnings	20,000	12,000
	$ 95,000	$ 85,000

Additional Information:
Net income for 19B was $9,000.
No equipment was disposed of during the year.

24. For Bojangles Company, what amount of cash was generated by normal operations during 19B?
a. $ 5,000
b. $ 7,000
c. $11,000
d. $15,000
e. $19,000

(handwritten: 9,000, 4,000, -5,000, -4,000, 5,000)

25. **Assuming** that cash provided by normal operations was $10,000, the total sources of cash during 19B amounted to:
a. $ 6,000.
b. $10,000.
c. $11,000.
d. $14,000.
e. $15,000.

(handwritten: 10, 4, BP-LT)

26. What was the total **uses** of cash during 19B?
a. $ 5,000
b. $ 6,000
c. $ 9,000
d. $10,000

(handwritten: I B-D, 9+12 -1 = 20, 21)

27. XYZ Corp. had revenue of $200 and expenses of $175 during 19A. Also, accounts receivable decreased by $20, accounts payable increased by $25, long-term bonds payable increased by $30, and depreciation expense was $15. Assume no other changes in account balances are relevant. What was the net cash flow from operations?
   a. $ 5 net cash outflow
   b. $25 net cash inflow
   c. $35 net cash outflow
   d. $85 net cash inflow

28. Manchester Fish Company reported that during a recent accounting period its accounts receivable increased by $500, merchandise inventory decreased by $300, accounts payable increased by $200 and income tax payable decreased by $100. If the company reported net income of $10,000, the cash inflow from operations during the period was:
   a. $ 9,800.
   b. $ 9,900.
   c. $10,000.
   d. $10,100.

29. The Snowpac Co. had revenues of $150 and expenses of $100. The revenues consisted of cash sales of $75, credit sales of $50 (already collected), and credit sales of $25 (not yet collected). The expenses were all paid for in cash except for $10 of merchandise which was taken from inventory that was purchased last year, and depreciation expense of $25. The Snowpac Corp. also purchased a new truck for $15 during the year. It paid 1/3 cash and will pay the remainder next year. Compute the net change in cash during the year.
   a. $25
   b. $35
   c. $50
   d. $55
   e. $60

30. Net sales for Piggly Wiggly Stores were $2,000 during 19C. Accounts receivable and inventory **each** increased by $100 during 19C and accounts payable increased by $400 during that same period. During 19C, what was the total cash **collected from sales**?
   a. $2,200
   b. $1,900
   c. $1,800
   d. $1,400

PART B: Statement of Changes in Financial Position, Working Capital Basis

31. Calculate the change in working capital during 19B.

Balances at Dec. 31:	19A	19B
Cash	$1,000	$1,100
Accounts Rec.	500	300
Operational Assets	2,000	2,500
Land Investment	5,000	5,000
	$8,500	$8,900
Accounts Payable	$1,000	$1,200
L-T Note Payable	2,000	2,000
Stockholder's Eq.	5,500	5,700
	$8,500	$8,900

   a. $400 increase
   b. $400 decrease
   c. $100 decrease
   d. $300 decrease
   e. $300 increase

32. An operational asset having a book value of $2,000 was sold on January 1, 19C. The following amounts were received for it.

   ---$500 cash
   ---$1,000 of IBM stock (market value) to be held as a long-term investment
   ---$1,000 bond (market value) to be held as a short-term investment

   What is the effect on working capital from this sale?
   a. $ 500 increase
   b. $1,500 increase
   c. $2,500 increase
   d. $2,000 decrease

33. If there has been an increase in working capital for the period, which of the following must be **true**?
    a. total current assets must have increased
    b. total current liabilities must have decreased
    c. there must have been net income, not a loss
    d. cash must have decreased
    e. none of the above **have** to be true

34. In general, which of the following transactions would be a use of working capital?
    a. transactions that increase noncurrent assets
    b. transactions that increase noncurrent liabilities
    c. transactions that increase owner's equity
    d. transactions that increase current assets

35. Y Company purchased a truck for $20,000. Payment was as follows: $5,000 cash, $2,000 short-term note payable, and a $13,000 long-term note payable. What is the net change in working capital as a result of this transaction?
    a. $ 8,000 increase
    b. $20,000 decrease
    c. $ 7,000 decrease
    d. $ 5,000 decrease

36. How many of the following would be listed under "Other Sources" on a statement of changes in financial position (working capital basis)?

    --sale of a machine
    --payment of dividends
    --sale of common stock
    --payoff of long-term debt
    --sale of inventory
    --purchase of long-term investment

    a. one
    b. two
    c. three
    d. four
    e. five

37. Compute the net working capital provided by normal operations.

Depreciation expense	$1,000
Cash dividend declared	500
Net income	3,000
Common stock issued	1,000

    a. $ 500
    b. $1,000
    c. $2,000
    d. $4,000
    e. $5,000

38. Given the following information, calculate the working capital provided by normal operations.

Net income	$10
Depreciation expense	2
Sale of a machine	5
Exchange of common stock for land	10
Purchase of a building	5

    a. $10
    b. $12
    c. $17
    d. $22

39. The Cal Poly Company is preparing the statement of changes in financial position on a working capital basis. Which one of the following events would most likely be shown thereon?
    a. the payoff of a short-term bank loan
    b. the collection of an account receivable
    c. the declaration and distribution of a stock dividend
    d. a net loss from operations

40. Which of the following is **not** a source of working capital?
    a. operations
    b. borrowings on a long-term note
    c. disposal of short-term investments at cost
    d. sale of capital stock for cash

41. North Dakota Company reports the following.

Sales	$150,000
Income tax expense	40,000
Depreciation expense	80,000
All other Expenses	25,000

Further, $20,000 of common stock was issued for cash during the year. What was the amount of working capital provided by operations?
a. $ 5,000
b. $ 25,000
c. ($75,000)
d. $ 85,000
e. $105,000

42. Baez Co. reported net income of $25,000 during the current year. During that period, accounts payable increased by $25,000 and accounts receivable decreased by $20,000. If depreciation expense was $15,000, what was the amount of working capital provided by normal operations?
a. ($5,000)
b. $ 40,000
c. $ 55,000
d. $105,000

43. Kay Jones sold a fixed asset for $6,000 that had a book value of $6,000. Terms of sale were 1/5 cash, with the balance due in six months via a note receivable. Which one of the following would be reported on the statement of changes in financial position (working capital basis) as a result of this event?
a. a source of $6,000
b. a use of $6,000
c. a source of $4,800
d. a use of $1,200
e. a source of working capital of $1,200

44. Dividends that had been declared during the prior accounting period were paid during the current period. This payment would:
a. increase working capital from operations.
b. decrease working capital from operations.
c. increase uses of working capital.
d. have no effect on working capital.

USE THE FOLLOWING INFORMATION FOR THE NEXT TWO QUESTIONS.

A company's Statement of Changes in Financial Position (working capital basis) included the following items.

Funds provided by normal operations	$10,000
Working capital, end of year	8,000
Depreciation expense for the year	12,000
Increase in working capital for year	2,000

45. The company's net income (or loss), assuming only the information above, would be:
a. $22,000.
b. $10,000.
c. $ 2,000.
d. ($ 2,000).

46. If the company's total current assets were $10,000 at the beginning of the year, the total current liabilities at the beginning of the year were:
a. $2,000.
b. $4,000.
c. $6,000.
d. $8,000.

47. Which of the following events increases working capital?
a. declaration of a cash dividend
b. recording of depreciation expense
c. sale of temporary investments at cost
d. sale of fixed assets at a loss

48. The Akamai Company sold for $60,000 equipment that had a book value pf $25,000. If Akamai reported net income of $100,000 and depreciation expense of $10,000, total working capital provided by normal operations would be $_____ . Listed under "other sources" would be Sale of Equipment in the amount of $_____.
a. $110,000; $60,000
b. $145,000; $35,000
c. $ 75,000; $60,000
d. $110,000; $35,000

49. Sylvia Company exchanged one of its machines for 100 shares of IBM common stock. The stock was to be carried as a short-term investment by Sylvia Company. What effect would this transaction have on Sylvia's statement of changes in financial position?
   a. Defining funds as cash, no effect would be recognized because cash was not involved.
   b. Defining funds as cash, both a source and use of cash would be shown because of the all-resources concept.
   c. Defining funds as working capital, no effect would be recognized because working capital was not affected.
   d. The transaction would not be recognized using either a cash or working capital definition of funds.

CHAPTER FIFTEEN: ANNOTATED SOLUTIONS

1. b	8. a	15. c	22. b	29. d	36. b	43. a
2. d	9. c	16. a	23. a	30. b	37. d	44. d
3. d	10. c	17. d	24. b	31. d	38. b	45. d
4. d	11. a	18. b	25. d	32. b	39. d	46. b
5. b	12. d	19. d	26. b	33. e	40. c	47. d
6. d	13. a	20. b	27. d	34. a	41. d	48. c
7. d	14. d	21. a	28. b	35. c	42. b	49. b

> *The correct answer and the percentage of students answering the question correctly (when it was used on an introductory accounting examination) are shown in parentheses at the beginning of each annotated solution.*

1. (b,84) Response a describes an income statement while response c describes the balance sheet. Response d describes the retained earnings statement. Response b is a straightforward description of the statement of changes in financial position.

2. (d,74) Gross profit information comes from the income statement, while information about debts would come from the balance sheet. The statement of changes in financial position is designed to show where funds came from (financing activities) and where they went (investing activities).

3. (d,91) The statement of changes in financial position complements both the income statement and the balance sheet but is not a substitute for either.

4. (d,87) Liquidity relates to the inflow and outflow of funds. The statement of changes in financial position is designed to report the sources of funds (financing activities) and the uses of funds (investing activities) during the period. It reports, therefore, liquidity information that is not included in either the balance sheet or income statement.

5. (b,70) If long-term notes payable have increased, this probably means that more cash was borrowed. This would be a source. If land increased, this would probably mean that cash had gone out of the firm to buy it. A net loss usually consumes cash. A direct exchange does not involve cash.

6. (d,63) This is a direct exchange that affects neither cash nor working capital. Under the all-resources concept, however, this item must be shown on the statement of changes in financial position as **both** a source and a use.

7. (d,53) This is an example of a direct exchange that, under the all financial resources concept, must be reported on the statement of changes in financial position as **both** a financing activity (a source) and an investing activity (a use).

8. (a,83) A company can only sell stock, bonds or fixed assets for so long. Eventually, it has to start generating cash from operations in order to pay dividends, replace assets, and finance growth.

9. (c,50) This transaction is an example of a direct exchange. It is both a source of funds (issuance of stock) and a use of funds (paying off long-term debt). It is to be reported as both a source and use of funds.

10. (c,52) This transaction is a direct exchange. It does not affect working capital or cash but is to be reported on the statement of changes in financial position because it is both a financing activity (giving up the land to pay off the bonds) and an investing activity (paying off the bonds with the land).

11. (a,59) This is an example of a direct exchange. No cash was involved, but the issuance of 200 shares of stock is reported a source of funds (a financing activity) while the acquisition of the machine is reported as a use of funds (an investing activity).

12. (d,71) A direct exchange is shown on the statement of changes in financial position as **both** a source of funds and a use of funds. It has no effect on either cash or working capital but represents a significant financing activity and significant investing activity and, therefore, must be disclosed.

13. (a,82) Two events affected the accumulated depreciation account this period. (1) it decreased by $8,000 when the machinery was sold, and (2) it must have increased by $16,000 when depreciation expense was recognized in the current year. This would prove the **net** change of + $8,000. The $16,000 depreciation expense, then, must be added back to net income.

14. (d,25) In this problem, net cash flow from operations can be computed as follows: working capital provided by operations + the decrease in the noncash current asset. ($10,000 + $1,000 + $500) + $3,000 = $14,500.

15. (c,47) Cash sales were $300,000 (40% of $750,000). Since accounts receivable increased during the year by $25,000, all but $25,000 of the $450,000 in credit sales were also collected in cash. Total cash collections from sales, then, were $300,000 + $425,000 = $725,000.

16. (a,33) Net cash flow = net loss + depreciation + accounts payable increase - inventory decrease = ($600) + $400 + $300 - $100 = $0.

17. (d,31) Since stock dividends do not affect cash or (working capital) and because they are neither a financing activity nor an investing activity they are not reported on a statement of changes in financial position.

18. (b,36) Net cash flow = net income + accounts receivable decrease + trade payable increase - accrued wages decrease + depreciation. Therefore, net cash flow = ($12) + $1 + $5 - $3 + $8 = ($1).

19. (d,70) In the long-run a company cannot survive unless its operations are generating sufficient funds to finance replacement of assets, payment of dividends, and growth. Responses a and b are not sources and uses. Instead, they are merely part of the computation of "cash from normal operations." Response c is incorrect because depreciation expense should be **added** to net income.

20. (b,53) Only net income, depreciation expense, the increase in inventory and the gain on sale of equipment are relevant to this question. Net income ($52,000) + depreciation expense ($20,000) - increase in inventory ($2,000) - gain on sale ($5,000) = $65,000.

21. (a,36) Begin with net income ($300,000), add back depreciation expense ($31,500), subtract the increases in accounts receivable and inventories ($6,500 and $1,400) and subtract the decrease in accounts payable ($5,400) for the correct answer of $318,200.

22. (b,81) Depreciation expense is added back to net income because we are trying to convert "net income provided by operations" into "funds provided by operations." Depreciation is properly deducted from revenue on the income statement because it is an expense. It does **not**, however, decrease funds (either cash or working capital) and needs to be added back.

23. (a,46) Under the cash basis, the cash paid out for prepaid advertising and prepaid insurance would have been expense ($1,200 + $1,300 = $2,500). Also, the rent money received in advance ($1,800) would have been considered revenue. Net income, then, would have been $700 lower ($1,800 revenue minus $2,500 expense).

24. (b,49) Cash provided by operations is computed in this problem as follows: net income ($9,000) + depreciation expense ($4,000; as determined by inspecting the change in accumulated depreciation) - increase in inventory ($4,000) - decrease in accounts payable ($2,000). $9,000 + $4,000 - $4,000 - $2,000 = $7,000.

25. (d,45) Total sources would be the sum of operations (assumed to be $10,000) + the increase in bonds payable ($4,000) for a total of $14,000.

26. (b,33) Total uses would be the result of buying new equipment ($5,000; as determined by inspecting the change in the equipment account) and paying dividends ($1,000; net income was $9,000 but retained earnings only increased by $8,000 so dividends of $1,000 must have been paid). $5,000 + $1,000 = $6,000.

27. (d,46) Begin with net income ($25) and add depreciation expense ($15). Also, add the decrease in accounts receivable ($20) and the increase in accounts payable ($25). Ignore the change in long-term bonds. Cash flow from operations, then, is $25 + $15 + $20 + $25 = $85.

28. (b,56) Start with net income ($10,000) and deduct the increase in accounts receivable ($500); add the decrease in inventory ($300) and the increase in accounts payable ($200); deduct the decrease in tax payable ($100). To summarize, $10,000 - $500 + $300 + $200 - $100 = $9,900. (Since this problem didn't mention depreciation expense, it must be that the firm doesn't have any depreciable assets.)

29. (d,38) The net change in the cash account is equal to (cash sales + credit sales already collected - expenses paid with cash - purchase of assets). Therefore, (75 + 50) - (100 - 25 depreciation - 10 already paid for) - (1/3 x 15) = $55.

30. (b,46) Read this question **very** carefully. It asks for the cash collected from sales, **not** cash inflow from operations. Sales were $2,000, but accounts receivable increased by $100 during the year. Effectively, this means that $100 of this years' sales was not collected in cash. Therefore, cash collected from sales was $1,900 ($2,000 - $100). What happened to inventory and accounts payable is irrelevant to determining the amount of cash collected from sales.

31. (d,39) Working capital (WC) = current assets - current liabilities. WC = cash + accounts receivable - accounts payable. On December 31, 19A, WC = $500 ($1,000 + $500 - $1,000). On December 31, 19B, WC = $200 ($1,100 + $300 - $1,200). During 19B, then, WC decreased by $300.

32. (b,56) A non-current asset has been converted into part current and part non-current assets. The current portion is the cash + the bond that will be carried as a short-term investment ($500 + $1,000 = $1,500). The IBM stock will be a non-current asset. Current liabilities are unaffected.

33. (e,60) A net increase in working capital can occur through a combination of transactions. Therefore, none of the above **have** to be true. All **could** be true, but none **have** to be.

34. (a,38) A use of working capital causes working capital to decrease. In general, an acquisition of a non-current asset causes working capital to decrease since usually either (1) cash is decreased, or (2) a current liability is incurred.

35. (c,81) Analyze the journal entry that had to have been made to record this transaction. The debit to trucks (a noncurrent account) of $20,000 has no effect on working capital (WC). The $5,000 credit to cash decreases WC as does the credit of $2,000 to short-term note payable. The $13,000 credit to long-term note has no effect on WC. Total change in WC, then, is a $7,000 decrease ($5,000 + $2,000).

36. (b,73) Both the sale of a machine and the sale of stock would be listed under "other sources" on the statement of changes in financial position. The sale of inventory is included in working capital provided by operations. The other items listed are uses of funds.

37. (d,49) Net income must be adjusted for expenses that did not consume working capital. Therefore, working capital from operations = $3,000 (net income) + $1,000 (depreciation expense) = $4,000.

38. (b,48) Working capital provided by operations = net income + expenses that do not consume working capital. Therefore, working capital provided by operations in this problem = $10 + $2 (depreciation) = $12.

39. (d,57) Responses a and b would not appear on a working capital basis statement. Response c never appears on the statement of changes in financial position. If a company had a net loss instead of net income, the net loss would appear on the statement instead of net income.

40. (c,35) As long as short-term investments are sold either at cost (or below cost), the event is **not** a source of working capital.

41. (d,55) Net income was $5,000 (sales of $150,000 - depreciation of $80,000 - income taxes of $40,000 - all other expenses of $25,000). To determine working capital provided by operations, depreciation expense ($80,000) must be added back. $5,000 + $80,000 = $85,000.

42. (b,30) Working capital provided by operations is computed by simply adding net income ($25,000) and depreciation expense ($15,000) for a total of $40,000.

43. (a,63) Kay Jones converted a $6,000 long-term item into $6,000 worth of short-term items ($1,200 cash + $4,800 short-term note). This results in working capital being increased by $6,000.

44. (d,63) The **payment** of dividends has no effect on working capital. It is the **declaration** of the dividend that is the use. Upon payment of a previously declared dividend, a current liability is reduced (Dividends Payable) and a current asset is reduced (Cash). The change in working capital is zero.

45. (d,39) If net income (amount unknown) + depreciation expense ($12,000) = funds provided by operations ($10,000), then net income (or loss) must have have been ($2,000).

46. (b,40) Beginning working capital must have been $6,000 because ending working capital was $8,000 and it had increased by $2,000 during the year. If beginning current assets were $10,000, it means that beginning current liabilities had to be $4,000.

47. (d,63) Response a **decreases** working capital while responses b and c have no effect. In response d, we start with no current assets (just a long-term fixed asset) and convert it into cash (a current asset) which increases working capital. Whether there is a loss or not is irrelevant. While the loss reduces the **amount** of current assets (cash) we received for the fixed asset, we still received at least some cash (current assets).

48. (c,24) The gain on sale would be $35,000 ($60,000 - $25,000). To determine working capital from operations, add net income ($100,000) + depreciation expense ($10,000) and deduct the gain on sale ($35,000) for a total of $75,000. The total sale amount ($60,000) is shown under "other sources."

49. (b,53) This is an example of a direct exchange which must be reported on the statement of changes in financial position even though it affects neither cash nor working capital.

CHAPTER SIXTEEN: USING AND INTERPRETING FINANCIAL STATEMENTS

1. Which of the following is a true statement concerning "notes to the financial statements?
   a. Only unimportant information is found there.
   b. They are more important than the financial statements.
   c. Nothing is reported thereon that is not also reported on the face of the financial statements.
   d. They are an integral part of the financial statements.

2. Given the following information, calculate the return on owners' investment for Big Apple Company.

Current assets	$80
Non-current assets	70
Expenses	60
Long-term liabilities	40
Current Liabilities	20
Revenues	75

   a. 10.0%
   b. 16.7%
   c. 25.0%
   d. 50.0%
   e. 83.0%

3. The following information is available at year-end. Determine the return on owners' investment.

Total assets	$10
Total liabilities	6
Total revenues	5
Total expenses	3
Total dividends paid	1

   a. 25%
   b. 33%
   c. 50%
   d. 100%

4. If average liabilities are $40,000, total expenses are $50,000, average owners' equity is $60,000, and sales revenue is $65,000, what is the return on owners' investment?
   a. 108.3%
   b. 37.5%
   c. 25.0%
   d. 15.0%

5. Assume liabilities total $25,000; average owners' equity totals $80,000; expenses total $43,000 and the return on owners' investment is 12%. Revenues must total:
   a. $ 9,600.
   b. $33,400.
   c. $52,600.
   d. $77,600.

6. If a company has positive financial leverage, the:
   a. return on owners' equity will exceed the return on total investment.
   b. firm has current liabilities but no long-term liabilities.
   c. debt to equity ratio exceeds 1.00.
   d. return on owners' investment will equal the profit margin.

7. Paul Watkins Company reported net income of $10,000 and paid a cash dividend of $2 per share on each of 2,000 shares outstanding. What is Watkins' earnings per share?
   a. $5
   b. $4
   c. $3
   d. $2

8. Which financial ratio below yields information about liquidity?
   a. return on total investment
   b. price/earnings ratio
   c. debt/equity ratio
   d. working capital ratio

9. ABC Corporation has just completed the 19C income statement. There were no extraordinary items and net income was $50. There are 10 stockholders and 100 shares outstanding. Assuming that dividends totaled $20, what was earnings per share for 19C?
   a. $5.00
   b. $3.00
   c. $ .50
   d. $ .30

10. Assume that Rich White Company had the following account balances.

Land	$3,000 dr.
Current Liabilities	2,000 cr.
Accounts Receivable	1,000 dr.
Sales Revenue	5,000 cr.
Inventory	1,500 dr.
Cash	500 dr.

    What is Rich White's working capital (current) ratio?
    a. 1.5 to 1
    b. 2.0 to 1
    c. 2.5 to 1
    d. 3.0 to 1

11. Calculate the **amount** of working capital from the following information.

Working capital ratio	1.5 to 1
Current assets	$90
Long-term notes payable	$15

    a. $ 30
    b. $ 60
    c. $ 90
    d. $120

12. A company has a working capital ratio of 3 to 1. Which transaction will below will **decrease** this ratio?
    a. sale of merchandise on account
    b. issuance of long-term bonds at a discount
    c. declaration of a cash dividend
    d. sale of equipment for less than book value

13. If current assets total $2,750 and working capital totals $2,200, the working capital ratio is:
    a. 10.00 to 1.
    b. 5.00 to 1.
    c. .80 to 1.
    d. .20 to 1.

14. Alex Company has the following account balances:

Cash	$ 2,000 dr.
Accounts Receivable	4,000 dr.
Land	12,000 dr.
Sales Revenue	20,000 cr.
Inventory	6,000 dr.
Accounts Payable	8,000 cr.

    Alex Company's acid-test ratio (quick ratio) is:
    a. .50 to 1.
    b. .75 to 1.
    c. 1.00 to 1.
    d. 1.50 to 1.
    e. 2.00 to 1.

15. At the balance sheet date, Arrington Company reported the following balances. (All accounts have **normal** balances.)

Inventory	$3,000
Cash	1,000
Accounts Receivable	2,000
Current Liabilities	4,000
Land	6,000
Sales Revenue	10,000

    What is Arrington Company's acid-test ratio (quick ratio)?
    a. .50 to 1
    b. .75 to 1
    c. 1.00 to 1
    d. 1.50 to 1
    e. 2.00 to 1

16. Kiger Company has a current ratio of 2 to 1. Which of the following transactions will **increase** that ratio?
    a. declaring a cash dividend
    b. paying off long-term bonds payable
    c. paying off short-term debt
    d. obtaining a short-term bank loan

17. Jayhawk Corp. had a working capital ratio of 2 to 1 at December 31, 19C. Which of the following transactions would cause the ratio to **decrease**?
    a. sale of operational assets for cash
    b. exchange of machinery for land
    c. issuance of bonds payable
    d. borrow cash via a short-term note

18. At the beginning of 19E, the Severn Grabski Company had a working capital ratio of 2 to 1. Which of the following events would cause the ratio to **increase**?
    a. purchase of machinery for cash
    b. borrowing money from a bank on an eight month loan
    c. payment of a cash dividend previously declared
    d. exchange of land for a truck

19. If current assets exceed current liabilities, payments to short-term creditors will:
    a. decrease the working capital ratio.
    b. increase the working capital ratio.
    c. decrease working capital.
    d. increase working capital.

20. Code Company financial records reveal the following.

Net Sales	$180
Cost of Goods Sold	120
Ending Inventory	25
Beginning Inventory	35

    Assuming a 360-day year, what was the average days' supply in inventory?
    a. 60
    b. 70
    c. 75
    d. 90
    e. 105

21. If net credit sales were $100,000, cost of goods sold was $80,000, and average net trade accounts receivable were $20,000, the "average days to collect" would be:
    a. 5 days.
    b. 20 days.
    c. 73 days.
    d. 91 days.
    e. 292 days.

22. Sundance Company's net accounts receivable were $250 at 12-31-19C and $300 at 12-31-19D. Net **cash** sales for 19D were $100 and the accounts receivable turnover for 19D was 5.0. What were Sundance **total** net sales for 19D?
    a. $1,350
    b. $1,375
    c. $1,475
    d. $1,500
    e. $1,600

23. If average inventory was $80,000, sales were $560,000, and cost of goods sold were $480,000, what would be the average day's supply in inventory?
    a. 150
    b. 61
    c. 52
    d. 14
    e. 7

24. Assume that total assets are $80,000 and owners' equity is $60,000. In addition, it is known that current liabilities total $10,000. What is the debt to equity ratio?
    a. .75 to 1
    b. .33 to 1
    c. .17 to 1
    d. .13 to 1
    e. cannot be determined from the information given

25. Coolidge Computerware has the following balance sheet information.

Current Assets	$4,000
Current Liabilities	1,000
Long-Term Assets	8,000
Long-Term Liabilities	2,000
Common Stock	4,000
Retained Earnings	5,000

    There was no interest expense and no dividends were declared. What is the debt/equity ratio at year-end?
    a. 400%
    b. 300%
    c. 75%
    d. 50%
    e. 33%

USE THE FOLLOWING INFORMATION FOR NEXT EIGHT QUESTIONS.

	19B	19A
Income Statements:		
Sales (25% credit)	$400,000	$390,000
Cost of Goods Sold	220,000	218,000
Gross Margin	$180,000	$172,000
Operating Expenses	147,000	148,000
Pretax Income	$ 33,000	$ 24,000
Income Taxes	9,000	7,000
Net Income	$ 24,000	$ 17,000
Balance Sheets:		
Cash	$ 25,400	$ 2,700
Acc./Rec. (net)	24,000	30,000
Inventory	30,000	24,000
Prepaid Expenses	600	500
Fixed Assets (net)	120,000	130,000
Total Assets	$200,000	$187,200
Accounts Payable	$ 19,000	$ 20,000
Income Tax Payable	1,000	1,200
Bonds Payable (5%)	50,000	50,000
Com. Stk. ($10 par)	100,000	100,000
Retained Earnings	30,000	16,000
Total Lia. & Equity	$200,000	$187,200

Other Information:
1. Market price of common stock during December 19B was $24 per share.
2. Total cash dividend paid in 19B was $10,000.
3. No fixed assets were acquired or sold during 19B.
4. Interest expense (net of tax) was $1,800 each year.

26. What was the return on total investment for 19B?
    a. 18.5%
    b. 13.3%
    c. 12.4%
    d. 10.0%
    e. .9%

27. The return on owners' investment (equity) for 19B was:
    a. 14.6%.
    b. 19.5%.
    c. 24.0%.
    d. 33.0%.

28. What is the financial leverage for 19B?
    a. zero
    b. positive
    c. negative
    d. cannot be determined from the information given

29. The net change in working capital during 19B was:
    a. $16,700.
    b. $22,800.
    c. $24,000.
    d. $29,400.
    e. $60,000.

30. The working capital ratio (current ratio) at the end of 19B is:
    a. 1.14 to 1.
    b. 1.63 to 1.
    c. 2.47 to 1.
    d. 2.85 to 1.
    e. 4.00 to 1.

31. What was the accounts receivable turnover for 19B?
    a. 1.66 times
    b. 3.70 times
    c. 4.16 times
    d. 13.33 times
    e. 16.67 times

32. The price/earnings ratio at year-end 19B was:
    a. 5 to 1.
    b. 4%.
    c. 10 to 1.
    d. 54%.
    e. 24 to 1.

33. What was the dividend yield ratio for 19B?
    a. 4.2%
    b. 10.0%
    c. 18.4%
    d. 24.0%
    e. 40.0%

USE THE FOLLOWING INFORMATION FOR THE NEXT THREE QUESTIONS.

At a balance sheet date, Eppley Company had 100,000 shares of common stock outstanding. Also,

Net sales for the year	$1,000,000
Current assets	62,000
Income before taxes (tax rate = 60%)	40,000
Inventory	12,000
Stockholders' equity	150,000
Average total assets	200,000
Total liabilities	50,000

34. What is Eppley's return on total investment?
    a. 8%
    b. 11%
    c. 20%
    d. 50%

35. What is Eppley's profit margin?
    a. 1.6%
    b. 2.4%
    c. 4.0%
    d. 10.7%

36. What is Eppley's book value per common share?
    a. $1.50
    b. $2.00
    c. $2.62
    d. $2.74

37. A prospective investor in Taco Tech, Inc. wishes to know whether the firm is using leverage. Which of the following ratios would yield information about Taco Tech's use of leverage?
    a. current ratio
    b. price earnings ratio
    c. dividend yield ratio
    d. inventory turnover ratio
    e. debt to equity ratio

38. Spendthrift, Inc. has ordered goods on credit from Prudence Co. Before Prudence ships the goods, however, it would like to be sure that Spendthrift is likely to be able to pay the bill when due. Assuming Prudence has access to Spendthrift's financial statements, in which of the following ratios will Prudence be most interested?
    a. current ratio
    b. price earnings ratio
    c. dividend yield ratio
    d. profit margin percentage
    e. debt to equity ratio

CHAPTER SIXTEEN: ANNOTATED SOLUTIONS

1. d	8. d	15. b	22. c	29. c	36. a
2. b	9. c	16. c	23. b	30. e	37. e
3. c	10. a	17. d	24. b	31. b	38. a
4. c	11. a	18. c	25. e	32. c	
5. c	12. c	19. b	26. b	33. a	
6. a	13. b	20. d	27. b	34. a	
7. a	14. b	21. c	28. b	35. a	

> *The correct answer and the percentage of students answering the question correctly (when it was used on an introductory accounting examination) are shown in parentheses at the beginning of each annotated solution that follows.*

1. (d,76) The notes are an integral part of the financial statements. Often a sentence to this effect is printed on each page of the financial statements to alert the reader that a complete understanding of the firm's financial situation cannot be achieved without also carefully reading the accompanying notes.

2. (b,60) Return on owners' investment = net income/average owners' equity. Net income = $15 (revenues of $75 - expenses of $60), while owners' equity = $90 (total assets of $150 minus total liabilities of $60). $15/$90 = 16.7%. (It is preferable to use **average** owners' equity, but it was not available in this problem.)

3. (c,63) Return on owners' investment = net income/average owners' equity. If revenue was $5 and expenses were $3, then net income = $2. If assets = $10 and liabilities = $6, then equity must equal $4. ROI = $2/$4 = 50%.

4. (c,75) Return on owners' investment is computed as "net income divided by average owners' equity." Net income is $15,000 ($65,000 - $50,000) and average owners' equity is $60,000. Hence, ROI = 25%.

5. (c,62) Return on owners' investment is computed as "net income/average owners' equity." Therefore, in this problem:

$$\frac{\text{net income (which is unknown)}}{\text{average owners' equity (\$80,000)}} = 12\%$$

Net income, then, had to be 12% of $80,000 (which is $9,600). Revenue minus expense equals net income. Let X = revenue. X - $43,000 = $9,600. Therefore, X = $52,600 ($52,600 - $9,600 = $43,000).

6. (a,58) Positive leverage means that the rate earned on borrowed assets exceeds the rate paid for the privilege of borrowing. These "excess" earnings accrue to the owners, increasing their return. Their return, then, is greater than the overall rate earned on all assets. Responses b,c, and d are all nonsense.

7. (a,82) Earnings per share is "net income/number of shares outstanding." Net income = $10,000 and the number of shares is 2,000. EPS, then, is $5 ($10,000/2,000 shares = $5). Cash dividends neither increase nor decrease EPS. Dividends are a **distribution** of earnings.

8. (d,74) Liquidity is a measure of how able a firm is to pay its bills as they become due. The working capital ratio measures the relationship between current assets (assets that will be turned into cash to pay bills) and current liabilities (the bills coming due).

9. (c,84) Earnings per share = net income/number of shares outstanding. In this problem, net income = $50 and there were 100 shares outstanding. $50/100 shares = $0.50 earnings per share.

10. (a,73) The working capital (current) ratio is computed as "current assets/ current liabilities." Current assets were cash ($500), accounts receivable ($1,000) and inventory ($1,500) for a total of $3,000. Current liabilities were $2,000. $3,000/$2,000 = a ratio of 1.5 to 1.

11. (a,31) The working capital (current) ratio is obtained by dividing current assets by current liabilities. If the ratio is 1.5 to 1, this means that current assets ($90) are 1 1/2 times the amount of current liabilities. $90/1.5 = $60. Working capital, then, is $30 ($90 - $60 = $30).

12. (c,57) Assume that before declaration of the dividend the current assets = $3,000 and current liabilities = $1,000 (a 3 to 1 working capital ratio). If a $1,000 dividend is declared, current assets will still = $3,000 but current liabilities will now = $2,000. The new working capital ratio will be 1.5 to 1; a decrease.

13. (b,50) Current assets - current liabilities = working capital. In this problem, $2,750 - X = $2,200; X = $550. The working capital (or current) ratio is computed as "current assets/current liabilities." Therefore, current assets ($2,750)/current liabilities ($550) = a ratio of 5 to 1.

14. (b,63) The formula to compute the acid-test (quick) ratio is "quick assets/current liabilities." Quick assets are cash, short-term investments and receivables ($2,000 + $0 + $4,000 = $6,000). The only current liability is accounts payable ($8,000). $6,000/$8,000 = .75 to 1.

15. (b,77) The acid-test ratio is computed as "quick assets/current liabilities." Quick assets are cash ($1,000), short-term investments ($0) and accounts receivable ($2,000) for a total of $3,000. If current liabilities are $4,000, the resulting ratio is .75 to 1 ($3,000/$4,000).

16. (c,39) Assume Kiger had $2,000 current assets and $1,000 current liabilities. Paying off $500 of short-term debt would result in having $1,500 current assets and $500 current liabilities; and a new ratio of 3 to 1. This would be an increase from the original ratio of 2 to 1.

17. (d,53) Assume that, before borrowing, the firm had current assets of $2,000 and current liabilities of $1,000 (a 2 to 1 ratio). **After** borrowing $1,000, the firm would have current assets of $3,000 and current liabilities of $2,000 (a 1.5 to 1 ratio). The ratio decreased.

18. (c,61) Assume current assets = $2,000 and current liabilities $1,000. If a previously declared cash dividend of $500 were paid, both a current asset (cash) and a current liability (dividends payable) would decrease by $500. The resulting current assets would be $1,500 and current liabilities $500 for a ratio of 3 to 1; an increase.

19. (b,48) As a proof, first assume that before making a payment to short-term creditors a firm has $2,000 in current assets and $1,000 in current liabilities. Working capital is $1,000 ($2,000 - $1,000) and the working capital ratio is 2 to 1 ($2,000/$1,000). Now assume that a $500 payment is made to a short-term creditor. Current assets will then = $1,500 and current liabilities will = $500. Working capital is still $1,000 ($1,500 - $500) but the working capital ratio has increased to 3 to 1 ($1,500/$500).

20. (d,31) Cost of goods sold ($120) divided by average inventory (($35 + $25) /2 = $30) yields an inventory turnover of 4 times. 360 days /4 inventory turns = 90 day supply of inventory.

21. (c,61) If net credit sales were $100,000 and average net trade receivables were $20,000, the receivables turnover would be five times per year ($100,000/$20,000). 365 days divided by 5 yields an average collection period of 73 days.

22. (c,27) The formula for accounts receivable turnover is "net credit sales/average accounts receivable." Stated alternatively, "net credit sales (unknown) = average accounts receivable ($250 + $300/2 = $275) x accounts receivable turnover (5 times)." This means that net credit sales were $1,375 ($275 x 5). Adding in cash sales of $100 yields total sales during 19D of $1,475.

23. (b,55) Inventory turnover would be 6 times per year ($480,000/$80,000). Dividing the number of days in a year (365) by 6 yields 61 days sales in inventory.

24. (b,40) Remember that assets = liabilities + equity. If assets = $80,000 and equity = $60,000, liabilities must equal $20,000. The debt to equity ratio is "total liabilities/owners' equity." $20,000/$60,000 = .33 to 1.

25. (e,69) The debt/equity ratio is computed as "total debt (liabilities)/ total equity." Here total debt is current liabilities ($1,000) + long-term liabilities ($2,000) for a total of $3,000. Total equity is common stock ($4,000) + retained earnings ($5,000) for a total of $9,000. $3,000/$9,000 = 33 percent.

26. (b,69) The return on **total** (not owner's) investment is computed as "(income + interest expense net of tax)/average total assets." Net income + interest expense net of tax = $25,800 ($24,000 + $1,800); average total assets = $193,600 [($200,000 + $187,200)/2]. $25,800/$193,600 = 13.3%.

27. (b,58) The return on owner's investment (equity) is "net income/average owner's equity." Net income was $24,000 and average owner's equity was $123,000 ($130,000 + $116,000/2). $24,000/$123,000 = 19.5%.

28. (b,63) Leverage can be measured as the amount by which the return on owners' investment exceeds the return on total investment. The return on owners' investment is 19.5% ($24,000/$123,000). Return on total investment is 13.3% [($24,000 + $1,800)/$193,600)]. The difference is 6.2% in the positive direction.

29. (c,53) Working capital at the end of 19A was $36,000 (current assets of $57,200 - current liabilities of $21,200). Working capital at the end of 19B was $60,000 (current assets of $80,000 - current liabilities of $20,000). The change is $24,000 ($60,000 - $36,000).

30. (e,47) The working capital ratio (current ratio) = current assets/current liabilities. Current assets = cash + accounts receivable + inventory + prepaid expenses ($25,400 + $24,000 + $30,000 + $600) for a total of $80,000. Current liabilities are accounts payable + taxes payable ($19,000 + $1,000) for a total of $20,000. $80,000/$20,000 yields a current ratio of 4 to 1.

31. (b,31) Accounts receivable turnover is computed as "net credit sales/average net receivables." Net credit sales = $100,000 (25% of total sales) and average net receivables = $27,000 (($24,000 + $30,000)/2). $100,000/$27,000 = 3.7 times per year.

32. (c,67) The price earnings ratio is "market price per share/EPS." Year end market price was $24 (given) and the EPS was $2.40 ($24,000 net income/ 10,000 shares outstanding). $24/$2.40 = price earnings ratio of 10. (You can determine the number of shares outstanding by inspecting the common stock account balance. $100,000/$10 par value = 10,000 shares outstanding.)

33. (a,59) The dividend yield ratio is computed as "dividends per share/market price per share." The dividend per share is $1 ($10,000 total dividends/10,000 shares outstanding). The market price per share is $24. $1/$24 = 4.2%.

34. (a,93) The return on total investment is "(net income + interest expense)/average total assets." Net income (after taxes of 60%) is $16,000; interest expense = $0; and average total assets is $200,000 (given). $16,000/$200,000 = 8%.

35. (a,96) The profit margin percentage is "income/net sales." Income was $16,000 (after taxes) and net sales were $1,000,000. The profit margin percentage,then, was $16,000/$1,000,000 = 1.6%.

36. (a,83) The book value per share is "total owners' equity applicable to common shares/number of shares outstanding." Total owners' equity is $150,000; there are 100,000 shares outstanding (given). $150,000/100,000 shares = $1.50.

37. (e,55) Leverage involves the amount of debt in a company's capital structure. The debt to equity ratio, then, establishes the relationship of the firm's debt to equity. A low debt to equity ratio reveals that not much leverage is being used.

38. (a,49) One purpose of the current ratio is to yield information about the ability of a firm to pay its bills as they come due in the short run.

CHAPTER SEVENTEEN: FINANCIAL REPORTING AND CHANGING PRICES

PART A: Reporting the Effects of General Price Level Changes

1. Which one of the following statements is **correct**?
   a. General price level changes cause real value changes.
   b. A general price level index is used to estimate the current replacement cost of a particular item.
   c. A general price level index is intended to measure general inflation or deflation.
   d. A general price level restated financial statement reflects the current costs for the items presented.

2. In a period of decreasing prices (deflation), one would experience a purchasing power gain from which of the following?
   a. notes receivable
   b. bonds payable
   c. accounts payable
   d. common stock

3. Assume the GPL index at the beginning of 19A was 116 and that at the end of 19A it was 121. At what total amount would the following assets be listed on the year-end 19A GPL restated balance sheet?

	Historical Cost When Acquired	GPL Index When Acquired
Cash	$ 10,000	118
Receivables	20,000	118
Equipment	40,000	110
Land & Buildings	100,000	110

   a. $154,000
   b. $170,000
   c. $184,000
   d. $184,762

4. Which of the following statements is **true** with regard to financial statements adjusted for changes in price levels?
   a. GPL restatements involve recording transactions in the ledger to reflect price level changes.
   b. All financial statement items are multiplied by the end-of-period GPL index in preparing GPL adjusted statements.
   c. Monetary items appearing in the financial statements are restated to reflect changes in the GPL.
   d. Monetary items cause a GPL purchasing power gain (or loss) to occur.

5. Land was purchased for $10,000 when the consumer price index (CPI) was 125. At the end of the next two years, the CPI was 140 and 150, respectively. What is the amount of purchasing power gain (or loss) from holding this land?
   a. $ -0-
   b. $(714)
   c. $1,200
   d. $2,000

6. If a monetary asset of $42,000 was acquired when the appropriate price index was 120 and currently the same index is 140, at what amount would the asset be reported in a current price level adjusted balance sheet?
   a. $50,000
   b. $49,000
   c. $42,000
   d. $36,000

7. Which of the following statements is **false**?
   a. Nonmonetary items cause general price level gains or losses.
   b. Nonmonetary items cause fictional changes.
   c. Monetary items are not restated on general price level financial statements.
   d. Monetary items can cause a real gain or loss during a period of inflation or deflation.

8. Exco, Inc. purchased equipment on January 2, 19A for $60,000. The equipment has a five-year life and no residual value. It is being depreciated on a straight-line basis. Assume that the general price level was 125 when the equipment was purchased, and that it was 175 at the end of 19C. What is the general price level restated depreciation expense for 19C?
   a. $21,000
   b. $16,800
   c. $15,000
   d. $12,000
   e. $ 8,570

9. Monetary items are usually:
   a. assets or liabilities.
   b. revenues or expenses.
   c. assets, expenses, or liabilities.
   d. assets, liabilities, or revenues.

10. Which underlying assumption of generally accepted accounting principles is apparently not holding true in order for price-level accounting to be of concern?
    a. continuity
    b. unit-of-measure
    c. separate entity
    d. time period

11. Penn Co. had the following selected balances on its historical cost balance sheet at December 31, 19D. (Assume all assets were acquired when the price index was 100.)

Cash	$40,000
Accounts Receivable	20,000
Land	70,000

    The general price level index was 100 for 19C and 110 for 19D. In a constant dollar balance sheet (adjusted for price changes) at December 31, 19D, these selected account balances should be shown at what amounts?

	Cash	Accounts Receivable	Land
a.	$40,000	$20,000	$77,000
b.	$40,000	$22,000	$77,000
c	$44,000	$20,000	$70,000
d	$44,000	$22,000	$77,000

12. Which of the following is **true** concerning monetary items?
    a. During a period of deflation, one benefits by holding monetary items.
    b. Cash, accounts receivable, and inventory are monetary assets.
    c. During a period of inflation, one benefits by holding nonmonetary assets.
    d. During a period of constant prices, one gains from holding monetary liabilities and loses from holding monetary assets.

13. During a period of deflation, a price-level gain will result from which of the following?
    a. bonds payable
    b. equipment
    c. inventory
    d. cash

14. Arkie Yaulagist purchased some very old bones for $6,000 in 1936. In 1968 she sold them to A. Mew Zeeum for $30,000. Price index history is as follows: 1936 = 52.3; 1968 = 125.8; 1936-1968 average = 90.0. What is the purchase price of the bones expressed in 1968-size dollars?
    a. $14,432
    b. $10,325
    c. $ 8,387
    d. $ 2,494

15. A price-level gain can arise from holding:
    a. nonmonetary assets during a period of inflation.
    b. monetary liabilities during a period of deflation.
    c. nonmonetary liabilities during a period of deflation.
    d. monetary assets in a period of deflation.
    e. nonmonetary assets during a period of deflation.

16. Which combination of factors below would generate a price-level loss?
    a. a monetary asset held during deflation
    b. a nonmonetary liability held during inflation
    c. a monetary liability held during inflation
    d. a nonmonetary liability held during deflation
    e. a monetary asset held during inflation

17. In 19A, Ronnie Rancher purchased a Malibu Canyon ranch for $500,000 when the price level index was 125. By 19M, the price level index had climbed to 175. The average price index over those 12 years was 150. What is the original cost of the ranch, stated in 19M-size dollars?
    a. $357,143
    b. $416,667
    c. $583,333
    d. $600,000
    e. $700,000

18. Orian Associates purchased a building in 1937 for $600,000. In 1969, the building was sold for $1,500,000. General price-level indices have been as follows:

    1937 = 44
    1969 = 110
    1981 = 212

    What was the selling price of the building expressed in 1937-size dollars?
    a. $ 311,321
    b. $ 600,000
    c. $1,500,000
    d. $3,750,000

19. Brother's Peanut Factory was purchased in 19A for $85,000. In 19U, it was sold for $300,000. During those 20 years the price index climbed from 110 to 185. The average price index during those years was 150. What is the selling price of the peanut factory expressed in 19A-size dollars?
    a. $178,378
    b. $220,000
    c. $243,243
    d. $370,000
    e. $409,091

20. During a period of inflation, a price-level loss will be incurred on which one of the following?
    a. land
    b. notes payable
    c. inventory
    d. accounts receivable

21. Which of the following statements is **true** concerning the effect that inflation has on a company's financial statements?
    a. The true cost of depreciation is usually overstated.
    b. Sales revenue is usually overstated.
    c. Cost of goods sold is usually understated.
    d. Wages expense is usually understated.

22. Technical equipment was acquired in 1969 for $100,000. In 1975, it was sold for $40,000. Assume the following price index history.

    1965 = 110
    1969 = 130
    1975 = 165
    1981 = 190

    What is the sales price of the technical equipment in 1981-size dollars?
    a. $69,091
    b. $50,769
    c. $46,061
    d. $34,737

23. Polyco Manufacturing reports the following balance sheet.

Assets	
Cash	$12
Accounts Receivable	32
Inventory	13
Equipment (net)	41
Total	$98
Liabilities & Equity	
Accounts Payable	$15
Notes Payable (LT)	20
Capital Stock	40
Retained Earnings	23
Total	$98

    The number of **monetary item** accounts on this balance sheet is:
    a. 3.
    b. 4.
    c. 5.
    d. 8.

24. Restating historical cost financial statements to a constant dollar basis requires the use of:
    a. the continuity principle.
    b. general price level index numbers.
    c. specific price level index numbers.
    d. current replacement cost information for all nonmonetary items.

25. Wyler had a GPL purchasing power gain of $124 on $1,400 of accounts receivable held throughout the recently completed year. Assume the average GPL index during the year was 135. Which one of the following **could** have been the year-end GPL index number?
    a. 123
    b. 147
    c. 150
    d. 162

26. Which one of the following statements concerning price-level accounting is **false**?
    a. Historical cost financial reporting ignores changes in the general price level.
    b. The Consumer Price Index for all Urban Consumers is a commonly used index in general price level accounting.
    c. Journal entries are used at year end to restate historical cost financial statements to dollars of a common size.
    d. Monetary items are not restated on price-level adjusted financial statements.

27. Compared to a base year index of 100, a current price-level index of 600 means that:
    a. each current dollar will buy 1/6th as much in real goods and services as in the base year.
    b. each current dollar will buy 6 times as much in real goods and services as in the base year.
    c. the historical cost amount for an asset must be multiplied by 600 to obtain its restated price-level amount.
    d. the purchasing power of the dollar has remained constant but there are more goods and services available to buy.

28. Monetary items may include:
    a. assets and liabilities.
    b. assets and revenues.
    c. assets, liabilities and expenses.
    d. assets, liabilities, revenues and expenses.

29. Which of the following is a nonmonetary item?
    a. inventory
    b. accounts receivable
    c. accounts payable
    d. notes payable

30. Edith and Company purchased a piece of land in 19A for $45,000 when the GPL index was 110. Today, the GPL index is 121. What is the cost of the land expressed in today's dollars?
    a. $45,000
    b. $49,500
    c. $54,450
    d. $57,820

31. Which of the following statements is correct during a period of declining prices?
    a. A debtor will incur a real purchasing power gain.
    b. A debtor will incur a real purchasing power loss.
    c. The owner of a piece of land will incur a real purchasing power gain.
    d. The owner of a piece of land will incur a real purchasing power loss.

PART B: Reporting Current Cost Changes

32. Select the **false** statement below.
    a. The acceptance of current cost accounting has been slow because of the difficulties associated with measuring current cost.
    b. Current cost/constant dollar financial reporting requires that certain adjusting entries be recorded in the ledger.
    c. For monetary items, historical cost and CC/CD amounts are usually the same.
    d. The CC/CD real holding gain (or loss) is the difference between HC/CD and the current cost of nonmonetary items.

33. Which of the following is **not** one of the concepts used to describe current value?
    a. book value
    b. present value
    c. net realizable value
    d. current cost

34. John purchased land for $10,000 when the GPL index was 125. Today, the general price level index is 135. If John were to sell the land today and was able to recognize a **real** gain of $1,000, at what price would the land have to sell?
    a. $10,259
    b. $10,800
    c. $11,800
    d. $12,000

35. Under which reporting system(s) below is it necessary to adjust historical monetary items on the balance sheet?

	HC/CD	CC/CD
a.	Yes	Yes
b.	Yes	No
c.	No	Yes
d.	No	No

36. How many of the following are appropriate techniques for determining the current cost value of various assets?
    --current price lists
    --prices for comparable used assets
    --specific price indexes
    --professional appraisals
    a. one
    b. two
    c. three
    d. four

CHAPTER SEVENTEEN: ANNOTATED SOLUTIONS

1. c	8. b	15. d	22. c	29. a	36. d
2. a	9. a	16. e	23. b	30. b	
3. c	10. b	17. e	24. b	31. b	
4. d	11. a	18. b	25. a	32. b	
5. a	12. a	19. a	26. c	33. a	
6. c	13. d	20. d	27. a	34. c	
7. a	14. a	21. c	28. a	35. d	

> *The correct answer and the percentage of students answering the question correctly (when it was used on an introductory accounting examination) are shown in parentheses at the beginning of each annotated solution that follows.*

1. (c,67) The primary purpose of a **general** price level index is to measure the general rate of price changes in the economy. Sometimes **specific** indexes are used to yield information regarding individual items, but general price level indexes are not. General price indexes measure the broad level of price change across an entire economy.

2. (a,62) During a period of **deflation**, holding monetary assets will result in a purchasing power gain. Notes receivable is a monetary asset.

3. (c,44) The four items would be stated as follows:

Cash (monetary; no restatement)	$ 10,000
Receivables (monetary; no restatement)	20,000
Equipment ($40,000 x 121/110)	44,000
Land & Buildings ($100,000 x 121/110)	110,000
	$184,000

4. (d,72) Response a is incorrect since GPL adjustments are not recorded in the journal or ledger. Responses b and c are both false because monetary items are **not** restated to reflect changes in the general price level. By definition, they are already stated in dollars of current size.

5. (a,32) Nonmonetary assets do **not** cause the holder to experience purchasing power gains or losses. It is the holding of **monetary** items that causes such gains and losses.

6. (c,24) Monetary assets are **not** restated on a price level adjusted balance sheet. Therefore, the monetary asset in this question would be listed at its original amount of $42,000.

7. (a,48) Only **monetary** items cause general price level (purchasing power) gains or losses; nonmonetary items do not.

8. (b,80) Depreciation expense = $60,000/5 years = $12,000 per year. The restated depreciation expense at the end of 19C is $16,800 ($12,000 x 175/125).

9. (a,50) Monetary items are those that are denominated in a fixed number of dollars and apply only to balance sheet categories. Assets such as cash and receivables are monetary as are most liabilities because of the obligation to pay a fixed number of dollars.

10. (b,54) The unit-of-measure assumption states that the dollar is the common denominator in the measurement process and that it remains constant in size (value). If inflation or deflation exists, the assumption of a constant size dollar is not holding true.

11. (a,55) Cash and accounts receivable are monetary assets and are not adjusted for changes in the general price level. The adjustment for land = $70,000 x 110/100 = $77,000.

12. (a,60) During a period of deflation money becomes **more** valuable. That is, the purchasing power of money increases. Monetary assets, then, also become more valuable during a period of deflation and the holder is "better off" having held them.

13. (d,62) During a period of deflation, price-level gains occur from holding monetary assets. In this question the only monetary asset given is cash (the correct answer). Equipment and inventory are **nonmonetary items** and and bonds payable is a monetary liability.

14. (a,72) The conversion factor for converting dollars of one size to dollars of another size is always "the price index you are converting **to**/ the price index you are converting **from**." In this problem, then, the conversion factor is 125.8/52.3 = 2.4053. The original purchase price times the conversion factor = restated cost; $6,000 x 2.4053 = $14,432.

15. (d,39) Nonmonetary items have absolutely **no** effect on price-level gains and losses. Responses a,c, and e, therefore, cannot be correct. Monetary liabilities held during deflation would result in a loss since "less valuable" dollars were borrowed and now "more valuable" dollars must be repaid. If monetary assets, though, are held during deflation, they become more valuable each day and a price-level gain results.

16. (e,73) Responses b and d must be incorrect since price-level gains and losses are unrelated to nonmonetary items; they are caused **exclusively** by holding monetary items. If a monetary asset (such as cash) is held during a period of inflation, it becomes less valuable each day and a price-level loss occurs.

17. (e,72) The original cost (of $500,000) is to be restated into 19M-size dollars. The conversion factor is always "index you are converting **to** /index you are converting **from**;" or in this case 175/125 = 1.4. So, $500,000 x 1.4 = $700,000.

18. (b,63) The selling price (of $1,500,000) is to be restated into 1937- size dollars. The conversion factor is "index you are converting **to**/index you are converting **from**." In this case, 44/110 = .4 so $1,500,000 x .4 = $600,000.

19. (a,76) The selling price of $300,000 is to be converted into 19A-size dollars. The conversion factor is always "index you are converting **to**/index of year you are converting **from**. In this problem it is 110/185 = .594594. $300,000 x .594594 = $178,378.

20. (d,72) During a period of inflation, price-level losses occur from holding monetary assets. The only monetary asset in this problem is accounts receivable. Land and inventory are nonmonetary; notes payable is a monetary **liability**.

21. (c,44) The "value" of goods sold is often understated in that those goods were purchased with older, larger dollars. When sold, the price level has increased and it takes more (smaller) dollars to represent the sacrifice necessary to replace the goods sold. If, for example, goods costing $12 were sold, it would take more than $12 to replenish the inventory; hence, cost of goods sold is understated.

22. (c,71) The selling price ($40,000) needs to be converted into 1981-size dollars. The conversion factor is 190/165 = 1.151515. $40,000 x 1.151515 = $46,061.

23. (b,52) The following are monetary items: cash, accounts receivable, accounts payable, and notes payable. A total of four items.

24. (b,59) When restating historical cost financial statements to dollars of a common size, general price-level index numbers are used.

25. (a,49) The key to this problem is to notice that there was a purchasing power **gain** from holding accounts receivable (a monetary asset). This means that prices had to be declining during the year. If the average index for the period was 135, the ending index had to be less than 135. Only response a meets this criterion.

26. (c,39) The journals and ledgers of a firm are **not** used in the restatement process. Those records continue to be maintained on an historical cost basis. Only the resulting financial statements are modified for the effects of changing prices.

27. (a,74) Stated another way, if the price index has changed from 100 to 600 it means that it now takes $6 to buy what $1 would buy during the base period. The purchasing power today is only 1/6 of what it was in the base period.

28. (a,64) Generally, monetary items are composed of certain assets and most liabilities. Revenues and expenses are not monetary.

29. (a,77) By definition, inventory is a nonmonetary asset.

30. (b,75) Since land is a nonmonetary item, its cost can be restated into today-sized dollars. The conversion is as follows: $45,000 x (121/110) = $49,500.

31. (b,56) Price-level gains and losses result from holding monetary items. If prices are declining, a debtor will have to pay back more purchasing power than was originally borrowed; hence, the loss.

32. (b,63) CC/CD financial **reporting** does not require entries in the accounts since only HC amounts are maintained there. HC amounts from the ledger are adjusted to yield CC/CD amounts but these new numbers are merely reported, **not** recorded via journal entries.

33. (a,80) Book value is defined as "cost minus accumulated depreciation." It bears no specific relationship to current value.

34. (c,55) A **real** gain is one after adjustment for the effects of inflation. Converting the historical cost of the land to current-size dollars yields a GPL restated cost of $10,800 (135/125 x $10,000). To obtain a **real** gain of $1,000 (stated in today's size dollars), the land would have to sell for $11,800 ($11,800 - $10,800 = $1,000).

35. (d,71) Historical cost based monetary items need not be adjusted under either HC/CD or CC/CD. They are already stated at CC in current dollars.

36. (d,83) Any of the four methods might be used, depending on what type of asset was being valued.

CHAPTER EIGHTEEN: STATEMENT OF CASH FLOWS

1. Which financial statement is specifically designed to report the events that caused a firm's assets, liabilities and equities to change during the period?
   a. income statement
   b. retained earnings statement
   c. balance sheet
   d. statement of cash flows

2. From which of the financial statements given below can information be obtained about the financing and investing activities that occurred during the period?

	Statement of Cash Flows	Comparative Balance Sheets
a.	Yes	Yes
b.	Yes	No
c.	No	Yes
d.	No	No

3. How many of the following items are cash equivalents?

   ---investment in money market fund
   ---short-term investment in bonds of Xerox Corp.
   ---treasury bills
   ---commercial paper

   a. one
   b. two
   c. three
   d. four
   e. zero

4. Bush-Wacker, Inc. reported cost of goods sold of $20, beginning inventory of $6 and ending inventory of $8. Beginning accounts payable was $4 and the ending accounts payable was $9. What amount of cash was paid out during this period to suppliers of inventory?
   a. $15
   b. $17
   c. $18
   d. $22

5. Antonia's Opera House had sales revenue this year of $70 and net income of $30. Beginning accounts receivable (from tour group sales) was $15 and ending accounts receivable was $12. Determine the amount of cash collected from customers during the current year.
   a. $73
   b. $70
   c. $67
   d. $33

6. What type of activity is the paying off of bonds payable?
   a. operating
   b. financing
   c. investing
   d. operating if short-term bonds were paid off; financing if long-term bonds were paid off.

7. Consider the following events.

   purchase of inventory
   payment of dividends
   issue of bonds payable
   purchase of treasury stock

   How many of the above are financing transactions?
   a. one
   b. two
   c. three
   d. four
   e. zero

8. Malotti Co. reported wages expense of $35,800 for 19B. Year-end 19A wages payable was $2,000 and year-end 19B wages payable was $3,500. How much cash did Malotti pay to employees during 19B?
   a. $32,300
   b. $34,300
   c. $35,800
   d. $37,300
   e. $37,800

USE THE FOLLOWING INFORMATION FOR THE NEXT FOUR QUESTIONS.

The Slippery Fish Company has the following comparative year-end balance sheets.

	19B	19A
Cash	$15	$10
Accounts Receivable	4	6
Inventory	16	22
Long-term Assets	12	9
	$47	$47
Accounts Payable	$ 7	$ 3
Wages Payable	8	13
Long-term Liabilities	9	12
Common Stock	10	10
Retained Earnings	13	9
	$47	$47

Additional information concerning 19B:

Income tax expense	$18
Cost of goods sold	26
Sales	180
Wages expense	35

9. What was the amount of cash paid for purchases during 19B?
   a. $22
   b. $24
   c. $26
   d. $28
   e. $30

10. Determine the amount of cash collected from customers during 19B.
    a. $172
    b. $178
    c. $180
    d. $182
    e. $188

11. What was the amount of cash paid to employees during 19B?
    a. $40
    b. $35
    c. $30
    d. $25

12. If a statement of cash flows were prepared for 19B, what amount would it report as the net change in cash?
    a. $0
    b. $5
    c. $8
    d. $120
    e. Cannot be determined from the information given.

13. Identify the item below that would be reported on the statement of cash flows as an investing activity.
    a. sold fully depreciated equipment
    b. purchased 100 shares of IBM as a short-term investment
    c. paid off bonds payable on their maturity date
    d. sold additional shares of common stock to outside investors

14. Consider the following transactions.

1. sale of bonds payable	$30
2. purchase of equipment	12
3. payment of dividends	6
4. payment of wages	4
5. purchase of treasury stock	8

    What is the net cash inflow from financing activities?
    a. ($12)
    b. zero
    c. $16
    d. $24
    e. $30

15. The Tylenol Co. reported a net loss for 19B of $600 using the accrual basis of accounting. The following information is available.

Depreciation expense	$400
Accounts payable increase	300
Inventory increase	100

    The net cash inflow (or outflow) from operating activities during 19B was:
    a. $ -0-.
    b. $ 600 outflow.
    c. $1,400 outflow.
    d. $ 200 inflow.

**USE THE FOLLOWING INFORMATION
FOR THE NEXT TWO QUESTIONS.**

The Belgian Waffle Co. reported sales of $26
during 19B and cost of goods sold of $14.
Selected comparative balance sheet amounts
were as follows:

	19A	19B
Accounts Receivable	$7	$9
Inventory	2	5
Accounts Payable	6	5
Wages Payable	4	0

16. What was the amount of cash collected
from customers during the year?
a. $24
b. $25
c. $26
d. $27
e. $28

17. What was the amount of cash paid to
suppliers of inventory?
a. $10
b. $12
c. $16
d. $17
e. $18

18. As the accountant for the Small Corp. you
are preparing the Statement of Cash Flows
at year end. While reviewing the general
journal you notice the following entry:

Bonds Payable, L.-Term   30,500
    Land   30,500

How should this transaction be reported on
the Statement of Cash Flows?
a. As an operating activity.
b. As either a financing activity or as an
investing activity.
c. As both a financing activity and as an
investing activity.
d. It should not be reported on the Statement of Cash Flows but on a separate
schedule.

19. The balance in the accumulated depreciation account of a company increased by
$8,000 during the year. During this period
the company sold machinery originally
costing $20,000 for $12,000 (its book value).
In determining cash provided by operating
activities:
a. $16,000 depreciation expense would be
added to net income.
b. $20,000 depreciation expense would be
subtracted from net income.
c. $8,000 depreciation expense would be
added to net income.
d. $8,000 depreciation expense would be
subtracted from net income.
e. $20,000 depreciation expense would be
added to net income.

20. Robert's Company is preparing the Statement of Cash Flows. An issuance of
common stock in exchange for the
acquisition of land would be:
a. reported as a financing activity.
b. reported on a schedule separate from
the statement of cash flows.
c. reported as an operating activity.
d. considered as both a financing and
an investing activity.

21. Calculate the "net cash flow from operating
activities."

Net income	$10,000
Depreciation expense	1,000
Patent amortization	500
Payoff of long-term note payable	5,000
Decrease in accounts receivable	3,000

a. $ 8,500
b. $ 9,500
c. $11,500
d. $14,500
e. $19,500

22. A firm's predominant recurring source of
cash over the long-run should be:
a. operations.
b. sale of noncurrent assets.
c. sale of capital stock.
d. borrowing.

23. Deep Purple Crawling Company had total sales in 19B of $750,000 of which 60% were on credit. The balance in accounts receivable was $100,000 at the end of 19A and $125,000 at the end of 19B. During 19B, what was the total cash inflow from sales?
    a. $300,000
    b. $450,000
    c. $725,000
    d. $775,000

24. Cactus Company reported revenue of $200 and expenses of $212 for the year ended December 31, 19C. During 19C, accounts receivable decreased by $1, trade payables increased by $5, accrued wages decreased by $3, and $8 in depreciation expense was recorded. Assuming there is no other relevant information, what is the net cash flow from operating activities?
    a. $1
    b. ($1)
    c. $5
    d. $7
    e. ($2)

25. Which of the following transactions will **not** be shown on a Statement of Cash Flows under either the direct or indirect method?
    a. cash dividends paid
    b. sale of an operational asset
    c. the amount of depreciation expense
    d. a stock dividend

26. Barry's Brake Shop just completed its first year in business and uses the accrual basis of accounting. Net income for the year was $30,000. The year-end balance sheet shows the following selected account balances:

Prepaid Advertising	$1,200
Prepaid Insurance	1,300
Rent Collected in Advance	1,800

    If Barry's Brake Shop had used the cash basis of accounting, net income of the year just ended would have been:
    a. $ 700 lower.
    b. $1,800 higher.
    c. $2,500 lower.
    d. $4,300 higher.

27. The Janice Stemmler Carr Company is preparing the Statement of Cash Flows using the indirect method. Which of the following is a **true** statement?
    a. A decrease in net accounts receivable should be added to net income.
    b. An increase in accounts payable should be deducted from net income.
    c. Depreciation expense should be deducted from net income.
    d. Over the long-run, the largest source of cash should be operating activities.

28. The accountant at ABC Company is preparing the Statement of Cash Flows and has gathered the following information:

Gain on sale of equipment	$ 5,000
Net Income	52,000
Common stock issued for cash	100,000
Depreciation expense	20,000
Sale of equipment	40,000
Increase in inventory	2,000

    Based only on the above information, the net cash inflow from operating activities during the year was:
    a. $ 32,000.
    b. $ 65,000.
    c. $ 72,000.
    d. $165,000.

29. Harriet Company reported net income of $300,000 for the year. Depreciation expense amounted to $31,500. The beginning and ending balances of current asset and current liability accounts were as follows:

	Beginning	Ending
Accounts Receivable	$50,000	$56,500
Inventories	75,200	76,600
Accounts Payable	45,800	40,400

    In a Statement of Cash Flows, the net cash inflow from operating activities would be:
    a. $318,200.
    b. $329,000.
    c. $334,000.
    d. $344,800.

30. The Snowpac Co. had revenues of $150 and expenses of $100. The revenues consisted of cash sales of $75, credit sales of $50 (already collected), and credit sales of $25 (not yet collected). The expenses were all paid for in cash except for $10 of merchandise which was taken from inventory that was purchased last year, and depreciation expense of $25. The Snowpac Corp. also purchased a new truck for $15 during the year. It paid 1/3 cash and will pay the remainder next year. Compute the net change in cash during the year.
    a. $25
    b. $35
    c. $50
    d. $55
    e. $60

31. Katie Corp. is preparing the Statement of Cash Flows. When doing so, depreciation expense for the year was added to net income. This was done because depreciation expense:
    a. is a source of cash.
    b. reduces reported net income but is **not** a use of cash.
    c. reduces net income for a period and represents an inflow of cash.
    d. represents an inflow of cash to a reserve account that is maintained for the replacement of assets.

32. XYZ Corp. had revenue of $200 and expenses of $175 during 19A. Also, accounts receivable decreased by $20, accounts payable increased by $25, long-term bonds payable increased by $30, and depreciation expense was $15. Assume no other changes in account balances are relevant. What was the net cash inflow from operating activities?
    a. $ 5 net cash outflow
    b. $25 net cash inflow
    c. $35 net cash outflow
    d. $85 net cash inflow

USE THE FOLLOWING INFORMATION FOR THE NEXT THREE QUESTIONS

Bojangles Company uses the indirect method of preparing the Statement of Cash Flows and reports the following comparative balance sheet information:

Balance Sheets	12-31-19B	12-31-19A
Cash	$ 15,000	$10,000
Inventory	40,000	36,000
Equipment	50,000	45,000
Accumulated Dep.	(10,000)	(6,000)
	$ 95,000	$ 85,000
Accounts Payable	$ 21,000	$ 23,000
Bonds Pay. (L-T)	24,000	20,000
Common Stock	30,000	30,000
Retained Earnings	20,000	12,000
	$ 95,000	$ 85,000

Additional Information:
Net income for 19B was $9,000.
No equipment was disposed of during the year.
Sales for 19B were $200,000
Cost of Goods Sold for 19B was $140,000

33. What was the net cash inflow from operating activities during 19B?
    a. $ 5,000
    b. $ 7,000
    c. $11,000
    d. $15,000
    e. $19,000

34. What was the net cash flow from investing activities during 19B?
    a. outflow of $5,000
    b. inflow of $3,000
    c. outflow of $6,000
    d. inflow of $4,000
    e. outflow of $2,000

35. What was the net cash flow from financing activities during 19B?
    a. inflow of $4,000
    b. outflow of $1,000
    c. inflow of $5,000
    d. outflow of $2,000
    e. inflow of $3,000

36. Net sales for Piggly Wiggly Stores were $2,000 during 19C. Accounts receivable and inventory **each** increased by $100 during 19C and accounts payable increased by $400 during that same period. During 19C, what was the total cash collected from sales?
    a. $2,200
    b. $1,900
    c. $1,800
    d. $1,400

37. Manchester Fish Company has no operational assets but reported the following for a recent accounting period. It's accounts receivable increased by $500, merchandise inventory decreased by $300, accounts payable increased by $200 and income tax payable decreased by $100. If the company reported net income of $10,000, the cash inflow from operating activities during the period was:
    a. $ 9,800.
    b. $ 9,900.
    c. $10,000.
    d. $10,100.

CHAPTER EIGHTEEN: ANNOTATED SOLUTIONS

1. d	8. b	15. a	22. a	29. a	36. b
2. a	9. a	16. a	23. c	30. d	37. b
3. d	10. d	17. e	24. b	31. b	
4. b	11. a	18. d	25. d	32. d	
5. a	12. b	19. a	26. a	33. b	
6. b	13. a	20. b	27. d	34. a	
7. c	14. c	21. d	28. b	35. e	

1. (d) By definition, the statement of cash flows is the best answer. Both the income statement and statement of retained earnings report **some** of the events that caused such changes, but it is the statement of cash flows which is specifically designed to report all of them.

2. (a) It is quite obvious that the statement of cash flows can be used to learn about a firm's financing and investing activities. At the same time, however, **some** of this information can also be determined by inspecting comparative balance sheets. For example, if the common stock account increased between balance sheets, it is likely that a financing activity (sale of stock) took place.

3. (d) A cash equivalent is a short-term, highly liquid investment. All four of the items listed meet this definition.

4. (b) Cost of goods sold ($20) - beginning inventory ($6) + ending inventory ($8) = accrual basis purchases ($22). Accrual basis purchases ($22) + beginning accounts payable ($4) - ending accounts payable ($9) = cash paid for purchases ($17).

5. (a) Sales ($70) + beginning accounts receivable ($15) - ending accounts receivable ($12) = cash collected from customers ($73).

6. (b) Borrowing via bonds payable (or paying off such borrowings) is defined as a financing activity . Whether the bonds payable happen to be classified as current or long-term at the time of payoff is irrelevant. (Note that **all** bonds payable are properly classified as current liabilities on their maturity date. Only if a bond is being paid off prior to maturity would it be a long-term liability.)

7. (c) There are three financing activities listed; payment of dividends, issue of bonds payable, and purchase of treasury stock. The first item is **not** a financing activity (purchase of inventory) but is an operating activity.

8. (b) Cash paid to employees is computed as wages expense ($35,800) + beginning wages payable ($2,000) - ending wages payable ($3,500) = $34,300.

9. (a) Cost of goods sold ($26) - beginning inventory ($0) + ending inventory ($0) = accrual basis purchases ($26). Accrual basis purchases ($26) + beginning accounts payable ($3) - ending accounts payable ($7) = cash paid for purchases ($22).

10. (d) Cash collected from customers is equal to sales ($180) + beginning accounts receivable ($6) - ending accounts receivable ($4) = $182.

11. (a) Cash paid to employees is equal to wages expense ($35) + beginning wages payable ($13) - ending wages payable ($8) = $40.

12. (b) The statement of cash flows is a proof of the change in the cash account during the year. For this firm, the change in the cash account was $5 (from $10 to $15). This means that the net sum of all inflows and outflows from operating, financing and investing activities was $5.

13. (a) Only the sale of fully depreciated equipment is an investing activity. (Technically, of course, we might call it a "disinvesting" activity since we are reducing our investment in these assets.) Response b is an operating activity since it involves a cash equivalent and responses c and d are financing activities.

14. (c) Items 1 (inflow of $30), 3 (outflow of $6), and 5 (outflow of $8) are financing activities. They net to an inflow of $16.

15. (a) Using the indirect method, net cash flow = net loss + depreciation expense + accounts payable increase - inventory decrease = ($600) + $400 + $300 - $100 = $0.

16. (a) Cash collected from customers is equal to sales ($26) + beginning accounts receivable ($7) - ending accounts receivable ($9) for a total of $24.

17. (e) Cash paid to suppliers of inventory is equal to cost of goods sold ($14) - beginning inventory ($2) + ending inventory ($5) + beginning accounts payable ($6) - ending accounts payable ($5) for an answer of $18.

18. (d) This transaction is a direct exchange in that it is both a financing activity (giving up the land to pay off the bonds) and an investing activity (paying off the bonds with the land). While a direct exchange does not affect cash, it is to be reported on a separate schedule accompanying the statement of cash flows because it involves financing and/or investing acitivites.

19. (a) Two events affected the accumulated depreciation account this period. (1) it decreased by $8,000 when the machinery was sold, and (2) it must have increased by $16,000 when depreciation expense was recognized in the current year. This would prove the **net** change of + $8,000 in the accumulated depreciation account for the year. The $16,000 depreciation expense, then, must be added back to net income when preparing the statement of cash flows using the indirect method.

20. (b) This is an example of a direct exchange that must be reported on a separate schedule accompanying the statement of cash flows.

21. (d) In this problem, net cash flow from operating activities can be computed by the indirect method as follows: net income ($10,000) + depreciation expense ($1,000) + patent amortization expense ($500) + the decrease in accounts receivable ($3,000) for a total of $14,500.

22. (a) A company can only sell stock, bonds or fixed assets for so long. Eventually, it has to start generating cash from operations in order to pay dividends, replace assets, and finance growth.

23. (c) Cash sales were $300,000 (40% of $750,000). Since accounts receivable increased during the year by $25,000, all but $25,000 of the $450,000 in credit sales were also collected in cash. Total cash collections from sales, then, were $300,000 + $425,000 = $725,000.

24. (b) Using the indirect method, net cash flow = net income + accounts receivable decrease + trade payable increase - accrued wages decrease + depreciation expense. Therefore, net cash flow = ($12) + $1 + $5 - $3 + $8 = ($1).

25. (d) Since stock dividends do not affect cash and because they are neither a financing activity nor an investing activity they are not reported on a statement of cash flows. (Depreciation expense would only appear on the statement if the indirect method were being used.)

26. (a) Under the cash basis, the cash paid out for prepaid advertising and prepaid insurance would have been expense ($1,200 + $1,300 = $2,500). Also, the rent money received in advance ($1,800) would have been considered revenue. Net income, then, would have been $700 lower ($1,800 additional revenue minus $2,500 additional expense).

27. (d) In the long-run a company cannot survive unless its operations are generating sufficient funds to finance replacement of assets, payment of dividends, and growth. Responses a, b, and c are stated backwards. For example, response c is incorrect because depreciation expense should be **added** to net income.

28. (b) Only net income, depreciation expense, the increase in inventory and the gain on sale of equipment are relevant to this question. Net income ($52,000) + depreciation expense ($20,000) - increase in inventory ($2,000) - gain on sale ($5,000) = $65,000.

29. (a) Begin with net income ($300,000), add back depreciation expense ($31,500), subtract the increases in accounts receivable and inventories ($6,500 and $1,400) and subtract the decrease in accounts payable ($5,400) for the correct answer of $318,200.

30. (d) The net change in the cash account is equal to (cash sales + credit sales already collected - expenses paid with cash - purchase of assets). Therefore, ($75 + $50) - ($100 total expenses - $25 depreciation expense - $10 expenses already paid for) - (1/3 x $15 truck) = $55 change in cash.

31. (b) Depreciation expense is added back to net income because we are trying to convert "net income from operating activities" into "cash from operating activities." Depreciation is properly deducted from revenue on the income statement because it is an expense. It does **not**, however, decrease cash and needs to be added back.

32. (d) Begin with net income ($25) and add depreciation expense ($15). Also, add the decrease in accounts receivable ($20) and the increase in accounts payable ($25). Ignore the change in long-term bonds. Cash flow from operations, then, is $25 + $15 + $20 + $25 = $85.

33. (b) Cash provided by operating activities is computed in this problem as follows: net income ($9,000) + depreciation expense ($4,000; as determined by inspecting the change in accumulated depreciation) - increase in inventory ($4,000) - decrease in accounts payable ($2,000). $9,000 + $4,000 - $4,000 - $2,000 = $7,000.

34. (a) The only investing activity that occurred was an apparent purchase of equipment. The equipment account increased from $45,000 to $50,000 implying that $5,000 of new equipment was purchased.

35. (e) There were two financing activities; a sale of bonds (bonds payable increased from $20,000 to $24,000 indicating an inflow of $4,000), and a payment of dividends (net income was $9,000 but retained earnings only increased by $8,000 suggesting an outflow from a dividend payment of $1,000). The $4,000 inflow minus the $1,000 outflow yields a net $3,000 inflow.

36. (b) Sales were $2,000, but accounts receivable increased by $100 during the year. Effectively, this means that $100 of this years' sales was not collected in cash. Therefore, cash collected from sales was $1,900 ($2,000 - $100). What happened to inventory and accounts payable is irrelevant to determining the amount of cash collected from sales.

37. (b) Start with net income ($10,000) and deduct the increase in accounts receivable ($500); add the decrease in inventory ($300) and the increase in accounts payable ($200); deduct the decrease in tax payable ($100). To summarize, $10,000 - $500 + $300 + $200 - $100 = $9,900. There is no depreciation expense in this problem because the firm had no operational assets.